Germany's other mo

MANCHEstER
1824
Manchester University Press

Germany's other modernity

Munich and the making of metropolis, 1895–1930

LEIF JERRAM

Manchester University Press
Manchester and New York

distributed exclusively in the USA by Palgrave

Copyright © Leif Jerram 2007

The right of Leif Jerram to be identified as the author of this work has been asserted by him in accordance with the Copyright, Designs and Patents Act 1988.

Published by Manchester University Press
Oxford Road, Manchester M13 9NR, UK
and Room 400, 175 Fifth Avenue, New York, NY 10010, USA
www.manchesteruniversitypress.co.uk

Distributed in the United States exclusively by
Palgrave Macmillan, 175 Fifth Avenue,
New York, NY 10010, USA

Distributed in Canada exclusively by
UBC Press, University of British Columbia, 2029 West Mall,
Vancouver, BC, Canada V6T 1Z2

British Library Cataloguing-in-Publication Data is available

Library of Congress Cataloging-in-Publication Data is available

ISBN 978 0 7190 9538 2 paperback

First published by Manchester University Press in hardback 2007

This paperback edition first published 2014

The publisher has no responsibility for the persistence or accuracy of URLs for any external or third-party internet websites referred to in this book, and does not guarantee that any content on such websites is, or will remain, accurate or appropriate.

Printed by Lightning Source

Contents

List of illustrations	vii
Introduction	1
Making sense of modernity	2
Cities, buildings and space	6
Historicising Germany, historicising buildings	10
Structure of the book	13

1 *Großstadtangst*: disorder and discomfort in the metropolis 20
  The culture of anxiety 24
  Metropolis as *Heimat* 25
  Producing *Heimat*: strategy and tactics 31
  Exhibiting the city: exhibiting anxiety 39
  Städtebau: building cities 47
  Conclusion 60

2 *Großstadtfreude*: joy in the metropolis 67
  Liberal mentality and the community of *Großstädte*, 1890–1914 69
  Liberal mentality and the community of *Großstädte*, 1918–30 78
  Urban selves and rural others: peripheries, edges and the colonial mentality 82
  The dysfunctional countryside and the useful city 90
  Modern signs, modern citizens: technological symbolism in the city 92
  Conclusion 100

3 The interior world of modernity 106
  The social state and the ungrateful citzen 110

	Domestic space and the modern citizen	126
	Conclusion	142
4	**The production of space and the execution of social policy**	149
	The politics of aesthetics	151
	Defining the problem, asking the question: the space of home	153
	Technologies of space: land versus architecture	161
	Technology, rent and construction	170
	From housing 'question' to design 'policy', 1917–30	172
	Conclusion	185
Conclusion: Germany, space and modernity		192
Bibliography		197
Index		219

List of illustrations

1.1 Wall paintings, Implerstraße School, Munich, 1900s. Author's photograph — 37
2.1 The Munich *Technisches Rathaus* – Technical Town Hall, 1920s. Author's photograph — 95
2.2 The Munich *Elektrizitätsverwaltung* – the Electricity Board, 1920s. Author's photograph — 96
3.1 The Frankfurt Kitchen, c. 1926 *Das Neue Frankfurt*, 5 (1926–27) — 129
3.2 The Munich Kitchen, c. 1927 GeWoFAG, *Die Siedlungen der Gemeinnützigen Wohnungsfürsorge AG München* (Munich, 1928) — 130
3.3 Christine Frederick's 'efficient' and 'inefficient' kitchens, 1919 Frederick, *Household Engineering* — 134
4.1 Typical 1890s Viennese Apartment Block, Eberstadt, *Handbuch des Wohnungswesens* — 157
4.2 Plans for model small flats for the poor, Vienna, 1900s Eberstadt, *Handbuch des Wohnungswesens* — 166
4.3 'Garden City' designs for housing reform, 1900s Eberstadt, *Neue Studien* — 167
4.4 Alte Heide Housing Estate, Munich, 1919. Author's photograph — 177

Introduction

You live in a big city,	Man lebt in einer großen Stadt,
And yet you're so alone.	Und ist doch so allein.
The man you yearn for,	Der Mann, nachdem man Sehnsucht hat,
Is nowhere to be found.	Scheint doch nicht da zu sein.
You don't know him at all ...	Man kennt ihn nicht,
And yet you know him so well,	Und kennt ihn doch genau,
And you live in angst,	Und man hat Angst,
That he'll pass you by.	Daß er vorüber geht.[1]

The opening lines of Marlene Dietrich's 1933 hit, *Allein in einer großen Stadt*, give an impression of life in a big city with which many would have been familiar in the first decades of the twentieth century – and may still recognise today. Yearning, desire, the frisson of contact and the potential for love and adventure are coupled with *Angst* and a fear of the unknown, and a sense that life is passing one by. Everything is pervaded by the paradox that one has never been so physically close to so many people, and yet so distant and detached. The quality of life in the city – quality in both its senses, that of the general attributes that city life possesses, and its material standard of living – was a subject of immense general interest across the West before and after 1900. Yet it concerned none more than those whose job it was to ensure that this quality, in these two senses, was as high as possible. The governors and administrators of any city had an interest in every aspect of urban life, from the economy to the emotional well-being of the citizens.

This book focuses on the ways in which German urban élites tried to mould German cities in the first thirty or so years of the twentieth century, between the 'birth' of modern planning in the 1890s and the complete cessation of building caused by the economic collapse around 1930. The book investigates the attributes which 'metropolis', or *Großstadt*, was given by early twentieth-century Germans. It examines the faith they had that in reshaping the life-world of the country's citizens it could make them happy, ordered, successful, contented and compliant: rounded, successful tenants of the modern world. It takes Munich as its 'still point in the turning world' of German urban development in particular, but makes arguments relevant well beyond the southern capital's city limits. One of the distinctive features of urban history is the way it challenges the nation state as a category of historical analysis. Munich stands as a representative metropolis – or *Großstadt*, in German. It functions as a case study of the urban landscape of modernity and modernisation which was increasingly characteristic of much European social, cultural and political life.

The objective, though, is not simply to trace a line of the 'rise' of planning, or even the 'rise' of the expert or rational discourse, important as both of these are. By assessing the ways that élite groups explored their faith in environmental determinism, by investigating their attempts to 'reconfigure urban order and identity',[2] the book will address other themes central to many contemporary debates in historical writing. It will directly address the historicisation of modernity and the ways historians use space, and thereby also offer indirect comment on the writing of German history in general.

Making sense of modernity

A working definition of modernity has been notoriously difficult to pin down. In part, this is because modernity has been characterised somewhat contradictorily. There is a necessity for simplification of some sophisticated arguments here, because otherwise it would be possible to write an entire book defining this idea alone. It is possible to divide the ways academics have characterised modernity into two contradictory (although not necessarily mutually exclusive) interpretations: modernity as 'ordering' and modernity as 'disordering'.

In its 'ordering' guise, modernity is ascribed a demonic logic which, for all its benefits, led to the gas chambers of Auschwitz–Birkenau. This 'catastrophist' model of modernity is represented (among others) by writers such as Zygmunt Bauman, Bruno Latour and Detlev Peukert.[3] Each argues in some form that the internal logic of how modern societies both produce and apply knowledge about themselves has led to some of modernity's most oppressive features. In this model, modernity is emplotted as an impersonal force or agent, an invisible *deus ex machina*. This model of modernity perhaps represents best the way it appears in some writing about the history of

German-speaking Europe. Both sociologist Bauman and historian of science Latour have emphasised the ways intellectuals since the seventeenth century have used their *partial* knowledge of the world to underpin *totalising* reformist plans. Each has highlighted the failures of producers of knowledge to recognise the Utopian, imaginary or dreamy nature of the remote social goals they identified, because they were unable to see the constructed nature of their 'objective' data. In particular, argues Latour, intellectuals began to extend the principles which underpin the 'laws of things' in order to construct equally firm 'laws of man' – a process which analogised two highly dissimilar things: the behaviour of, say, planets acting in relation to one another, and the behaviour of people doing the same thing.

Cultural historians, on the other hand, often characterise modernity somewhat differently; for them, modernity is a set of disordering and disorientating experiences, wisps and vapours. While acknowledging that modernity operates with internal logics (especially when they are influenced by Foucault or Marx), modernity as a character in urban historical narrative is often portrayed very differently, especially in late nineteenth- and early twentieth-century Europe and America. The influence on cultural and urban history of writers such as Charles Baudelaire, Georg Simmel, Walter Benjamin, Marshall Berman, Guy Debord and Matei Calinescu have stressed this experiential, incoherent modernity, which is about thrills, superficiality, danger, excitement, disorder.[4] Rather than representing an impersonal, ordering *deus ex machina*, it is highly subjective, accentuating the impressionistic, the fractured and the atomised; it is about bewildering change and subjective experience. For example, Debord (an important commentator on the culture of modernity) characterises modernity thus:

> In societies dominated by modern conditions of production, life is presented as an immense accumulation of *spectacles*. Everything that was directly lived has receded into a representation ... The images detached from every aspect of life merge into a common stream in which the unity of that life can no longer be recovered. *Fragmented* views of reality regroup themselves into a new unity as a *separate pseudoworld* that can only be looked at. The specialisation of images of the world evolves into a world of autonomised images where even the deceivers are deceived. The spectacle is a concrete inversion of life, an autonomous movement of the nonliving.[5]

Here modernity is emplotted as a sort of ghost-train ride – fantastic, dark, mysterious, potentially threatening, but also thrilling and alluring – maybe even a little daring or edgy. Baudrillard has gone on a stage further to argue that the primary category is the spectacle of spectacles, twice removed from reality, such that reality has become a series of simulacra.[6] Berman evokes Marx's characterisation of modernity, arguing that:

> As we read on [in the *Communist Manifesto*], however, if we read with our full attention, strange things begin to happen. Marx's prose suddenly becomes luminous, incandescent; brilliant images succeed and blend into one another; we are hurtled along with a reckless momentum, a breathless intensity.[7]

And in reading Marx's blend of brilliant images (although if the prose is that good, the chances are it may well have been Engels), we are not reading mere description but, for Berman, we are being taken to the heart of a persistently relevant set of truths about modernity. While Marx and Engels located urban modernity in the uncompromising *orders* of class and capital, cultural historians have often placed emphasis on the disorder of the chaotic impressions which this systematising produces in the individual psyche. Modernity for them is, above all, exciting and fragmentary.

The two narratives of modernity – ordered and disordered – are not, however, unrelated. Some cultural historians have directed scholarly attention (entirely appropriately) to the expert response to this fractured, atomised existence, by emphasising its role in producing the discourses of 'nerves' and psychic malaise said to be characteristic of metropolitan modernity.[8] As Anthony Vidler has noted, in the late nineteenth century: 'Metropolis rapidly became the privileged territory of a host of diseases attributed directly to its spatial conditions, diseases that took their place with in the general epistemology of Beard's neurasthenia and Charcot's hysteria, but with a special relationship to their supposed physical causes.'[9] While modernity in this narrative is not characterised as dangerous or pathological *per se*, it is typified as eliciting a certain anxious response in experts, governors and élites. The fragmentary, chaotic and superficial urban modernity caused disorder in the minds of citizens; contemporaries had to define this disorder, and repair it. The perceived experiential disorder of citizens produced the impulse to impose order among the personnel of the modern state. This pathologisation of the symptoms provides a bridge between the ordering and disordering characterisations of modernity.

If we recognise that we cannot separate the metropolis from modernity or modernisation, then this presents historians with a problem. Having abandoned long ago a Whiggish narrative of progress, and disenchanted as many have become with historical materialism, historians are often neutral (or silent) when it comes to positive aspects of modernity, such as antibiotics, clean water, personal freedom and human rights. However, we can be highly critical, through our selective scrutiny, of some of its concomitant negative aspects – such as ever more rigorous surveillance by those who 'help' us, or more effective genocides. This imbalance does great discredit to those voices from the nineteenth- and early twentieth-century city whom we so often privilege in our writing. Generally, all but the most extreme among German doctors, eugenicists, psychologists, planners, sociologists and so on (the people who produced and applied the social knowledges so characteristic of modernity) went out of their way to sing the praises of clean water, postal systems, international travel, universal education, personal freedom and modern medicine. This book tries to restore an emphasis on contemporaries' nuanced views of modernity and modernisation, and thus Chapters 1 and 2 explore the balanced construction of 'the city' in planners' world views.

This book sets about the task of recapturing this equitable world view by presenting the logical, ordering projects of the modern city and social state in the context of individual humans' beliefs, relationships and cultural discussions about the disordered aspects of the modern urban experience. It fixes on a relatively small group of people, but a group which represents a whole class and type: Munich's city planners and governors, and those in the wider Reich with whom they communicated, discussed and argued. Although the planners and designers and governors in this book did adopt most of the mentalities associated with the 'rise' of the expert and rational thought, they remained nameable individuals, with wills, personalities, friendships, anxieties and hopes of their own. They were not the simple servants of the historical narrative of the 'rise' of experts which has become so dominant in some recent historiography of the city.[10] Nothing precludes an expert or a scientist from also being a *flâneur* and a thrill-seeker. After all, they walked the streets they helped to design.

One of the most coherent definitions of twentieth-century 'modernity' I have encountered is by Detlev Peukert. With Peukert I:

> take the term 'modernity' to refer to the form of fully-fledged industrialised society that has been with us since the turn of the [twentieth] century until the present day. In an economic sense, highly rationalised industrial production, complex technological infrastructures

and a substantial degree of bureaucratic administrative and service activity ... characterise modernity. Socially speaking, its typical features include the division of labour, wage and salary discipline, an urbanised environment, extensive educational opportunities and a demand for skills and training ... In intellectual terms, modernity marks the triumph of western rationality, whether in social planning, the expansion of the sciences or the self-replication dynamism of technology.[11]

I would disagree with Peukert, though, when he continues that:

[a]s far as culture is concerned, ... continuity with traditional aesthetic principles and practices in architecture and the visual and other creative arts is broken, and is replaced by unrestricted formal experimentation.[12]

This view of culture is overly formal, and would be true only if one focused on a restrictive canon of Modernism, and casually associated Modernism with modernity – the unrelated nature of which is a key theme of Chapter 4. Furthermore, the historian in this model would have to discard the persistence of highly stable ideological constructs such as 'house', 'home' or 'street' which firmly constrained formal experimentation in building. It is to architecture which I will now turn, for the cultural production of the twentieth century is far from being one of 'unrestricted formal experimentation'.

Cities, buildings and space

It is difficult to discuss the city without addressing the issue of space – and, in fact, this book is an investigation of how urban space was 'invented' as a social category, described and understood by contemporaries and manipulated in the service of a large modernising project. Most attempts to define the nature of space have not been successful, because it is such an elusive concept. Yet most agree that it has been hugely important as a means for sorting, segregating, collating, enabling and directing a whole variety of social processes. I would redouble its importance as a category of historical analysis, for there are no a-spatial historical processes, and space and the technologies and ideas which underpin it have been just as much a factor in producing change and continuity over time as other epistemological categories familiar to the historian, such as gender, class, capital or ethnicity.

Henri Lefebvre is generally used as a starting point for discussions of space, although his ideas present significant problems. His major

Introduction 7

work, *The Production of Space*, offers a useful tripartite division of three types of 'space': [13]

1. 'Spatial practice' – by this, he means the ways space is used in order to produce social cohesion and reproduction.
2. 'Representations of space' – how space is schematised and described, usually by planners, architects, army generals in command rooms and so on. He refers to 'knowledge, to signs, to codes' as being crucial here.
3. 'Representational space' – the values ascribed to spaces by those who use them. By this, he means the values and beliefs which turn a material space with objective qualities into places, like 'home' or 'church' or 'market', and which serve as shorthand for whole social value systems and associated practices.[14]

The obvious problem here is that all three of these 'spaces' are located inside the human mind, and none in the 'real' world beyond it. If we conduct a brief thought experiment, we can see why this is so problematic. Imagine a factory owner who is threatened with bankruptcy because the factory buildings are too small to accommodate the new plant that the factory's competitors have acquired, thereby boosting their profitability and cutting their costs. Assuming the land around the factory is all occupied (or is bounded by rivers, cliffs, marshes, etc.), the factory will go bust and close. But it will not close because of people's spatial practice (for example, their tendency to congregate in the smoking room rather than the cafeteria for social interaction). Nor will it fail because of their schematic representations of space (i.e. because the managers cannot find a way to describe or quantify the space they need). Neither will the problem be the place-like attributes (such as sacredness) given to a physical feature such as, say, the cliff at the back. Its demise will not be because of people's beliefs about space, in the senses that Lefebvre meant them. It will close because of an incapacity to manipulate real, physical space. A big machine will not fit into a small space – it feels almost embarrassing to say it so baldly – so we need to approach space as an intersection of the imaginary and the real, not merely the sum total of a series of discourses.

It would seem that rather than a *more* sophisticated understanding of space, with ever more layers of theoretical nuance, scholars perhaps need a less sophisticated one. Unfashionable as it may be, there must be a way of asserting that there is a reality beyond the human mind, while also recognising the role of the mind in producing reality; which recognises the attributive aspects that Lefebvre highlights, but which also acknowledges the capacity of things like walls or forcible relocation to act in a very real, very 'un'-imaginary way. Historians, with some exceptions, have been slow to empiricise recent scholarship on space, and its dynamic, formative roles and functions.[15] For example, more ink has been spilled on the unbuilt Panoptikon than on the history of all the real prisons in the Western world put together. This book tries to focus more on the transition from imaginary space to real spaces, and privileging (once) real, nameable people over the processes they may represent. So, for example, it deals with schools as symbolic environments representing a certain social project, but also as individual buildings which are real and measurable and locatable, designed by nameable individuals with ideas accessible to the historian.

The book deals primarily with 'representations of space' by focusing on the activities of planners, architects and experts; secondarily with 'representational space', investigating metaphors of the city as a place, and the ideological constructs which constituted it – like 'home' and 'hospital'; and only glancingly with 'spatial practice' – largely because information about this is often so hard for the historian to recover. But it does this with an assumption that these were real life-worlds, and that experts and governors produced material, and often unalterable, environments imposed by and on social groups in order to structure social relationships and cultural practices. Frequently, citizens were forced to enter these real environments and spaces. Scholars need to address material effects as well as meanings for, as Chapter 3 shows in its discussion of hospitals, old people's homes and social housing, space could be a highly coercive tool for the social reformer, while Chapter 4 demonstrates how intellectual impasses in manipulating the technologies of space could have profound political consequences.

One of the major ways in which space is partitioned, added up, taken away, withheld and demarcated is through the activity of building. The ways that the built environment is currently used as evidence in historical writing are problematic, however. The major weaknesses are, first, that historians and art historians give insufficient weight to the analysis of the mundane constructions which dominate people's lives, and too much weight to a handful of iconic structures which belong to an art-historical canon;[16] and, secondly, they are preoccupied with how buildings look, rather than what they do.[17] Tournikiotis has highlighted the almost complete exclusion of 'historians *qua* historians' in understanding architecture since 1900. Instead, architecture has been investigated in a historiographical tradition dominated by three authorial personae, all alien to the 'doing' of history: the connoiseurial art historian, aiming to identify the most beautiful human creations; the 'architect/historian', ideologically committed to establishing the coherency and universal relevance of the 'Modern Movement' in the service of promoting his/her own activities; and the polemical 'architect/critic', keen to make broader political or cultural arguments using architecture as his or her material.[18] Mitchell Schwarzer has highlighted the obsession of architectural journals with the iconic structure or idea, rather than the typical.[19] A collection of essays edited by Mari Hvattum and Christian Hermansen aims to 'trace modernity' in the 'manifestations of the modern in architecture and the city' – precisely the sort of project with which a historian should be able to engage. However, 'modernity' in this context actually means Modernism, and the contributors confine themselves yet again to a cast of characters familiar to most educated readers: 'Greek' Thompson, Gilbert Scott, Gottfried Semper, the Great Exhibition, Le Corbusier, Walter Benjamin and Siegfried Kracauer.[20] This book treats modernity with little eye for Modernism.

In all of its forms, the investigation of twentieth-century building has been dominated – perhaps suffocated – by this obsession with star architects and a narrow canon of buildings. This fixation with the canon becomes all the more problematic in the context of German history because Modernist architecture (as opposed to simply modern, statist/capitalist, urban architecture) represents the yardstick of what is 'good' not only in architecture (thereby dominating the output of architectural historians), but also in a way which has served as a shorthand for that authentic, good, daring, humane Germany, in which the *NS-Zeit* should be seen as an anomalous interruption, appealing to a 'triumph leading to tragedy' narrative structure. While the Nazi period should certainly be seen as a tragedy, this still leaves Modernist buildings and design with an enormous burden to bear, as Paul Betts has argued in his book, *The Authority of Everyday Objects*.[21] Betts argues that Modernist design and words like 'functionalism' were used aggressively in Germany after the Second World War to suggest a continuity with the 'golden' (but imaginary) Germany of the Bauhaus, and to imply distance from the (actually, frequently Modernist) styles of the *NS-Zeit*. Thus on the all-too-rare occasions when historians fully engage with the built environment in Germany before 1933, there is sometimes almost a vague suggestion that every building which was simply banal, everyday, ordinary or conservative should in some ways be seen at best as a disappointing concession to unimaginative petty bourgeois philistinism, or at worst as another stumble on the steep path towards the National Socialist catastrophe.

Crucially for architectural historians, Munich's buildings, like the overwhelming majority of buildings in Germany – and, in fact, everywhere across the western world – were not Modernist 'with a capital M', for reasons this book will discuss. They were, however, modern, in Peukert's terms: industrialised, rational, technological, bureaucratic, urbanised, capitalist. Currently, a vast literature discusses the relatively small amount of Modernist building during this period. Conversely, a relatively small literature discusses the overwhelmingly mundane nature of almost all building form in historical context – be that the vast swathes of Tudorbethan housing in Britain, through the conventional tenements built by the Office d'Habitations à Bon Marché in Paris, to the blocks of flats built with pitched roofs in Germany. This book begins to address this deficit, not just by 'de-exceptionalising' Germany in the early twentieth century, but by de-canonising discussion of architecture and re-focusing on the types and ideologies of building which overwhelmingly dominated the social and spatial organisation of cities.

Historicising Germany, historicising buildings

While this book is primarily concerned with cities, spaces and modernity, discussing these has an interesting by-product. By focusing on cities and space, this book thereby makes an indirect argument about German history in general – the ways Germany is characterised in international comparison, and the way Berlin functions as a (misplaced) yardstick for assessing German culture in its own terms.

All too frequently, modern German historical enquiry addresses one particular singularity: National Socialism, or sometimes the Holocaust. This book offers a narrative of German history in which the National Socialist catastrophe is not the end-point, but exists only as an occasional 'structuring silence'. While almost all historians now clamour to assert their rejection of the idea that Germany had a 'unique path' into modernity, a *Sonderweg* which led so catastrophically to the Final Solution, the quantity of work on the period 1930–45 dwarfs that on the years before it.[22] The meaning of modernity for Germany continues to play a significant role in historical enquiry. For when historians approach the culture of German-speaking Europe in the hundred years before 1933 they are frequently tempted to detect a maladjustment to modernity which led to a terrible distortion of humane values. Since the 1980s, most historians have formally disavowed the persistent exceptionalisation of Germany associated with the '*Sonderweg* thesis', and yet still the question of German-speaking Europe's approach to modernity is a live one. Even when scholars have clearly asserted, as Thomas Rohkrämer has, and as Jeffrey Herf suggested before him, that in fact there was a widespread affection for modernity across the political spectrum in Germany, it is almost 'naturally' tied into the major end-point of much German history – Nazism. Both Rohkrämer and Herf link this friendliness to modernity to trying to explain National Socialism.[23] All roads of historical investigation combining culture, modernity and Germany, it seems, must lead to National Socialism. Germany's modernity and anti-modernity have both been used to explain it. Inasmuch as this is a specifically German history book (rather than a history of cities, space, or culture), its goal is not to dismiss or downplay the radical opposition to liberal humanism in German-speaking Europe, nor to underestimate the catastrophic results of how that opposition eventually came to express itself. The book's aim is to posit a Germany in the early twentieth century which can be examined un-teleologically – from its starting points, not its end-point. Echoing an eminent German historian, Thomas Nipperdey, I would argue that:

> The historian and his [*sic*] readers must give back to the past what it once had, what every period has, our own included: namely, an open future.[24]

Examining the symbolic and cultural life of the metropolis in this period in Germany allows real light to be thrown on this issue, because almost all contemporaries agreed that the city and its bureaucrats were key producers of modernity. Scholars in history, sociology, art history and cultural studies have concurred – the city stands at the heart of everything it means to be modern. Therefore, if we turn to German cities, and the ways they were described, related to as cultural objects, invested in, and manipulated, we shall be able to judge not just what the peripheral extremes of German-speaking cultural life felt about them. We shall be able instead to produce a meaningful historical perspective on what urban modernity meant to mainstream, educated, bourgeois Germany around the turn of the twentieth century. Crucially, we shall be able to recapture the ambivalence and proportion within which contemporary discourse framed discussion of the city.

Furthermore, there has been a second distortion in some German historiography, which has compounded the problems caused by the exceptionalisation of Germany in the international context, and that is the normalisation of Berlin in the German context. Berlin has figured prominently in scholarship on understanding German modernity, especially in the 1920s. In some ways this is fair – it was, after all, the capital. But it was not an uncontested capital in Germany. It certainly did not lead the way in manufacturing or labour politics, dominated by the Ruhr cities and Saxony; it was not the dominant commercial or bourgeois city, an honour which it shared with Hamburg, Bremen, Frankfurt and Munich. It was not the undisputed cultural capital of Germany, in any of the senses of the word 'culture'. It was not even, in many respects, the political capital of Germany, in the way that Paris was of France, because not only did other cities inside the Reich compete for status as the 'residence' of (albeit lesser) kings and governments, but Vienna, too, was an alternative pole to Berlin around which much in contemporary German-speaking life in Europe revolved. But Berlin does not represent 'Germany', just as claiming to discuss 'Germany' does not even begin to comprehend the diversities and contradictions of the national construct. Berlin has, however, proved a useful source of 'ethereal, sparky, edgy' narratives for the cultural historian – and emblematic works from the time like Walter Benjamin's *Arcades Project*, and the 'golden age before the catastrophe' narrative have reinforced that.

However, to understand the policies, practices and discourses of, say, medicine or theatre or journalism or education or healthcare or social security or housing or policing in Germany before 1918, a local focus is absolutely imperative; after 1918, it is only slightly less so.[25] Lastly, in common with most modern states before the 1930s, national governments intervened very little in the lives of their citizens relative to the increasingly vigorous intrusions of city governments. Thus when historians focus on the Reich, they over-privilege the significance of Reich politics. As Ben Lieberman found when he investigated local authority finance, as George Steinmetz showed when looking at varying urban welfare systems and as Anthony McElligott demonstrated with urban politics in general, to assume a coherent German polity pursuing coherent German policies is to overlook the fundamental diversity of pre-Second World War states.[26] In allowing Berlin to stand for Germany, an impression is created of a centralised culture, economy and polity which simply did not exist. Thus, this book looks for an urban German modernity outside Berlin, by focusing on a city which was German, but not Prussian; Catholic, but not Austrian. To focus on Munich is therefore to focus on the intersection of several dominant tropes in German history, and this makes the case study more, not less, relevant.

While much work in German history instinctively takes this localised approach, when it comes to discussing urban modernity, Berlin dominates.[27] Berlin has a totemic status in scholarship on modernity. In part, this is perhaps legitimate, as contemporaries often used 'Berlin' as a convenient shorthand for urban modernity.[28] But, more recently, scholars have accepted a specifically 'Berliner' modernity to stand for both urban modernity and Germany as a whole, often implicitly accepting the seductive idea of a 'golden era' of expressivity and freedom, pointing to a legitimate German modernity 'before the deluge'.[29]

This study will therefore shift the focus of investigation elsewhere; in particular, to Munich, which was a fairly typical large city in German-speaking Europe in this period. With a population of roughly 500,000 in 1900 and 750,000 in 1930, it was similar in size to the Manchester–Salford conurbation. It was not the same as Vienna or Berlin on the one hand, or identical to Hamburg, Essen, Leipzig, Cologne, Düsseldorf or Chemnitz on the other – but all of them had much in common, and their expert and political élites shared much in their understandings of the world. As recent research in 'discourse' and 'governmentality' has demonstrated, in modern systems experts, managers, governors, planners, scholars and other allied personnel behave remarkably homogeneously, operating to a distinctively 'modern' set of logics.[30] Equally, the whole point about modernity and 'the' city is that it addresses the universal nature and features of urban modernity. While the historian should certainly respect the particularities of specific times and places, the urban historian cannot help but be impressed by what is common to all (or at least, most) urban experience at a given time.

Structure of the book

The book addresses three major themes in contemporary historical debate: the historicisation of modernity; the role of space in organising, ordering, producing and reproducing society; and the writing of German history. The first half of the book (Chapters 1 and 2) focuses mostly on the ways the city was constructed intellectually by the bureaucrats and governors trying to administer it: the emotional and psychological features of urban life and space, positive and negative, which contemporaries chose to highlight when formulating their policies on urban design and management. The second half of the book (Chapters 3 and 4) focuses more specifically on the built environment as a material artefact, and the ways contemporaries used it (or failed to use it) to regulate social relationships and implement social policy.

Chapter 1 investigates the central issue of cultural criticisms of the city. Under the rubric '*Großstadtangst*' – or 'anxiety about the metropolis' – it tackles German critiques of urban modernity. It begins by examining two poles of contemporary debate, *Großstadt* (or 'metropolis') and '*Heimat*' (or 'homeland'), because much discussion situated itself on the continuum between the two. It goes on to explore how contemporaries sought to reconcile the psychic 'distress' of the big city with the goal of emotional contentment with architecture, stressing the reconciliatory potential of building projects for contemporaries. It then turns to one of the dominant methods in which the German expert and governing class engaged the public with their ideas on modernity, reform and urban life: through their design and management of exhibitions. Attendance at these spectacles was a hugely popular leisure pastime in Germany, and across the West. The focus here is on two exhibitions in Munich, one in 1908, celebrating the city's 750th anniversary, and the other twenty years later, on the theme of 'Home and Technology'. The final part of Chapter 1 addresses contemporaries' 'action plans' as responses to the problems of modernity, and characterises these actions as themselves distinctly modern. While modernity may have stimulated the anxiety, modernity would also be the solution. It focuses on the paradigms of planning developed to respond to less appealing aspects of urban modernity – and in particular, on the writings of a hugely influential thinker on urban design and urban space, Camillo Sitte. Sitte's ideas were first published in the 1880s, but his conclusions influenced urban design right through the period in question, and the discussion of planning paradigms in the 1920s tried to address many of the issues he raised. In particular, the Weimar Republic's planners developed housing design solutions to address anxieties about the atomisation of urban society and, conversely, the clumping together of urbanites into indistinguishable human 'lumps' – two of the distinctive features of contemporaries' assessments of modern social order.

Chapter 2 aims to challenge the general picture of turn-of-the-century German (or, in fact, Western) culture as being anti-urban and anxious. It explores contemporary experts' and governors' joy in the city, under the title *'Großstadtfreude'* – the celebratory instincts which metropolitan life aroused in them. It begins by looking at the ways that urban governors and experts envisioned a world ordered around a humane, modern, successful network of metropoles, and set about eagerly participating in modern, urban governmental projects and systems. The focus here is on how experts and governors began to be aware of the universal, rather than local, nature of the ambitions which underpinned their activities, understanding that they were part of a community of big cities, and how they explored and assembled this community. It then goes on to examine a set of debates about how the city of Munich – an old royal capital city – should define itself with regard to the new industrial world on the one hand, and to the rural kingdom/state which surrounded it on the other. In particular, attitudes towards a rural other show not a romantic view of the countryside, but a contemptuous one, in which the un-urban was seen as redundant, pointless and in some ways peculiarly 'empty'. It shows the changing ways that the frontier between city and country was managed, and the growth of a sort of 'colonial' mentality, in which urban experts increasingly sought to over-run and 'civilise' the land. The chapter concludes by showing how technocratic urban infrastructures of electricity, gas and planning sought to make themselves more present and purposeful by manipulating the cityscape, by transforming a mediaeval town centre oriented towards churches to one dominated by the rational institutions of modern social order, governance and service provision.

Chapter 3 leaves the macro-level of the city as a whole and turns to interior space, focusing on what Lefebvre calls 'representational space', exploring how users and producers of interior spaces infused them with meaning and significance. It opens with a discussion of how experts hoped to produce a compliant, contented citizenry, fully 'at home' in the helping projects of the modern state (like health, policing and education). It examines how this desire to produce both health and compliance influenced the ways the interior spaces of institutions such as hospitals, care homes for the elderly and orphanages were developed. The second half of the chapter focuses on one 'representational space' in detail: the kitchen, with all its heavy ideological baggage. It excavates an encounter between 'representational space' – the value-laden world of the private kitchen, the 'home and hearth' – and 'representations *of* space', as planners and politicians struggled to produce designs which could coercively reform the individual woman in the ways they hoped, while still retaining enough of the essential values of 'kitchen-ness' to be recognisably part of Germans' understandings of 'home'.

Chapter 4 expands the theme of encounter between 'representational space' and 'representations of space' into a discussion of the production of housing. Experts, designers and planners in the late nineteenth and early twentieth centuries struggled to produce a formal representational system which could both address coherent, stable ideological habits of spatial practice (namely, the conventions underpinning the building of homes), while also adapting to new political imperatives to produce ever greater amounts of housing for ever lower costs. The state's ambition to produce a healthy population which invested the state with legitimacy was severely hampered by the lack of plausible design options for describing and producing the space of the home. This meant that the spatial practices which underpinned poorer people's housing had to be defined for the very first time by experts. Then they had to formulate a set of solutions and responses – and, finally, they had to apply them. This issue of finding a representative language to first describe the spaces of the home, then reproduce them, was not a marginal issue in the early twentieth century – either in Germany, or anywhere else. Contemporaries were not slow to realise that poor housing in big cities was intimately related to many of the things which distressed them most, ranging from socialism and unruly women, through disease and incest, all the way to the collapse in political stability and order in the period after 1918. Thus the problems of how to design housing were in no wise peripheral to the themes which feature in more conventional histories of Germany of this period, such as political violence and social change. It was in these attempts to define representations of space that an entire class of experts engaged most vigorously in an attempt to produce an ordered, calm, clean, happy environment which would engender a citizenry which shared similar qualities – a citizenry which would be as successfully and comfortably modern as they were.

Notes

1 Lyrics by Max Kolpe, music by Franz Wachsmann, written some time between 1928 and 1930. Dietrich began singing the song c. 1930, and had her hit with it in 1933.
2 Nancy Stieber, *Housing Design and Society in Amsterdam: Reconfiguring Urban Order and Identity, 1900–1920* (Chicago, 1998).
3 Zygmunt Bauman, *Modernity and the Holocaust* (Cambridge, 1989); Bruno Latour, *We Have Never Been Modern* (London, 1993); Detlev

Peukert, 'Das Janusgesicht der Moderne', in *Max Webers Diagnose der Moderne* (Göttingen, 1989), pp. 55–69; *The Weimar Republic: The Crisis of Classical Modernity* (London, 1991); 'The Genesis of the "Final Solution" from the Spirit of Science', in *Re-Evaluating the Third Reich*, eds. Thomas Childers and Jane Caplan (London, 1993), pp. 234–252.

4 Charles Baudelaire, *The Painter of Modern Life and Other Essays* (London, 1995); Marshall Berman, *All that is Solid Melts into Air: The Experience of Modernity* (London, 1982); Walter Benjamin, 'On Some Motifs in Baudelaire', in *Illuminations* (London, 1970), pp. 152–196; *The Arcades Project* (London, 1999); Georg Simmel, 'The Metropolis and Mental Life', in *Simmel on Culture*, eds. David Frisby and Mike Featherstone (London, 1997), pp. 174–185; Guy Debord, *The Society of the Spectacle* (London, 1992 [Paris, 1967]); Matei Calinescu, *Five Faces of Modernity: Modernism, Avant-Garde, Decadence, Kitsch, Postmodernism* (Durham, NC, 1987).

5 Debord, *The Society of the Spectacle*, p. 1.

6 Jean Baudrillard, 'Simulacra and Simulations', in Jean Baudrillard, *Selected Writings*, ed. Mark Poster (Stanford, CA, 1988), pp. 166–184.

7 Berman, *All that is Solid*, p. 91.

8 Joachim Radkau, *Das Zeitalter der Nervösität: Deutschland zwischen Bismarck und Hitler* (Munich, 2000), pp. 204–265.

9 Anthony Vidler, 'Agoraphobia: Psychopathologies of Urban Space', in *Warped Space: Art, Architecture and Anxiety in Modern Culture*, ed. Anthony Vidler (London, 2001), pp. 25–50 (pp. 25–26).

10 For example, Patrick Joyce, *The Rule of Freedom: Liberalism and the Modern City* (London, 2003).

11 Peukert, *The Weimar Republic*, pp. 81–82.

12 Peukert, *The Weimar Republic*, p. 81.

13 First English edn. trans. Donald Nicholson-Smith (Oxford, 1991 [Paris, 1974]).

14 Lefebvre, *The Production of Space*, p. 33.

15 For example, some of the essays in Alan Mayne and Tim Murray (eds.), *The Archaeology of Urban Landscapes: Explorations in Slumland* (Cambridge, 2001) or Jennifer Robinson, *The Power of Apartheid: State, Power and Space in South African Cities* (Oxford, 1995).

16 Such as Sarah Williams Goldhagen and Réjean Legault, *Anxious Modernisms: Experimentation in Postwar Architectural Culture* (London, 2000), Margaret Kentgens-Craig, *The Bauhaus and America: First Contacts, 1919–1936* (Cambridge, MA, 2001) or Eric Mumford, *The CIAM Discourse on Urbanism, 1928–1960* (Cambridge, MA, 2000).

17 For example, William Whyte's attempt to theorise building largely confines himself to a discussion of buildings' appearances, qualified by Hegel's reminder that buildings fail to be pure art because they have function. William Whyte, 'How do Buildings Mean? Some Issues of

Interpretation in the History of Architecture', *History and Theory* 45 (2006), pp. 153–177. Much more interesting are the possibilities opened up by Thomas Gieryn in 'What Buildings Do', *Theory and Society* 31 (2002), pp. 35–74.
18 Panayotis Tournikiotis, *The Historiography of Modern Architecture* (Cambridge, MA, 2001).
19 Mitchell Schwarzer, 'History and Theory in Architectural Journals: Assembling Oppositions', *Journal of the Society of Architectural Historians* 3 (1999), pp. 342–348.
20 Mari Hvattum and Christian Hermansen (eds.), *Tracing Modernity: Manifestations of the Modern in Architecture and the City* (London, 2004).
21 Paul Betts, *The Authority of Everyday Objects: A Cultural History of West German Industrial Design* (Berkeley, CA, 2004).
22 For an introduction to the problems this dominant trend poses, see Jürgen Kocka, 'Asymmetrical Historical Comparison: The Case of the German *Sonderweg*', *History and Theory* 1 (1999), pp. 40–50.
23 Thomas Rohkrämer, 'Antimodernism, Reactionary Modernism and National Socialism: Technocratic Tendencies in Germany, 1890–1945', *Contemporary European History* 1 (1999), pp. 29–50; *Eine andere Moderne? Zivilisationskritik, Natur und Technik in Deutschland 1880–1933* (Paderborn, 1999); Jeffrey Herf, *Reactionary Modernism: Technology, Culture and Politics in Weimar and the Third Reich* (Cambridge, 1984). Much work has continued to interrogate German modernity with one eye on the *NS-Zeit*: see Paul Betts' review article, 'The New Fascination with Fascism: The Case of Nazi Modernism', *Journal of Contemporary History* 4 (2002), pp. 541–558 and Peter Fritzsche's discussion, 'Nazi Modern', *Modernism/Modernity* 1 (1996), pp. 1–22.
24 Thomas Nipperdey, *Deutsche Geschichte 1866–1918, Band I: Machtstaat vor der Demokratie* (Munich, 1992) cited in Richard Evans, *Rereading German History, 1800–1996: From Unification to Reunification* (London, 1997), p. 24.
25 To explore the contradictions between being a metropolis (*Großstadt*) and being 'metropolitan' in the way Paris or London has been, see Alfred Zimm, 'Berlin als Metropole: Anspruch, Wirklichkeit, Tendenzen', *Beiträge zur Geschichte der Arbeiterbewegung* 3 (1992), pp. 3–15; Detlef Briesen, 'Berlin – Die überschätzte Metropole: Über das system deutscher Hauptstädte zwischen 1850 und 1940', in Gerhard Brunn and Jürgen Reulecke (eds.), *Metropolis Berlin : Berlin im Vergleich europäischer Hauptstädte, 1871–1939* (Bonn, 1992), pp. 39–78.
26 Ben Lieberman, *From Recovery to Catastrophe: Municipal Stabilisation and Political Crisis in Weimar Germany* (Oxford, 1998); George Steinmetz, *Regulating the Social: The Welfare State and Local Politics in Imperial Germany* (London, 1993); Anthony McElligott, *Contested*

City: *Municipal Politics and the Rise of Nazism in Altona, 1917–1937* (Ann Arbor, MI, 1998).

27 A good recent example would be Jennifer Jenkins, *Provincial Modernity: Local Culture and Liberal Politics in Fin-de-Siècle Hamburg* (Ithaca, NY, 2003).

28 Ralf Thies and Dietmar Jazbinsek, 'Berlin – das europäische Chicago: Über ein Leitmotiv der Amerikanisierungsdebatte zu Beginn des 20. Jahrhunderts', in Clemens Zimmermann and Jürgen Reulecke, *Die Stadt als Moloch? Das Land als Kraftquell? Wahrnehmungen und Wirkungen der Großstädte um 1900* (Basel, 1999), pp. 53–94.

29 Otto Friedrich, *Before the Deluge: A Portrait of Berlin in the 1920s* (New York, 1995). See, for example, the essays in Katharina von Ankum (ed.), *Women in the Metropolis: Gender and Modernity in Weimar Culture* (London, 1997); Janet Ward, *Weimar Surfaces: Urban Visual Culture in 1920s Germany* (London, 2001); Maria Tatar, *Lustmord: Sexual Murder in Weimar Germany* (London, 1995); Peter Fritzsche, *Reading Berlin 1900* (London, 1996); Peter Jelavich, *Berlin Cabaret* (London, 1996).

30 For example, see Graham Burchell, Colin Gordon and Peter Miller (eds.), *The Foucault Effect: Studies in Governmentality* (London, 1991); Dean Mitchell, *Governmentality: Power and Rule in Modern Society* (London, 1999); Timothy Mitchell, *Rule of Experts: Egypt, Technopolitics, Modernity* (Berkeley, CA, 2002).

1

Großstadtangst: disorder and discomfort in the metropolis

The phenomenon of urbanisation challenged a sense of belonging to place because urban populations were either migrant, or the product of that migration, and they existed in a landscape novel in its forms, functions and scale. In early twentieth-century Germany, as elsewhere, these changes caused extensive comment, and proved to be the focus of much discussion – on both a technical level and a more emotional and spiritual one. Some saw the agglomeration of the city in the light of an economic dynamic and a growth in personal freedom. Others saw in it a menace, in which (to use a very loose analogy) a sort of inversion of a Newtonian law took place: the closer human beings came to each other, the greater the mass of humans living together, the weaker the attraction and bonds between them were. The urban individual had become separated from his or her political system, from his or her culture and from other individuals. Moral and physical disease was the result. Under the heading *Großstadtangst* – 'anxiety about the metropolis' – I want to posit some ways in which these problems could be translated into, and also read from, the material fabric of the urban environment in early twentieth-century Germany. This process of translation reflects the traffic between the 'ordered' and 'disordered' models of modernity, as the archetypal 'orderers' (here, bureaucratic planners) attempted to relate themselves and their work to the *disordered* aspects of modernisation.

The word *Großstadtangst* is in some ways slightly uncomfortable because it is not a German word, and nor do the two halves of it sit together particularly easily as a compound. Yet it describes a situation very well, without aligning itself with some of the better-known (and more spectacular) German critiques of modernity, which more generally fall under the banner of *Großstadtfeindlichkeit* – hostility towards the metropolis. The situation which needs to be outlined in the case of Germany is significant, because it allows a revision of models suggested by the extremist authors from this period that have so often formed the focus of the study of late nineteenth-century German 'thought' (as if a society or a time can possess a coherent 'thought') – authors like Langbehn, Lagarde, Spengler, Nietzsche and Chamberlain. This move away from the 'star turns' of German 'cultural pessimism' leads to a more nuanced position, reflected by the mainstream of German culture. George Mosse's and Fritz Stern's classic studies of the phenomenon of 'cultural pessimism' are of immense value, but are in need of constant revision as the historiographical imperative to provide an aetiology for Nazism diminishes.[1] Assumed binary opposites such as 'cultural pessimism' and 'faith in progress' such as those suggested by Arthur Herman in his popular study designed to discredit 'declinism',[2] or by Stern in his 1961 classic or by Walter Laqueur in his 1996 article on the *fin-de-siècle* mentality,[3] do not help in identifying the real and highly subtle picture of *Großstadtkritik* – critical discussion of the metropolis – within German society. They do not tackle the teleological underpinnings of German historiography, moving away from regarding Germany as a 'special case' because of events which took place thirty or forty years later. British planners are held up as a paradigm of liberal, humanistic social reform (albeit with occasional asides about their controlling ambitions), while German ones are chastised for being racist.[4] While many German town planners certainly *were* racist, so were their British counterparts. Spotting racialised discourse in German expert thought and writing in the early twentieth century is like shooting fish in a barrel; but so it is in French, British and American writing and practice. Models of selective breeding and racial decline were present in Ebenezer Howard's writings and also in much of the 'heroic', 'liberal' Modernism of 1920s *Neue Sachlichkeit*.[5] Indeed, ideas about an ideal England, and a mystical attachment to the soil, were of central importance to much early twentieth-century British discussions of cities, citizens and urban geography.[6]

As Charles Masterman, a prominent British Liberal politician, social reformer and academic, wrote in a hugely influential volume on urban problems in Britain and threats to the British Empire at the turn of the last century: 'The England of the past has been an England of reserved, silent men, dispersed small towns, villages and country homes.' However, new cities, he argued, were soaking up the healthy rural populations to sustain themselves, such that: 'the second generation of the immigrants has been reared in the courts and crowded ways of the great metropolis, with cramped physical accessories, hot fretful life . . . . The problem of the coming years is just the problem of the New Town type; upon their development and action depend the future progress of the Anglo-Saxon Race', corrupted by 'twice-breathed air' and 'thirty years of school education.'[7] Here he characterises urban life as 'fretful', echoing the nerves and anxiety discussed in Chapter 1; he attacks universal education, a central feature of the modern state's plans to 'improve' its citizens. Indeed, Volker Welter shows that biological metaphors underpinned much British town planning, and Patrick Geddes, one of the most influential planning theorists, had his academic training in biology.[8] Such words, such sentiments, in German mouths have been given a metanarrative significance which, when in British ones, they do not have. Only a teleological insistence on a fundamental fissure in the geological make-up of German responses to modernity can justify this.

This chapter will focus on the difficulties which the modern metropolis posed the élites of knowledge and politics in Germany, but develop the idea that it did not cause panic. While Germans, like their counterparts in all Western societies, did develop a *Großstadtkritik* there was no generalised pessimistic response. These men (and they were almost all men) never lost their faith in their ability to intervene 'modernistically' in the difficulties which they identified in modernity. They retained the belief that, although modern social, economic and cultural phenomena – made conspicuous and thrown into sharp relief by their intersection in the metropolis – were distressing in some ways, the distress could be relieved. More importantly, this relief was not to be cured by any sort of flight into a cultural, pre-modern nostalgia for authentic *Gemeinschaft* (community), and a rejection of a desolate *Gesellschaft* (society). Instead, thoroughly modern means were advocated to retrieve what it was thought had been lost – personality, character and warmth. This chapter approaches these themes using the writings of Munich's expert élites as a case study, in order to focus on the human, individual aspect of this process, and provide a fuller picture of the ways the city could excite contemporaries.

In some of its aspects, this *Angst* proved exceptionally difficult to name, but it had a constellation of features, all of which were regarded as distinctive characteristics of life in the big city. These would typically range from the relatively culturally constructed alienation, atomisation, sensory over-stimulation, loneliness, spiritual collapse, or subsumation into the mass, to more formal 'medical' categories such as agoraphobia, neurasthenia or kleptomania. For those involved in the nascent discipline of town planning, it seems that *Angst* could be relieved in two ways. First, it could be brought under control by developing interpretative or ideological methods to apply to describing the metropolis which made the city less nervousness-inducing, strange and chaotic by rendering it manageable and 'familiar' to the experts themselves. Put simply, the more one knows about something, the less one might fear it. The second method lay in adopting specific strategies for the management of the appearance and arrangement of the material metropolis to regulate more closely the citizen's own experience. Contemporaries had a strong faith in environmental determinism, and so to recast, re-explain or reform the life-worlds and action-spaces of urbanites would be to reach into their psyches and reorder them.

The first part of the chapter focuses on the nature of the *Angst* which the city induced in intellectuals and experts. It then goes on to investigate the ways the city could be described and narrated to make it *seem* less threatening – without necessarily reconfiguring urban space at all. One ideological reformulation which could render the metropolis unthreatening without requiring a massive challenge to it as an irreversible inevitability of modern life was the conceptual transformation of the metropolis into a *Heimat*, a central concept for describing place in early twentieth-century Germany. This part of the chapter considers the modernity (or otherwise) of *Heimat* discourse, before going on to examine its use by architects and city administrators. *Heimat* is a very complex concept, or constellation of concepts, in German, to which there is no direct analogy in English and which will require some substantial explanation. The second part of the chapter addresses how German governors and experts resolved to teach Germans how to interpret their cities and the technological, social and spatial principles around which they were organised. They did this by entering into the world of exhibitions, in which a perfectly structured environment could be created for the public to experience – part didactic, part leisured. In the exhibition park, planners, designers, politicians, industrialists and clubs and associations could design a world which both critiqued the present and marketed a future. In short, they could enter into a dialogue with the people they hoped to reform – and make money out of it. The final part of the chapter focuses on how this anxiety was linked to the application of a very modern set of practices – *Städtebau*, or 'town planning' – with which to address it. So, while modernity could produce anxiety, explicitly modern solutions were sought to resolve it.

The culture of anxiety

This distress at seeing the problems of the metropolis – its disease, squalor, despair, poverty and potential for political, sexual and gender disorder – was felt in an intellectual sense by governors and experts across the Reich (and beyond). As already mentioned, Anthony Vidler argues that, in the late nineteenth century: 'Metropolis rapidly became the privileged territory of a host of diseases attributed directly to its spatial conditions, diseases that took their place with in the general epistemology of Beard's neurasthenia and Charcot's hysteria, but with a special relationship to their supposed physical causes.'[9] Frequently, the élites who could get their ideas printed and discussed generalised this distress, and extended it to a very real, day-to-day unease which they attributed to the citizens of the town; it was so generalised as to qualify for the category of *Angst*. They translated physical ills into psychic distress and environmental degradation into mental disease. This fed into, and in turn fed from, an obsession with 'nervousness' identified in some of the key texts used in recent discussions of modernity, most notably Simmel's essay, 'The Metropolis and Mental Life'.[10] Simmel's essay forms a cornerstone of much current discussion of the metropolis, and crops up on countless reading lists.[11] Written in 1903, though not widely read at the time, it shows a middle-class German intellectual trying to integrate the new academic disciplines of psychology, economics and sociology into a more general reflection on urban life.[12]

On the positive side of the metropolis, Simmel described the unparalleled freedoms which urban life offered. In the city, one could be, and associate with, whoever one wanted. However, this freedom was paradoxical in nature, for while one could infinitely reinvent and re-present oneself, and journey to discover new possibilities of self-expression in the diverse subcultures of the modern metropolis, the urbanite was also uniquely constrained. This was because the modern city produced new forms of dependence on a social infrastructure in which the individual played no social part – on water providers, building and food hygiene inspectors, supply chains of goods and services simply irrelevant in pre-modern or small-town existence. On the down side, the city could be a lonely place. It engendered a high level of sensory stimulation, with its deafening clatter of steel-rimmed wheels on cobbled streets, glaring colours of advertising hoardings, the stench of human and animal excrement, smoke and pollution. This sensory (over-)stimulation caused, according to Simmel, the human brain to filter out most sensations, such that the urbanite became blasé and detached. Thus Simmel's work was a piece of *Großstadtkritik* in the best sense of the word 'critique'; it was fair, balanced, and incisive – it was not polemical. In this, it was typical of much contemporary discussion of the city.[13]

This use of material urban problems to diagnose the human psyche was widespread. Joachim Radkau's work interprets the decades either side of the turn of the century as a 'nervous epoch' for Germany, obsessed with neurasthenia, hysteria, worry, nerves, panic, agoraphobia, insanity and *Angst*, particularly in relation to the nascent discipline of psychology.[14] Across Germany (and the wider West), there emerged a general preoccupation with nerves, anxiety and stress – and concomitantly, a set of strategies was devised by doctors and administrators to describe and manage it. Such discussions pervaded not just German-speaking culture, but western culture as a whole. Similar discourses can be found in Britain, the USA and France, and many such discourses drew a connecting line between modernisation and individual nervous distress.[15] This line almost always, at some point, ran through the city – whether it be the moral insanity of the streetwalking prostitute, the impulsiveness of the kleptomaniac in department stores, or the agoraphobia 'discovered' in people (overwhelmingly women) when experiencing urban public spaces. As will be discussed below, such anxieties about 'nerves' drove much urban governance, and the intention was that the planner might acquire a similar professional status, moral authority and curative capacity with the 'nerves' of modern urban life as the medical doctor. But, first, planners had to find a vocabulary to describe the 'place' of the city as non-threatening, and central to this was the German concept of *Heimat*.

Metropolis as *Heimat*

Heimat is a word of enormous complexity in German. It is difficult to define satisfactorily, without wanting to return to it to refine the definition, to add something or take something away. At its most basic level, it means 'emotional homeland', the geographical place in which one might see one's character reflected, the landscape to which one might look for one's own spatial and cultural conditioning. Furthermore, it is deeply preoccupied with ideas of organic, often transcendental, 'connectivity' and 'belonging', and is intimately bound up with a model of the past as a rich seam to be mined. For urban planners and governors to discuss *Heimat* was a method of engaging in *Großstadtkritik* which discussed the city in terms of loneliness and estrangement: estrangement from nature, estrangement from the past and estrangement from the warm, personal relationships with other human beings which it was assumed characterised the pre-modern world. As Heynen has argued: '*Heimat* is seen as the place where utopia is achieved, the homeland where human beings and the world are reconciled and where the dream of a better life is finally realised. This *Heimat* does not yet exist – nobody dwells there – but as children, we have all had a glimpse of it: an existence without deprivation, without alienation, and without appropriation.'[16]

Heimat is an 'authentic' place, on some levels, and in its own discourse regards itself as a distinctively 'authentic' environment, contrasted with the artificial aspects of the modern city. And yet in practice, *Heimat* has often been deeply *in*authentic – as anyone who has watched the *Heimat* television programmes which dominate German Saturday-night schedules will confirm, with their folk dress, plaited wigs and synthesiser songs about falling in love in the spinneys/copses/valleys/mountains of whichever German region has the honour of hosting that week's edition.[17] This issue of nostalgia and authenticity is crucial to a discussion of the project of making the urban environment into a *Heimat*, an emotional homeland, and the idea of forming a distinctively urban, distinctively German antipathy to modernity. One of the most dominant themes in discussions of the city and modernity since the mid-nineteenth century has been that the city is alienated, lonely and disconnected and that citizens lack rootedness and belonging. Seen like this, the city was not *Heimat* – and this was a problem for contemporaries. They suggested that *Heimatlosigkeit* – the lack of *Heimat* – led to a variety of problems, such as socialism, criminality and such like. This meant that if a *Heimat* could be created in the city, such problems would be reduced. For example, Munich's Mayor Borscht outlined the plan he had for the municipality's early venture into housing provision in 1900:

> We intend that through safer and more comfortable housing, especially among the growing youth of this city, the feeling for the *Heimat* will be won back and strengthened, and that thereby the growing youth criminality problems will be most effectively tackled.[18]

In some way the urban environment would have to become organic; it would have to address the past in some way; it should acquire the trappings of historical authenticity if this enormous faith in environmental determinism could be translated into action.

The *Kitsch*, so-called 'backward-looking' aspect of the paraphernalia and trappings of *Heimat* discourse in German culture over the last 130 years is crucial. This is because its utterly inauthentic glances backwards to a past which never was are sometimes used to associate it with a certain *Volkstümlichkeit* – a para-racist folksiness – which, yet again, is assumed to feed into the 'catastrophist' narrative of German history, in which Germany and Germans could not reconcile themselves to modernity. It certainly does not belong there: Germans who pursued a discussion of the modern world through the metaphor of *Heimat* in the early twentieth century were sometimes conservative, but also often liberal progressives. Indeed, recent work on the *Heimat* movement has begun to argue more explicitly that discourse about nature, tradition, belonging and landscape had no special relationship with the political right. When discussing nature campaigners and their attempts to secure legislation in the Weimar Republic, Lekan has characterised their efforts as 'a middle ground of cautious technological optimism tempered by the desire to protect the aesthetic textures and ecological integrity of the landscape'.[19] Often the Heimat League members' desire to preserve landscapes and environments led them to a position which is now currently called 'environmentalism' – not at all associated with the right. Indeed, in 1998, the German Heimat League changed its name to the League for the Heimat and the Environment in Germany. As such, members were often viewed by contemporaries as being highly progressive. Indeed, in a collection of essays by leading scholars on the *Heimat* movement, the editor is forced to concede that: 'it is a remarkable outcome, that none of the authors in this collection can support the general accusation of anti-modernity.' This despite the title of her collection: *Antimodernismus und Reform* – anti-modernity and reform.[20] It is a habit that must be broken: to critique modernity is not to reject it.

And despite academics' own antipathies to the 'bad taste' of *Kitsch* (contrasted with the 'good taste' of the *avant garde*), there is nothing un- or anti-modern about *Kitsch*, about nostalgia, about false re-creations of tradition. In fact, they are supremely modern. '*Kitsch* is the contemporary form of the Gothic, Rococo, Baroque', wrote playwright Frank Wedekind in 1917.[21] One author on *Kitsch*, Matei Calinescu, argues that since the early nineteenth century intellectuals have been claiming that there has been a unique form of artistic and cultural decline – a corollary of which was the rise of the cult of artistic originality. Where Calinescu diverges from this connoiseurial tradition is that he does not attach value judgements to these critiques. Only possible after Romanticism, *Kitsch* is modern culture's commercialisation and commodification of the past; it is the rendering of great ideas into affordable knick-knacks, and functions as a critique of connoiseurial visions of taste. It is irredeemably bourgeois, based around particular forms of cultural reproduction and consumption.[22] In short, looking backwards in this way is distinctively modern, not anti-modern, and Calinescu is issuing a plea to look at the underlying actions and practices of nostalgia, not its superficial claims.

David Gross echoes this view in his discussions of 'tradition'. Only fundamentally modern societies can discuss 'tradition' or 'preservation', because only fundamentally modern societies need to. Premodern societies may well refer to the past for a variety of reasons (the English legal system is a good example of this), but tradition can be used to justify or explain or manage innovation only in a modern, un-traditional society. This is because in genuinely 'traditional' societies, 'tradition' is what one instinctively does, not what one used to do.[23] As Alon Confino, one of the leading authors in the burgeoning field of 'memory' in recent historiography, has commented:

> Germans like to think of the *Heimat* idea as unfathomable, mysterious, and, above all, peculiarly German. In fact, the *Heimat* idea was not an inherent attribute of the German nation, but came to appear as such after the 1880s . . . *Heimat* became immemorial because memory is short: an alleged timeless national memory, invented at the second half of the nineteenth century, for an alleged timeless nation, unified in 1871.[24]

According to Confino, *Heimat* is modern. It is a functional tool of a modern society, and his discussion of the ways Württembergers discussed their 'past' echoes that of Celia Applegate's investigation of the idea in the Palatinate, between the middle of the nineteenth and the middle of the twentieth centuries.[25] Both of these studies are clear about their rejection of the *Heimat* discourse as merely a symptom of an inevitable German historical course, or a distinctively German historical category. They acknowledge that *Heimat* discourse could be progressive or conservative – it was a 'language' or a 'code', which could be used in the exposition of any one of a variety of political, social or cultural positions.

It was as equally prevalent in the language and writings of *avant garde* modernists as among more conservative or progressive reformers. For example, Karl Scheffler, Modernist architect and author of *Architektur der Großstadt* ('Architecture of the Metropolis'), complained in the *avant garde* journal *Die Neue Rundschau*:

> To [urbanites] the places where they work or live are almost accidental; therefore, the city offers them no feelings of home [*nichts Heimatliches*],

nothing symbolic, and no morally elevating sense of community can take root in them.[26]

As Lees concludes, 'a conservative could not have said it better'. Another *avant garde* contemporary, a lawyer, hugely popular travel writer and pacifist, Armin Wegner, wrote a cycle of expressionist city poems between 1909 and 1913. In one, 'Song from the Streets of the City', he wrote:

There glows the sky up above the houses,
As over the peaks of distant mountains,
There reddens the cloud, leading, promising,
And for a moment the crowd stops and stands,
And the eyes of men search upwards in the pale sky,
Search upwards towards the red flame which burns in the slits between roofs,
As on the slopes of an icy mountain:
'Show us the path which leads out of these ravines,
Further than the gateway to this street,
The way to the land of children, the way to the *Heimat*,
The way to joy, to a breathing earth!'[27]

Heimat vocabulary could serve any position – modernist, *avant garde*, conservative, moderate. The rest of this poem, and Wegner's oeuvre, is a paean of praise and wonderment for the metropolis. And yet still it locates a world of childhood purity, of fundamental human wholesomeness and truth, in a place beyond the city. Thus, the yearning for *Heimat* could be *avant garde* and Expressionist, just as much as it could be nostalgic and reactionary.

Confino and Applegate both examine *Heimat* discourse primarily in the context of German nationalism and nation-building. Here, I want to discuss some of the other social and cultural positions that could be articulated through the *Heimat* vocabulary. This vocabulary came together as a distinctive corpus in institutional form in Germany around the turn of the century, in the Bund Heimatschutz – the League for the Protection of the *Heimat*. The institution (or, really, network of institutions, walking clubs, restoration projects, naturalists and lifestyle reformers) was a populist, not academic, response to industrialisation and urbanisation. It was one of the first movements to advocate systematic environmental protection and the preservation of natural landscapes, and man-made 'treasures', both rural and urban. As such, it emerged at a similar time, and often advocated similar 'progressive' policies to, for example, the National Trust in Britain, and the National Parks legislation in the USA.[28] Similar motives inspired the British state to extend the obligation to provide allotments to urban authorities in 1908,[29] and Patrick Geddes, perhaps the most influential planning theorist in the early twentieth century British Empire, placed the conservation of 'historic' town centres at the heart of his vision – and in doing so, created much of the Royal Mile in Edinburgh which is so central to that city's tourism 'industry'. *Heimat* was, in Applegate's view, a project about commercialising nature and commercialising the past – and as such, conforms to Calinescu's model of *Kitsch* as being about consumption.[30]

When not concerned with such worldly things as lifestyle reform and tourism, the concept of *Heimat* in German was predicated on an indefinable, but inescapable, profound emotional link between the individual and his or her environment. It was a way of locating identity and belonging in something as intangible, but less controversial, than more politicised categories such as 'class' or 'nation'. Instead of divisive issues of class, or religion, or gender, it proposed that Germans were bonded together through their origins in a specific place; all Germans came from somewhere, and this 'coming from somewhere' could bind them together. It was a spatialised form of identity.

While the *Heimat* idea turned diversity of origins into a source of unity and shared experience, this posed a problem for cities and city planners. Contemporary continental planning paradigms tended to model the city as one regulatory whole, with one centre, which should have one, coherent, visual identity – the final section of this chapter, on Central European planning paradigms, will discuss this. Whereas in Britain the polycentric city is quite normal, in continental Europe monocentric cities were more common. This meant that Central European metropoles were in a difficult situation, because they are rather homogeneous – streets were of universal widths, buildings of universal heights and dimensions, and European cities after the mid-nineteenth century were often, in their built forms, the product of the working-out of an algorithm. It is often impossible to distinguish between a street from the centre of Berlin, Vienna, Paris, Milan, or St Petersburg. Indeed, homogeneity was one of the main charges levelled at the 'baroque' model of city planning, based around geometric lines, axial arrangements and aesthetic consistency. August Endell, a fashionable designer and pioneer of Art Nouveau and expressionism, commented in 1908 on this. In his polemic, *Die Schönheit der Großstadt* (*The Beauty of the Metropolis*), he turned this critique on its head, while still persisting with a natural, landscape metaphor:

One can walk for hours through the new parts of Berlin, and indeed get the impression that one has made no headway at all. Everything appears uniform, despite the loud attempts to call one's attention, to stand out from one's neighbour. And yet even here, in the dreadful heaps of stone, beauty is alive. Here too, there is nature, landscape. The changing weather, the sun, the rain, the fog form remarkable beauty out of the hopeless ugliness.[31]

Homogeneous cities on this scale lacked the diversity to be 'places' as, crucially, they were inorganic in arrangement. Even when fêting their bizarre aesthetic appeal, contemporaries reached for metaphors of landscape and weather.

Thus, to give the citizen the experience of *Heimat* in the metropolis operated both to relieve the ideological and intellectual *Angst* felt by some urban governors and experts, and also (they felt) act as a restorative tonic for those citizens who perhaps had least stake in some of the possible economic advantages of life in the metropolis – the poor, disadvantaged children, orphans, the sick, the elderly in need of care. The ideology of *Heimat* would not suffice alone, though, and with this in mind experts, bureaucrats and governors promoted means which would allow them to control the shape and also the uses of the metropolis in a much more solid and real sense through town planning. Agoraphobia, loneliness and fear underpinned their actions. Challenging the fractured and disjointed nature of modern city design was, it was thought, a way of addressing the fractured nature of individual experience, of restoring wholeness to the human mind and soul. Expanding on Radkau's thesis, it is perhaps possible to identify a parallel between the references to fragmentation in the city and the distress felt when certain aspects of the self-fracture in mental illness; such nerve-related metaphors and ideas of psychiatric disorder were linked by leading planning theorists explicitly to the planning of the city, and others in urban government frequently made this connection.

Producing *Heimat*: strategy and tactics

City councils as institutions were compelled to address the issue of place by a desire and a responsibility to ensure the physical, spiritual and economic well-being of the citizens of the town. The scope of city governments' activities boomed in the final years of the nineteenth century, along with their populations, as urban governments had taken on myriad functions – welfare, education, housing, transport, energy provision, policing, water purification, food inspection, care of the old and young and so on. This had led cities – again, across the West – to be far less deadly than they once had been, although a new breed of social investigator in the last years of the nineteenth century found that for most of their inhabitants, they were still far from pleasant.

If one turns to a more specific case study, one finds that one of the founders of the Bund Heimatschutz was Hans Grässel, an energetic figure in the Munich Municipal Building Office. He was the city's most prolific and popular architect in the first twenty years of the last century, and will serve as the main example in this section. Broadly representative of many of these trends before the First World War might be the Implerstraße school, built by Grässel between 1910 and 1911. It represents the culmination of many strands of thinking about the role of the built environment by councillors, educationalists and architects. It was one of the schools of which Grässel himself was most proud and, coincidentally, is one of the very few schools in which the original interior decoration and room usage has survived renovation, war and educational reform. It was one of eleven schools designed by him between 1898 and 1914, and his contribution represents a third of the thirty-three new schools built in Munich in this period. Educationalists in Munich had devised a revolutionary educational programme for the city – one which would eventually become accepted across Germany. It focused on small-class teaching (35 instead of 70–100 children), and on practical, vocational training for boys and girls, instead of just teaching the 'liberal' educational curriculum, which emphasised knowledge for knowledge's sake. It added vocational education in subjects such as hairdressing, tailoring, car maintenance and technical drawing as an option for two years after 14, when most children in the West left school. This required a comprehensive building programme of schools, replete with smaller classrooms, and also workshops, shower rooms, delousing facilities, kitchens and sports halls – in fact, the modern school building. The package of school reconstruction and pedagogical reform was so momentous that in fact both became renowned throughout not just the Reich, but beyond. The Director of Schools the city appointed in 1895, Georg Kerschensteiner, and the architects hired for the city's comprehensive replanning project appointed at the same time (particularly Hans Grässel, Theodor Fischer, Robert Rehlen and Wilhelm Bertsch) achieved renown through both professional literature and speaking tours in Britain, France and the USA.[32]

Georg Simmel's essay, 'The Metropolis and Mental Life,' commented on precisely this sort of 'modern' project to intervene and structure the lives of the individual, and argued that:

the person resists being levelled down and worn out by a social–technological mechanism. An inquiry into the inner meaning of specifically modern life and its products, into the soul of the cultural body, so to speak, must seek to solve the equation which structures like the metropolis set up between the individual and the super-individual contents of life. Such an inquiry must answer the question of how the personality accommodates itself in the adjustments to external forces.[33]

The school would be just one of the 'social–technological mechanisms' of modern existence established to manage the relationship between 'the individual and the supra-individual contents of life' but, as Simmel noted, 'the person resists'. Indeed, Simmel, in the same essay, singled out rational state buildings as agents in this process, pointing out that:

> Here in buildings and educational institutions, in the wonders and comforts of space-conquering technology, in the formations of community life, and in the visible institutions of the state, is offered such an overwhelming fullness of crystallised and impersonalised spirit that the personality, so to speak, cannot maintain itself under its impact.[34]

While it is probable that Hans Grässel had never read – or even heard of – Simmel, and vice versa, this generalised concern with the levelling effects of the technologies of modern rule and the desire to overcome resistance to it was crucial to people trying to describe, understand and manipulate the metropolis.

The Implerstraße school lies in the heart of what was Munich's poorest, most industrial quarter, the Sendlinger Unterfeld. It stands between the central goods railway terminus, the southern power station, the municipal wholesale market and the municipal abattoir. This was unremittingly urban; precisely the sort of landscape characterised by poverty, industry and urban squalor which generated most fear and *Angst* in contemporary critiques. This was the environment which many wanted to transform into *Heimat*; by filling the void of good taste and wholesomeness, one need have no fear either of being sucked into it, or of what terrifying phenomena and tumults might come out of it. The municipality in this case seems to have believed it could do that architecturally by intervening in a discourse about nostalgia *and* modernity (not nostalgia *instead of* modernity).

The discourse involving nostalgia *and*, rather than *versus*, modernity, and the essentially moderate position of a city government like Munich's, can perhaps best be reflected by contrasting the exterior with the interior of the school. When contemporaries talked in terms of cultural–political or socio-economic criticism, modernity implied any of the following negative themes – haste, nervousness, alienation, unrootedness, impermanence, fashion, mass-production, fear, luxury, placelessness, meaninglessness, speed, shallowness, novelty, greed, mean-spiritedness, loneliness, exploitation – and several positive ones, such as education, freedom, wealth, choice, fun, pleasure, leisure. More could be added here, but these are key tropes culled from police chiefs' writings, Mayors' speeches, tourist guides, council debates, doctors' reports, educational programmes, newspaper articles and the like. Grässel, as were many others, was clear in aligning this sort of criticism with the metropolis, lamenting that 'after all this artistic decay and the general degeneration of taste finally came the effect of the rapid growth of the metropolis', characterised by financial speculation, bad taste, fashion and a mobile population.[35] The exterior of the Implerstraße school was displayed to an industrial area: Grässel would have to formulate a response which both expressed his critique of this particular form of urban environment while also fulfilling his commitment to making structures belong to, rather than contradict, their surroundings.

Grässel believed that every building should reflect the functions for which it was designed; its interior life should clearly define its exterior form. He wrote:

> Only in the most recent period have people finally begun to grasp that every decorative form must proceed from the very nature and function of the thing, and that when we are building, we must create from the interior outwards to the exterior, not the other way around as previously, from a pre-determined external style inwards to the interior.[36]

Put in other words, he believed that form followed function. His greatest quarrel with 'Heroic' Modernism – that formal, canonical form of Modernism in art and architecture which dominates the historiography – was that he felt a building should reflect the character of the place. If we think back to the discussion of *Heimat* above, this meant that the building should reflect the characteristic features of the landscape, in which landscape was very broadly defined. In turn, this would mean that the building would also reflect the characteristics of the people, as both would be products of their interaction with the landscape or environment. If the surroundings were semi-rural and dominated by an extant eighteenth-century palace, then that would be reflected in his work, as in the Municipal Orphanage and Heiliggeistspital old people's home in Neuhausen; if the surroundings were industrial, unadorned and Spartan as here in the Sendlinger Unterfeld, his response would be in keeping with that landscape. 'All buildings must be subordinated to the demands of functionalism', he argued, 'and that includes the demands of the positioning and surroundings of the school building, and of the obligatory example of the past'.[37] The past was seen by Grässel as very much the *Heimat* or landscape from which the present was derived.

This school's stripped-down character matches the 'functional' nature of the suburb it serves, and seems to complement the vast municipal wholesale market, built entirely in reinforced concrete behind it, the new goods railway terminus and the new electricity generating station at the end of the street. Significantly, this intentional clarity of form in the Implerstraße school was regarded by Grässel as appropriate, as it fitted in with the 'character' of its surroundings, and shows that the municipality was prepared to countenance the development of quite an 'industrial' aesthetic for this area. It is worth expanding on Grässel's previous comment to emphasise how important this sense of continuity of character was:

> Every school building should not have an alienating effect but instead should be attractive in a *heimatlich* way. The historical uniqueness and the earlier buildings of a place or a town should find union and evolution in all public buildings of the present, especially school buildings, as they, along with churches, most often form the focal points of any particular part of town.
>
> A school building will be all the less alienating the less it deviates from the usual type [*Art*] of the place. Therefore it should be built with particular attention to the native [*heimischen*] building materials, local roof forms and local types and customs, and by doing this it will be most attractive in general, and through its matter-of-fact [*sachliche*] beauty, build up the pride of the citizens.[38]

This school exterior, in following these rules, should be viewed as an accommodation with the metropolis as *Heimat*. The exterior was slick, clear, unadorned – in keeping with the industrial setting. However, if we turn to the interior a different, and contradictory, set of preoccupations becomes visible.

The contrast is stark. One of the key requirements which preoccupied many contemporary architects was that interiors of 'rational' projects like hospitals or schools should not be 'cold' or 'scientific', a theme which is enlarged upon in Chapter 3. This was particularly important in schools, hospitals, old people's homes and the orphanage – that is to say, in places where the citizen and the state engaged in an intimate, protracted encounter, predicated on the weakness or need of the citizen and the strength and/or beneficence of the state. In the case of the Munich orphanage, for example, it was felt the building could challenge this massively depersonalising experience (the loss of a parent) and mitigate it into something *Heimatliches*, and thereby rescue the personality and the individual from the growing, impersonal, bureaucratic but caring state apparatus. One commentator wrote of this orphanage that it altered the whole *Stimmung* (mood, atmosphere, disposition, attitude) of the individual:

> In the rooms, halls and corridors the builder [*Erbauer*] constantly set himself the task of avoiding all cold, barrack-like sobriety; all spaces should be a beloved *Heimat* to their occupants, and remain as such for them in happy memory for the whole of their lives.[39]

The use of the word *Erbauer* is important here, because whereas the *Architekt* or *Ingenieur* was book-learnt, rational, inauthentic, the *Erbauer* (builder–creator) was creative, dynamic and worldly. The same author concluded that the building and the fittings within it could lift children out of anonymity and give them something personal to belong to: children 'that had lost their home, lost everything, would be rewarded and consoled with a *Heimat*'.[40] While the children of the typical German municipal school could not be described as having 'lost their home, lost everything', they would be rewarded with a *Heimat* nonetheless. Grässel's main technique for inspiring this mood-altering atmosphere in building interiors had two prongs: first, to buy very cheap, mass-produced furniture and get unemployed local artists and craftsmen (many of whom were studying in the new vocational schools) to decorate it in the folk tradition at a low price; and, secondly, to paint the walls with frescos (Figure 1.1).

The frescos in the Implerstraße school covered many themes: protection of plants, protection of songbirds, care of patriotic sentiment, respect for the ruling house, care of religious folk traditions, care of the folk song, care of those who like rambling ('Pflege der Wanderschaft') and cultivation of a sense of *Heimat* ('Pflege des Heimatsinns').[41] As such, the early form of mass-tourism embodied in the rambling movement was linked directly to *Heimat* discourse, as well as regional politics (the ruling house here was the Bavarian Wittelsbach dynasty, not the Reich's Hohenzollerns). On an abstract level, one might think that these themes might have had little or no relevance to the children of this smoky suburb. Of course, there is no concrete way of knowing, but the number of children who would have belonged to the *Wanderschaft* in this area would have been low;

1.1 Wall Paintings, Implerstraße School, Munich, 1900s.
The paintings on the wall are entitled, 'Protect the Song Birds' and 'Protect the Plants', and are typical of the ways the council tried to 'humanise' institutional buildings. They were used as teaching aids in a period when textbooks were uncommon.

it is absolutely certain that their exposure to the twenty-four species of songbirds which they were supposed to protect and the same number of wild flowers would have been next to none. This area of Munich does not impress for its birdsong, even despite a massive tree-planting programme over the last few years. However, the wall illustrations were used extensively in pedagogy, particularly in the subject of '*Heimatkunde*', which was a combination of biology, natural history, local history, music and some religion.

On a more practical level, Figure 1.1 shows how relevant these illustrations must have been to the children of this area. The base of the paintings – in this case 'Schützet die Singvögel' ('Protect the Songbirds') and 'Schützet die Pflanzen' ('Protect the Plants') on either side of the main boys' entrance – are at approximately the same height as the tops of the door – about 6ft 6in. up the wall. They reach their completion near the ceiling, around 13ft high. Children would have left this school at around the age of 14, so before they would ever have been big enough to truly appreciate these images and, as already stressed, one might reasonably question whether their response would have been positive anyway. The images are textually and visually dense, not offering easy access at a distance – although their use in day-to-day classroom teaching was heavy in a period with no textbooks and few colour illustrations. However, metaphorically and literally, these images must have passed over many of the children's heads.

In this particular example, it would be tempting to view the contrast between the interior and exterior experiences of this municipal building as negating one another. This is how one of the most prominent historians of building between the wars in Germany, Barbara Miller Lane, approached the question of contrasts in a structure or set of structures. She argued that, in the case of National Socialist-approved architecture, the contrasts between its different elements, Modernist one minute, bland the next, bombastic somewhere else, *völkisch* ('ethnically traditional', backward-looking, typical) in the next place meant that it was meaningless and contradictory, and could not function for the transmission of ideas; specifically, for the transmission of an ideology.[42] This is an error of judgement as it ignores the subtlety inherent in any dialogue; it underplays the awareness that the person with the message has of the person who has yet to hear it, and vice versa. This school shows that two messages could be simultaneously projected, though with varying degrees of success: the first, that buildings should embody ideas of visual and emotional continuity with their surroundings, the second that urban residents should reappraise their relationship to wildlife, nature, the country and tradition. Meanwhile, it indirectly embodies a third idea, namely that an expert, and the state apparatus which stood behind him, were both able to suggest this reappraisal and justified in attempting to do so. For all that such responses might seem naïve or dreamy looking back, creating environments of order, calm, cleanliness, warmth and good health were regarded by contemporaries as significant achievements in cities characterised by cramped conditions, disease, dirt, noise and poverty.

Exhibiting the city: exhibiting anxiety

It was not enough for city governments to tackle these issues; they also wanted to be *seen* to be tackling them, and they felt a missionary drive to persuade others of their ideological convictions. They did this most often through exhibitions, which were enormously popular in the early twentieth century across the West. At these events, city governments would give their 'diagnoses' of the sicknesses of the modern world, and outline the cures they proposed. German cities were no exception, and governors and experts paraded themselves and their beliefs as a form of rational leisure to a public eager to consume them. Therefore to enter the world of the urban exhibition in early twentieth-century Germany is to eavesdrop on two conversations. One conversation was between German cities themselves – their governors, their experts, their paradigms, their knowledges, their discourses. But there was a second conversation – perhaps slightly more one-sided: between those same people, and 'ordinary' Germans, whoever they may have been. Indeed, Keith Lilley has argued that when it came to the built environment, exhibitions operated somewhere on the interface between propaganda and consultation.[43] They were dialectical and discursive.

It is important to understand the scale of exhibition-going and exhibition organising in this period, from the 1890s until after the Second World War. These were not peripheral events, hastily thrown together. They were important leisure facilities, major engines in the growth of twentieth-century tourism and central to discussions of both the past and the future. There were many exhibitions and events aimed at professionals and experts in the relatively new areas of public health, pedagogy, housing, electrification and such like. They were enormously influential, helping to produce and define the discourses which, before, during and after the Great War, would solidify into the central fields of activity of the modern state. But the ones that had the greatest impact on the public were the massive exercises in futurology that took place on a local, national and international scale – from the World's Fairs of St Louis, Chicago and Paris, to the Ideal Home exhibition in London's Earl's Court.[44] They were part theme/pleasure park, part didactic experience, where whole life-worlds could be constructed on a small scale a by experts working in a 'social laboratory', and experienced by a public eager to engage in accessible 'futurology'.

Model streets, communities, homes, ideal futures and pasts were created at these exhibitions – *Ausstellungen* in German – and they were set alongside vast fairgrounds and pleasure palaces. The Chicago World's Fair of 1883 attempted to posit a variety of 'perfect cities', for example. Alongside 'Old Vienna' stood a model military camp, a German village and a Javanese village. They were arranged around the Ferris wheel, and the 'Middle-Eastern Pleasure Palaces'.[45] Berlin's exhibition of 1896 attracted 7.5 million visitors. It was supposed to be an industrial exhibition, but only the parts which recreated 'Olde Berlin' and 'Ancient Cairo' made any money.[46]

But alongside these more fantastical – perhaps, phantasmagoric – 'perfect cities', could stand something like Pullman's model industrial city, built with prefabricated units designed and produced by Pullman's railway works. It was a city which would exterminate disease, and engender rational, orderly subjects. Contemporaries argued variously that it would produce a new sort of manhood, a new urban culture, material well-being, orderly behaviour and social improvement. In particular, it would restore social harmony, and overcome class division.[47] Thus, when an exhibition-goer – in Germany or elsewhere – saw a model apartment or an ideal street, they read a phrase or a paragraph written out in a language in which they were probably well versed or fluent. They expected to see model worlds, and expected those model worlds to posit solutions in future realities. Such remodelling of urban space in an exhibition environment in the early twentieth century was almost something of an impulse, an instinct. The exhibition – whatever its scale – was a forum in which experts, commercial manufacturers and 'their' publics could liaise with and inform each other – preach, persuade and consume. While the over-arching metaphor which dominated their presentation was frequently didactic, their practice was far less rigid, and buying, selling and enjoying were common bedfellows with teaching and learning. Little has been written on such exhibitions in Germany in the early twentieth century. What work has been done on the production of 'perfect cities' in exhibition culture has tended to focus on the Weißenhof exhibition in Stuttgart in 1927, organised by the German design pressure group, the Deutscher Werkbund. It was intended to explore the idea of '*Die Wohnung*' – the dwelling. This exhibition, however, was something of an anomaly, as it was not an 'event' in the way others were. It has earned its predominance in the historiography because it drew together many of the dominant 'masters' in the canon of Modernism, such as Le Corbusier, J.J.P. Oud, Mies van der Rohe, Peter Behrens and Hugo Häring. This has given the exhibition the air of being a 'moment', a singular coherent event at which the course of history changed when, in fact, it was no such thing.

It is time to rectify this, with two examples taken from far more popular German exhibitions than the Weißenhof – one from before the Great War, one from after. The city of Munich's Municipal Building Office organised two major exhibitions in this period – in 1908, they celebrated the city's 750th anniversary, and attracted 3,000,000 visitors. In 1928, they held the 'Home and Technology Exhibition', which attracted 1,500,000 visitors – twice as many as the Weißenhof exhibition in Stuttgart the year before. The two large exhibitions (there were many small ones in between) which the city government organised twenty years apart offered the perfect opportunity for the municipality both to clarify its own objectives, and also publicise them. They could do this secure in the knowledge that millions of Germans would visit the places, and engage with the themes set out there – and that hundreds of column-inches would be secured for their ideas in both newspapers and women's magazines. The two exhibitions proved massively popular, and each focused on the built environment and the ideologies the municipality was interested in promoting as underpinning it. In 1908, municipal facilities provided the centre-point – surprising to us, perhaps, but at this period new schooling, electricity and hospitals were cutting-edge achievements. In 1928 it was housing, yet in each presentation the Council demonstrated its obsession with providing a reasoned account of their worries about the modern world, rejecting any notion that either they were powerless to reform it, or that it should be destroyed in its entirety. These exhibitions were so significant because they offered the means of developing both a critique and a solution in parallel, and presenting both to the public without veering off into extreme, pessimist positions, remaining firmly in the cultural mainstream.

The exhibition 'München 1908' marked the Corporation's entry into a field of both cultural manipulation and economic activity which was relatively novel for German municipalities at that time: *Ausstellungswesen*, or the exhibition industry. Key figures in the municipality regarded the possibilities presented by *Ausstellungswesen* as an element of the town's 'cultural mission', and throughout this period it presented the Council with a special opportunity, first for the generation and presentation of a cultural summary or précis and, secondly, for the Corporation to mark its own place in relation to that summary. Experts in taste, hygiene, education, planning, design and sport would provide a 'digest' of recent cultural, visual, social and economic 'progress' for the citizen; and the Corporation would cast itself as the cipher and oracle of that very progress. It is worth stressing that both exhibitions were products, to a large degree, of the Municipal Building Office – urban design, urban criticism, urban reform and exhibition-holding were intimately linked, conceptually and administratively. The Municipal Building Office's architects and engineers were in charge of buildings, goals, advertising and exhibits at the exhibitions, and the office for exhibitions (*Ausstellungsamt*) was a subsection of the Municipal Building Office. But the Council as a whole, and the Magistrat (executive) and the Mayors in particular, took a close interest in the smallest details of the exhibitions, and every exhibit and exhibitor had to be approved by the body of the Council, the Magistrat and the Municipal Building Office. What would be in these exhibitions was not rubber-stamped; it was debated in several institutional contexts exactly which presentations would reach the public.

The emphasis at the 1908 exhibition was to be on *Schlichtheit* and *guten Geschmack*: simplicity and good taste, in contrast to the complexity and bad taste of modern culture, and its vehicle, the metropolis. The exhibition was conceived as part of the city's cultural mission, and at the centre of the whole exhibition stood building, in the form of both the structures of the exhibition area itself and the exhibits within them. It should also be mentioned that all this took place in the midst of an enormous fun-fair. All exhibits, whether municipal or not, were to be subordinated to a set of aesthetic principles developed and defined by the Municipal Building Office. The exhibition was to be a *Gesamtkunstwerk* (a complete work of art), in which every detail from the toilets to the uniforms to the programmes to the buildings to the exhibits would conform to a single set of principles which would develop a sense of *Schlichtheit*, *Nüchternheit*, *Sachlichkeit* and *guten Geschmack* – simplicity, sobriety, plainness and good taste: 'Thus the whole should serve to enlighten in an economic as well as an art–political [*kunstpolitischer*] regard, . . . because the whole exhibition in all its parts should be nothing short of one piece of applied art.'[48]

The picture of a troubled urban society requiring a cultural cure was at the heart of the exhibition. The organising principle behind this propagandistic or enlightening mission would be *Baukunst* – not élitist architecture, but the far more accessible art of building. Bauamtmann Robert Rehlen – another member of Munich's building team – was responsible for the selection, order and layout of the exhibits, and he arranged that the entire main hall (and approximately some 30% of the remaining exhibition space) would be given over to the built environment.[49] The chain of representation was completed: architecture was brought to a public both through its lived existence in the streets of Munich and through its more mediatised life in the exhibition, and the municipality fully aligned itself with its architects and their drives to address the themes thrown up by 'modernity'. For example, describing the role of sport at the exhibition, one Hans Uebel wrote:

> Our age sickens with hurry and body and soul-rotting nervousness. Superficiality and lust for pleasure are the signature of everyday life . . . This is a universal: in commerce, in industry, in art. The same goes for the care of the soul and the body.[50]

Mayor Borscht, at the opening speech, said that the only way problems like these could be tackled was through the approach the Municipal Building Office had taken of the *Gesamtkunstwerk*; transforming the life of the *Großstadtmensch* – the 'big city type' or 'metropolitan individual' – so that the individual saw himself or herself as part of a wider (and here I paraphrase), more organic whole. City governments were uniquely placed to return the individual back to this sort of wholeness through the fulfilment of their immense '*kulturellen Aufgabe*' (cultural mission) he maintained, and that was how the exhibition should be viewed.[51]

One of the problems that the municipality identified which both architecture and the exhibition could address was that many of an urban governments' services and achievements – electricity, education, social care – were invisible. But they took on a tangible and experiential life in the buildings in which they took place. Education was essentially invisible, Kerschensteiner argued, until buildings called it forth into three dimensions and stamped its presence into the *Stadtbild*, or 'urban landscape'. Therefore it was essential that models of school buildings (and the radical reconceptualisation of educational practice they represented) took pride of place in the main hall of the exhibition.[52] It seems that Kerschensteiner was arguing that building was a way of asserting control where there had been none, of making a firm social and cultural statement of order, imposed on a worrying city of uncontrolled chaos. Through displaying the municipal architects' work in school-building, it was intended that the exhibition would doubly educate the citizen in the virtues of simplicity, sobriety, plainness and good taste, love of the *Vaterland*, the city, art and each other.

Three million people visited the exhibition; it was estimated that about 500,000 of these were tourists, which means that there were around five visits to the exhibition for each citizen of the town.[53] All the local, national and foreign press coverage confirms that the show was a huge success, and that it led to the city government, cultural developments and thinking on the built environment to be tied tightly together for the journalists sent to cover it. An unknown paper summed up in an article:

> On these broad cultural foundations the Magistrat [the executive of German city governments] has raised up a culture for the likes of which we all yearn, and which this Ausstellung 'München 1908' portends. Here we encounter the spirit of an epoch exalting in the future.[54]

It was, however, a future of a calm antidote to the 'soul-rotting nervousness' of everyday modern life. This entire process of the fulfilment of this yearning was ordered in and around municipal building projects. The modern metropolis was described, criticised and analysed, and municipal administration in the form of building was, at least in part, the solution. While some of the metaphors critiqued the present, almost all of them 'exalted in the future': Germans had found a coherent way of critiquing modernity, without rejecting it.

The 1928 exhibition on 'Home and Technology' was a direct attempt to sell to Germans a model of social housing provision and social housing organisation, devised in Munich and intended to compete with the models offered by Berlin, Frankfurt and Vienna. Called the '12,000-Programme', it was a bold attempt to double the rate of construction and engineer a 'totalising' environment which would produce the ideal modern citizen – while directly confronting many of the key ideological features of the housing projects of other German-speaking cities which have so dominated the historiography. The full ideological underpinnings of the '12,000-Programme' can be understood only in the light of the criticism offered of modern urban life at the huge exhibition organised by the Council in 1928. This demonstrates the way the municipality aligned their housing policy, a moderate *Großstadtkritik* and themselves together with regard to the '12,000-Programme'. They did this through taking control over the Ausstellung 'Heim und Technik' in Munich in 1928 – the year the housing programme was pushed through the Council; indeed, it was part of the function of the exhibition to promote the new mass-housing policy to citizens, councillors and Reich government alike.

The exhibition catalogues and newspaper articles reveal several themes which show how the Corporation regarded modernity as a whole and the city in particular, and how they set about putting housing to work to repair the damage to the individual which both caused. The entire exhibition was founded on what were regarded as two binary opposites: *Heim* – the elemental home or dwelling, and *Technik* – technology and science. *Heim* operated as a shorthand symbol for a pre-modern world, and shared many of the emotive connotations (and linguistic roots) with *Heimat*; *Technik* was modern, cold, inhuman and impersonal. As Mayor Scharnagl wrote in the introduction to the catalogue:

> 'Home' and 'Technology' – two words, two fundamentally different worlds. Fundamentally different in their basic meaning, in their significance for each and every one of us, and in the effects they have on human society. But they are also synonymous in the following sense: they reach out and touch every modern human; they grasp him and force him to take a position.[55]

He continued, linking this to the housing debate at large:

> What technology can bring to the ultimate completion of the home must be constantly displayed to each and every one of us, especially to women, who are the soul of the family home. This city enthusiastically recognises the importance of this process. We have undertaken the tricky task of showing how to make technological successes contribute successfully to the perfection of the home, and to do so in a way which does justice to the circumstances of our own varied forms of social life.[56]

This theme is more fully explored in the second half of Chapter 3, on the design of kitchens in competing German social housing projects. Others continued this theme, that the city government must take the lead in reconciling these two strands. The thrust was, however, constantly that the theme of *Technik* must be made to serve that of *Heim*. It was not an equal partnership; the one was deployed not to defeat but to manage the other. Karl Mantel, the Police Chief of Munich, echoed a rhetoric familiar to many, and repeated the critiques presented in the 1908 exhibition, when he allied the municipality's exhibition to the combating of the exact same elements identified as characteristic of 'modern life' which have already been sketched out:

> In these days of hustle and bustle, agitated hurry and the constant pressure of dreadful demands and expectations which attack the health and the nerves of each individual, whoever wants to refresh his vigour and joy in creation must have one thing above all: Refreshment in a comfortable home.[57]

Again and again the exhibition's catalogue drew the attention of the visitor to the practical applications of the technologies they saw at the exhibition in the resolution of the city's own housing emergency. The documentation surrounding the exhibition as a whole repeatedly dwelt on how the Munich municipality would build to restore a sense of wholeness to the individual and the city in its housing policies and thereby end the attack on 'the health and nerves of each individual' caused by 'hustle and bustle, agitated hurry and the constant pressure of dreadful demands and expectations'.

The high point of the whole summer of the exhibition year was the firework show, 'The End of the World', which received much national press coverage; the description here is taken from a syndicated article. In this firework show, with 69,612 paying spectators (10% of the city's population), and hundreds of thousands more throughout the city on rooftops and in streets, the following scenario was played out on wires above the crowd's heads, stretched across the Theresienhöhe – the high peak right behind the Theresienwiese, the enormous gravelled area where the Oktoberfest is held. The Earth appeared, geographically accurate, flanked by Mars, Jupiter, Saturn and Venus, surrounded by thousands of firework stars. Martians and Moon-men flew past. In the middle of the Milky Way, 'fliers' (*Flieger*) and rocket ships passed each other, one of which collided with a huge comet. This technological intervention caused the calamity on Earth below. The explosion led to a meteor shower on Earth, and an army of stars hurtled towards our planet causing a '*Welteinsturz*' – a collapse of the world, or Armageddon (and causing, it would seem, the plot of countless subsequent movies). Chaos ensued, and the metropolises of the earth were paraded across the sky on wires; Paris, London and New York burned. The collapsing Eiffel Tower 'characterises the chaos on our planet'. Trumpets of doom sounded, alongside thunder and lightning, as fire rained down from the sky and destroyed the cities, causing the very Earth to fragment. As the Earth exploded, rockets were released all round the spectators, and water-bombs were exploded over their heads to simulate the weather catastrophe as the elements of Earth, Wind, Fire and Water entered into their final conflict which would destroy all humanity. Not unsurprisingly, this caused a panic, and there were many injuries.[58]

The message seems distinguishable, if not altogether clear. I do not wish to suggest that anyone in the municipality devised this display to conduct an explicit debate about the destruction of cities, the fragmentation of the earth and the annihilation of mankind. They neither yearned for, nor anticipated, either. There is no evidence that anyone interpreted the display so simplistically. But it does demonstrate that the municipality could be viewed as engaged in a set of diverse media – expressed through building, exhibitions and firework displays, to name but a few – characterising the city as being in some way problematic, volatile, unstable and liable to disintegration. The Council which mounted this show and the exhibition which gave its context were demonstrating an awareness of the problems of the city and technology, and a sympathy with those who regarded these developments with some trepidation. They were displaying, in the case of the exhibition, a carefully presented solution to these problems, and they allied this display in time with the development and adoption of a massive building programme to restructure the city and bring it together again, ending its fragmentation but without creating an anonymous, indistinct and impersonal mass.

The exhibition was a resounding success. With 1.5 million visitors, it attracted over twice as many visitors as the Werkbund's Weißenhof exhibition in Stuttgart of the previous year. Scharnagl's pique at Stuttgart's fame, and his and Küfner's sense of Munich's decline and fragmentation, caused them to embark on an ambitious housing and exhibition programme.[59] The exhibition transformed the widespread worries in the Council Chamber that the building programme and the exhibition would be 'an architectural exhibition like the one in Stuttgart',[60] into unanimous support for the '12,000-Programme', thereby reconciling the councillors with a moderate Modernism and a largely unreformed modernity.

Städtebau: building cities

The idea that the city was volatile, fractured and uncontrollable has already been touched on, and the firework display showing the disintegration of the earth and its metropoles seems a clear expression of that idea. However, few contemporaries concluded that the city was not capable of being healed. In fact, their thoughts veered between anxiety about social, cultural and personal fracturing on a large scale on the one side, and clumping together into de-individuated, amorphous, anonymous masses on the other, which meant that the conclusions that they offered tried to steer a middle road between these agglomerative and disintegrative models.

Iconic as it has become, the subterranean world of Fritz Lang and Thea von Harbou's film *Metropolis* (1927) far from created these metaphors of agglomeration and disintegration, but it does show how widespread such metaphors were. While *Metropolis* is often viewed as a vision of a futuristic dystopia and a critique of modernity, in fact it would seem more likely to be a deeply conservative retelling of the story of Jesus. In it, Maria and Joseph (the Father's assistant) bring the Son down from the Father, enticing him to leave the garden of pleasure 'High in the Heavens', as the caption has it, and go to the underground world of the Workers, consumed in serried ranks by the Moloch (a Canaanite god) of industry. Mary preaches to the workers, as John the Baptist did, that one day someone will come and save them. Mary's increasing band of followers meet in the catacombs under the residential city, just as early Roman Christians did. Freder Fredersen, the 'Son', is curious to understand what Maria has to say about the world, so lives among the workers as one of them, appalled by their suffering, and their alienation from his Father. As he works almost to death, he cries out, 'Father! Father! I never knew ten hours could be so long!', echoing Christ's plea to His Father from the cross. However, misled by the robotic creation of a duplicate, but more sexual Mary (part Eve, part Mary Magdalene) designed by a corrupt scientist and former employee of the Father yearning for a lost love, the workers riot and turn to disorder. Led by this false prophet, the underground world cracks and fractures. In the flood which is unleashed on the city as it collapses into disorder, the Son saves the children from doom. He leads the children to safety, and then leads the workers to reconciliation with his Father in front of the cathedral. The themes of a frightening underworld – homogeneous and terrifyingly lumpen on the one hand, ever in danger of splintering, fracturing and rupturing on the other – were not themes invented by Lang or *Metropolis*' writer, Thea von Harbou. Instead, they were responding very directly to dominant metaphors and tropes which pervaded discourse on the city, class and space.[61] On a social level, commentators across Europe – from Gustave le Bon's study on the crowd to Freud's writings on agoraphobia to Nordau's texts on degeneration to Simmel's investigations into economics and psychology to Stewart Chamberlain's work on racial decline to Howard's and Geddes' writings on urban design – singled out the tendency of urban life to polarise individuals' experiences into either a levelling down and banding together into amorphous masses, or a sharp, lonely individuation.

David Frisby, a critical theorist of modernity, has argued that modernity produces tensions between:

> the desire to give to the modern world new modes of *ordering* and *regulating* it and the recognition of the *disintegration* of the basic categories through which we interpret and experience that world (such as time, space and causality replaced by the transitory, the fortuitous and the arbitrary); between tantalisation and fragmentation; between the emergence of the masses and the crisis of individual identity; between the ancient and the eternally new . . . [T]hese same tensions and contradictions will be apparent in all dimensions of modern experience, including our experience of the social spaces and built environment of modernity.[62]

Recent work on the ways that industrial quarters were described and recounted and understood across Europe have emphasised the demonic nature of their portrayal when the bourgeoisie came to describe them to itself. The working-class suburb 'appeared in contemporary reports . . . as the disorder inherent and hidden in urban order, as a cosmos of social and cultural marginality and as the epitome of urban alienation'.[63] Indeed, discussions of the urban underworld (in which 'under' means 'poor') were littered with the metaphors of wild, untamed nature and discovery and exploration across western culture – jungles, swamps, strange species, caves, races, caverns and deserts abounded. Such a territory invited exploration, categorisation and the imposition of order. And yet, before the turn of the century, those who wished to address these problems struggled to define a usable theory which combined both the manipulation of space and the restructuring of society. The algorithms of the new American city, or the Viennese and Parisian redevelopments of old ones, managed space, but did not provide a technique for micro-managing social activities in a universalising way. Such was the task which early planners, like Olmstead in the USA, Geddes and Howard in Britain and Garnier and Hénard in France were struggling to manage. In German-speaking Europe, the key figure in this struggle was Camillo Sitte.

Camillo Sitte is a remarkably under-researched figure in the history of planning and urban analysis compared to a character like Ebenezer Howard, given his defining role in producing a distinctly Central European model in this era. Little English-language literature on him exists and, Vidler aside, most readers in the academy will have encountered him in Schorske's *Fin-de-Siècle Vienna: Politics and Culture* (if they have encountered him at all).[64] Schorske used Sitte largely as a sort of nostalgic, reactionary foil to fellow Viennese architect, Otto Wagner. Wagner sits much more comfortably in the heroic narrative of the rise of canonical Modernism,[65] and I might caricature Schorske's use of Wagner as the noble voice of liberal, healthy early twentieth-century high-cultural production, in opposition to the 'retrograde nostalgia' of Sitte. Leaving Wagner to one side, Sitte is crucial here, and so it will be worth establishing what, exactly, his critique of urban modernity was, before going on to specify how it was indirectly transformed into a programme of action by an urban governmental élite.

Sitte was the director of the Museum of Applied Arts in Vienna in the 1880s and, although a trained architect, he never went into architectural practice. He remained in the service of the state as an administrator, although he frequently sat on panels of judges in architecture and urban design competitions across the Austro-Hungarian and German empires.[66] His twin obsessions were: first, the critique of the modern city by comparison with the urban spaces, forms, functions and proportions of older cities; and, second, the emotional, spiritual life of the modern urbanite. He argued that the purely technical problems of urban design – such as the prevention of water-borne diseases, or the provision of fire-safe dwellings – had already largely been resolved. He argued that what was missing from town planning was a focus on the human, rather than the technical problem. Only by adopting a more humane, artistic set of principles could the residual social problems of the metropolis be resolved. From these twin obsessions came a book, *City Building According to its Artistic Principles*, in 1889. The book was an overnight success throughout Central Europe, both in its field and beyond, reprinted sixteen times in the next six years. It is written in graceful, engaging, involving German, and always proceeds by demonstrating mastery of the technical aspects of planning before going on to offer devastating critiques of the way humans responded to 'rationally' produced spaces. Frisby classes it as a polemic, but it is not.[67] While it has a firm argument, it is patient and measured. It is certainly far less polemical than the visionary canon of writings by the 'Great Modernists' whom he privileges in his analysis – men like Otto Wagner or Walter Benjamin. It is a plea to restore the other half of town planning, which centred it on the individual human rather than agglomerated social problems. It effectively demolished the logic which underpinned Haussmannesque design and the Vienna Ring, and remains a convincing assault on the sufficiency of reason alone to produce happiness or contentment. In it, Sitte argued:

> No-one cares any more to approach town planning as an artistic problem; instead, the question is seen as a technical one. When subsequently the artistic effects do not fulfil expectations, we stand there astounded and bewildered, but at the next opportunity everything will be handled in just the same way: only from the technical stand-point, as if it was nothing more than a question of laying out a railway line, in which art has no role.[68]

Through its adoption as a planning 'bible' throughout the Austro-Hungarian and German Empires, *City Building* transformed both the perception of urban space in Central Europe, as well as the paradigms of how that space would be produced and arranged.

Crucially, Sitte and his large band of disciples in German-speaking Europe defined the city not as a series of technical problems such as sewerage, transport and health, but as a series of emotional and experiential qualities – loneliness, confusion, over-stimulation, agoraphobia, privacy, thrill-seeking, freedom, happiness and contentment. While he often worked from ancient, mediaeval and baroque models, he also pleaded that we start planning for the *'Millionenstadt'*, the city of millions, which would grow over the next fifty years. In doing so, he used precisely the same metaphors of millions that dominate many of the 'Heroic' Modernists' early plans – people like Garnier, Hilbersheimer and Le Corbusier. He staked bold claims for what planning should do:

> Planning [*Der Städtebau*] is the union of all technical and applied arts into one large, complete whole; planning is the monumental expression of the true pride of citizens, and the seed-bed of true love for the *Heimat*; planning regulates traffic, arranges the foundations of healthy and comfortable living of the vast majority of people – modern people – who have moved to big cities; it must cultivate and accommodate industry and trade, and must support the reconciliation of social conflicts.[69]

The German word for planning, *Städtebau*, translates literally as 'city building', and is therefore capable of sustaining a far greater rhetorical presence than the English 'town planning', which lacks the dynamic urban, constructive attributes of the German. While commentators have focused on Sitte's use of old examples, thereby branding him a reactionary or nostalgic, they have glossed over this bold set of ambitions which rings through his whole work; ambitions which were expert, governmental, statist, helping, reforming and regulatory – ambitions which were, in short, modern, but which responded to a critique of modernity.

Sitte's emphasis on the 'emotional life of planning' implied a revolution in both the training of the experts who managed urban life and the application of their knowledge. Experts (and here Sitte singled out his nemesis, Reinhard Baumeister, professor of engineering at Karlsruhe, and his standard 1876 text book *Urban Growth in its Technical, Regulatory and Economic Dimensions*[70]) had previously applied algorithms to determine, say, the width of a street in relation to the anticipated volume of traffic using it: x number of carriages requires y width of street. Criticising 'our mathematically encircled modern life, in which man himself becomes formally a machine' (p. 115), Sitte argued instead that:

> It is not true that modern traffic forces us to do this; it is not true that hygiene makes all this necessary. It is simply thoughtlessness, complacency and lack of good will which condemns us modern city dwellers to a life sentence in shapeless areas for the masses consisting of views of endlessly repetitious tenements, in endlessly repetitious geometric street alignments. They kill the soul, they kill pride, they kill all sense of belonging.[71]

Besides providing a rhetorical drive to stimulate bureaucrats, experts, urban governors and cultural critics to change the way city space was conceived, Sitte provided a carefully worked-out methodology which, if followed, would produce a series of urban spaces which would comfort the citizen, instil in them a sense of wholeness and make them feel that they belonged to the city and that – crucially – the city belonged to them. It would also address the needs of traffic circulation, hygiene and fire prevention. Sitte wanted to destroy the infinite vistas of the city of Haussmann, and replace them with a city consisting of a series of 'rooms', through which the citizen moved, always able to locate himself or herself as a person, both social and individual, and always enjoying the comfort of defined space. The city, he argued, should be about enclosure and density of settlement.

Few examinations of attempts to put Sitte's writings into practice exist – although such attempts were widespread. The first city to attempt to do so comprehensively was Munich. The Corporation there underwent what might be called a 'spasm' of radical reform in the mid-1890s, and one symptom of this was the announcement in 1893 of a large competition to plan both the projected growth of the metropolitan area, and also to zone and regulate the extant city – the first such universal plan, applying to old and new parts of the city. They employed both the technocratic Baumeister and the more humanistic Sitte to be judges, aided by the head of planning at Cologne and recent victor in a planning competition in Vienna, Josef Stübben. Why the city embarked on such a radically new way of describing, regulating and designing itself is something historians have struggled to explain.[72] A neat historical explanation would be the death of the head of the Municipal Building Department, Arnold von Zenetti. Zenetti had been a firm adherent of the Viennese and Parisian types of urban design, in which the main role of the state was the parcelling up of land to make it more rentable for private developers. At the same time, Bauamtmann Carl Hocheder was involved in laying out a station in south Munich; he had given a lecture on Sitte's work in 1890 and designed the area around the station clearly on Sittesque lines.[73] However, why all this should prompt the administration to announce a competition to devise a complete, holistic plan to manage both the extant city and any subsequent expansion, in both form and function, with zoning, remains unknown.

What is known, however, is that out of this came a set of principles for describing and delineating urban space known as the *Staffelbauordnung* – Tiered Building Regulations – which set out principles for laying out cities (essentially, a summary of Sitte) but, furthermore, pledged to intervene in the extant city, against the inclinations of liberal political and economic theory. It also set out functional principles regulating the interior lives of buildings, and stipulated the establishment of industrial zones, separate from living ones. Outside these zones, it went on to stipulate that electrical power had to be used for most industrial functions, in order to limit smoke pollution. It is possible to interpret this as environmental planning (this is how it was presented), but the city government was also the monopoly provider of electricity and was keen to secure a market for the risk it had taken on in building hydro-electric power stations on the Isar. This set of regulations was enthusiastically administered by Theodor Fischer, a young, unheard-of architect whom the city controversially employed. Under his stewardship, Sitte's ideas were firmly embedded in the administration, to such an extent that when large-scale building resumed after the Great War they continued to provide the guiding principles.

In the case of Munich, experts and governors there, following Sitte, continued after the Great War to work with *fin-de-siècle* metaphors of the atomised individual and the impersonal mass. Politicians and experts stressed both the splintering and inconsistency of urban vision (*Stadtbildzersplitterung*), and the clumping together of individuals into characterless masses (*Menschenzusammenballung*). For each of these emotional challenges to the modern subject, they posited spatial solutions which would cosset the individual, reconcile him or her to the helping projects of the modern state and make modernity and urban life seem warm and fulfilling. They posited no retreat from modernity or the city, only rational technocratic management to manipulate its more problematic aspects.

Sitte had elucidated clearly how he felt that 'mathematically encircled' planning had destroyed the individual's instinctive sense of attachment to place:

> The size of blocks and the width of streets are generally agreed at some sort of committee meeting. Once that is done, the actual details of the layout are decided by bureaucrats and clerks, assuming that there is not to be any real artistic input. The artistic value of the plan is thereby nil, and therefore the joy of the inhabitant in their city is also nil, their attachment to it is nil, their pride in it is nil – in one word, their entire sense of belonging [*Heimatgefühl*] is nil, and one can actually observe this in any inhabitant of any of the new, artless, boring cities.[74]

If the experience of urban space corroded *Heimatgefühl*, this would indeed be a serious problem. The question which remained in the 1920s was how restructuring urban space could remedy the deficiencies the Mayor and Sitte had identified. The major housing programme developed at the end of the 1920s in Munich, the 12,000-Programme, was, in part, intended to address this issue.

Planning new housing developments in the 1920s was an unmistakable political imperative. It also offered urban governments in both Austria and Germany the possibility of exercising a new level of control over the spaces which constituted the 'urban continuum' from the level of the most private, domestic spaces of the home, through the block, to the housing estate, to the area and finally to the city as whole. It was a level of formal state control, of regulation and spatial structuring of private life, which Sitte in the 1880s could never have imagined. It would have been inconceivable to him that the psycho-spatial analysis on which he based his theories could be transformed into such an elaborate regulatory construct on both the micro- and the macro-level. In effect, planners and governors after the war were left without established theoretical guidance on how to organise the new urban spaces they set out to create, and instead had to re-interpret some of the principles of turn-of-the-century planning – this applied as much to the so-called innovative Heroic Modernists, as to less famous (but more numerous) examples like the 12,000-Programme. In Central Europe, this normally took two forms: either the British Garden City satellite model, in which housing estates would be built on the peripheries of cities, or even outside them; or a re-interpretation of Sitte, who constantly emphasised the advantages of increasing population density within the extant city, so long as this population's experience of urban space was improved.

That housing construction was a political and social imperative in post-war Germany and Austria, few denied – an imperative which is explored more fully in Chapter 4. Almost every major European city east of France experienced extreme political violence in the years 1917–23, and much of this violence, when it acquired a coherent political voice, focused on housing. The objectives of subsequent housing policy in Munich – and, indeed, most European cities – were not, however, solely to do with improving the standard of living for urbanites or averting revolution. The old preoccupations of experiential quality and emotional well-being remained. This can be seen by focusing on the two joint Mayors of Munich from 1923 onwards, Karl Scharnagl of the Centre Party and Hans Küfner, a politically independent career civil servant. In a meeting of the Housing Committee Scharnagl established a strategy for Munich which set out to overcome the major obstacles to the successful inhabitation of the metropolis described in some contemporary housing theories:

> The execution of [housing] projects in Munich will distance themselves just as much from the clumping together in one mass [*Menschenzusammenballung*] of many hundreds of households in the smallest dwellings in one block, as is the practice in Vienna, as from the expansion at this time – a luxurious tendency – of low-rise housing estates.[75]

Scharnagl explicitly rejected Viennese models, such as Karl-Marx-Hof, and implicitly rejected the plans of Frankfurt City Council, dismissing them as an example of the 'luxurious tendency of low-rise housing'.

These objectives were intended to reconcile the individual to scientifically organised planning of space (internal and external), while preserving individual autonomy and personality. When City of Birmingham councillors asked the Munich Corporation what 'typical' housing solutions they favoured for 'the worker', the Council's Planning Department told their study tour:

> No real dwellings for workmen as such have been built, which would crowd people together into a narrow space, and furthermore, which would unite them in crowded dwelling blocks. [The design of our housing] is due to the diverse habits and desires of the population, which had to be considered. The experiences up to this time have shown that this principle is right, and answers the local wants.[76]

This particular vision of urban space, focusing on a fear of clumping people together into a de-individuated mass, was primarily a reaction to the development of large housing estates in Vienna – which the study trip from Birmingham had just visited. While superficially the Corporation's housing estates seemed to resemble Vienna's, in fact they were organised around very different principles. In Vienna, they were laid out in open forms, not around small spaces, and though they had similar population densities when viewed as a whole the scale of the buildings on the Munich estates was worked out according to Sitte's principles of the emotional need for enclosure to prevent agoraphobia. In particular, the large open spaces in, for example, Vienna's Karl-Marx-Hof were avoided.

The second feature which differentiated Vienna's estates from Munich's was the provision of, and charges for, shared social facilities such as heating and laundry. Such charges were felt by the Munich Corporation also to remove individual freedom from citizens, and this was a type of urban freedom which they particularly prized. Whereas the Viennese focused on providing communal laundries and other facilities in their estates, and especially communal central heating, Munich's experts rejected this solution. Unfortunately, the records of the fact-finding mission to Vienna are lost, but Frankfurt (having employed several of Vienna's planners and architects) copied both central heating and central laundries. When the councillors and officials from Munich went to Frankfurt, they found much disquiet among aggrieved housewives who lived in collectively organised housing estates. Given the way that experts typically constructed their knowledge, it is quite remarkable that the councillors and experts bothered to find out these women's opinion at all, given both their gender and class. The Frankfurt women complained that in hard times when money was tight, they used to economise by having no heating and putting the whole family to sleep in one bed or one room. Equally, they complained that the standard laundry charges were an irritation, as many families did not have enough clothes to make weekly laundry worthwhile. It also meant they had to walk through the snow to the wash house, and it took away a substantial source of income from 'taking in', which enabled many women not to have to work outside the home.[77]

However, it was precisely practices such as keeping girls off school to help with washing, and different sexes and generations sleeping in the same room, that the experts across German-speaking Europe wanted to eliminate through redesigning the spaces in which people lived.[78] And yet the projects in Munich were not nostalgic, backward-looking or lacking in planning: they did not reject modernity, although they did reject some of the more controlling ambitions of the modern state. Rather, they stressed an alternative aspect of modernity: personal freedom. It was precisely the liberties that urban life afforded the individual – liberties Simmel and countless others were so keen to emphasise throughout their work – which they wanted to enhance. '[T]oday, metropolitan man is "free" in a spiritualised and refined sense', argued Simmel, and most experts across Germany agreed.[79]

Of course, the Munich City councillors did not approve of girls being kept away from school either, but it seems they felt deeply committed to that strand of urbanised modernity which emphasised personal freedom and individual liberty alongside rational planning, and they wanted to produce spaces which facilitated it. Therefore, while Munich's solutions rejected the ambitious 'totalising' plans of the social state evidenced by 'Red' Vienna, they did not shy away from modernity and the city. They used the enhanced powers of the state to plan space to provide pockets of autonomy, however small, in the fabric of the city. Their commitment to expertise, to the social, to planning, to state activity matched Vienna's, but their goals in terms of the personal life of the individual were very different. As one of the Corporation's municipal architects concluded on planning for women in the home: '[I]t is the joy of the housewife to create in the home, to organise her home herself, to make it homely and cosy.'[80]

Patronising as this observation may seem, Munich's housing estates and domestic interiors offered far more scope for individual freedom than more meticulously planned environments, as will be discussed in the second half of Chapter 3, and explicitly ascribed agency to working-class women, rather than standardising *'the'* working-class woman as the object of helping interventions. Munich rejected solutions which emphasised the same-ness of people, refusing to design spaces for the 'typical' person, whether 'worker' or 'woman'. However, Munich may reasonably be considered more committed to the modern city than both Vienna's and Frankfurt's textbook Modernists, as the Viennese authorities always regarded their inner-city housing estates based on apartment blocks as second best, a crisis solution before peripheral Garden Cities could be built in the green belt.[81] And with regard to Frankfurt's *Trabantenstädte* (satellite towns), Munich's authorities never liked Garden Cities, always insisting that urban problems required urban solutions.

The great paradox here lies in the historiography. The urban spatial policies which are considered most modern, most Modernist, most closely related to modernity by much of the literature in this area are those of Ernst May's planning department in Frankfurt, and that of 'Red' Vienna.[82] Yet these were precisely the spatial policies which the Munich Corporation considered most detrimental to the individual's experience of the city, because they were based on a version of satellite Garden City principles (May, Frankfurt's director of planning, had spent a year working with Ebenezer Howard in Britain), or socialist principles. Crucially, the types of housing environments planned by Frankfurt's city government were outside the extant city. They were also very low density, often terraced houses, and usually required the inhabitant to take out a mortgage – according to British principles. While the Munich Corporation thoroughly approved of the way the Viennese had used housing projects to stamp orientation points and an identity into the extant fabric of the city, they thoroughly disapproved of the tendencies in Frankfurt to turn away from the city. Whatever the problems of the modern world were, they had to be solved in that world, and not by attempts to recuperate an ultimately illusory realm of emotional calm and spiritual peace in the countryside.

When the Bavarian councillors went to see the developments near Frankfurt they noted that although they had 'modern forms and colours, that was all that was modern about them'.[83] In particular, they noted that the low-rise, low-density, out-of-town solutions of the Frankfurt Planning Department offered no opportunity to influence the *Stadtbild* – the overall impression of the town. The Munich Corporation was keen to address the very fabric of the city, as the Viennese had done, but without their 'levelling' and 'clumping' aspects. Leading experts in the Munich Corporation emphasised in the mid-1920s that the city was becoming too visually diverse, and that activities like the school building programme were absent. This meant that the city was losing the visual and experiential homogeneity necessary to produce happy, proud, participative and compliant citizens.[84] Mayor Küfner, *ex officio* chairman of the Building Commission, argued that:

Before the war, Munich was recognised as paradigmatic in the shaping of buildings and the city [*Bau- und Stadtgestaltung*]; whether it still could claim this leadership today is another question. A study commission of the council has seen many buildings worthy of note in its travels to London, Amsterdam, Hamburg, Berlin, Frankfurt, Stuttgart, Cologne, Düsseldorf, Essen, Mühlheim-a.-Ruhr etc. Unfortunately, Munich after the war sadly fell prey to a certain fragmentation [*eine gewiße Zersplitterung*]; we built in too many places, on too small a scale, and the overall impression which the city makes on its inhabitants has not profited from this; in the exteriors of our buildings, and in the city as a whole, too much diversity has left a lot to be desired.[85]

In fact, after the war experts in Munich pursued a policy of *Lückenbebauung*, 'building in the gaps', in order to control land speculation and increase urban density. The opportunities offered by large-scale housing projects seemed to offer the perfect occasion to remedy this, and re-impose a unified homogeneous order on a fractured city. As Mayor Scharnagl argued, 'in the current building programmes, the city-building idea [*die städtebauliche Idee*] has not been allowed its full scope'. He went on: 'The estates should not be made up of individual buildings [as in Frankfurt], but appear as one, distinct block . . . [But the programme] should consciously oppose the Viennese block creations with a totally different concept of housing politics and space.'[86]

Mayor Scharnagl proposed that if the drive to end '*Zersplitterung*' (splintering) in the metropolis were to be successful, 'the whole process will be all the easier, the bigger the building programme is, the bigger the estates are; that is obvious'.[87] As the estates were to be built in the city, there would be limits on how large they could be; so in between these big projects of generally 1,500–2,000 flats each, smaller schemes of between 70 and 300 or so flats would be placed, permeating the city from mediaeval core to industrial suburb. This programme, called the '12,000-Programme', was brought to completion in three years from 1928 to 1931. What distinguished it from the existing, *ad hoc* Munich housing programme (which had also built an impressive 12,000 dwellings between 1925 and 1928) was its attempt to re-impose a visual and experiential order on the city, to create a coherent, homogeneous and imposing set of spatial experiences. Average occupancy of a dwelling in Munich in 1930 was approximately four people,[88] a figure likely to underestimate the occupancy in these dwellings as priority was given to large or extended families. Based on a crude average, this implies that at least 48,000 people were living in housing built under this scheme to end the splintered city. Put differently, one in twelve of the population of the city as a whole lived in these projects intended at once both to liberate and regulate the individual urbanite, to bring wholeness and satisfaction and contentment to both the people who lived in them, and the city which surrounded them.

Conclusion

The evidence in this chapter shows, then, that there certainly was a critique of modernity, and its agent, the metropolis, in the first decades of the twentieth century. Furthermore, this critique could be nostalgic and backward-looking. However, while authors and publicists – like Oswald Spengler – might develop from this an overarching critique of *all* modern culture, it would seem that the positions taken by those involved in managing the urban environment and the urban experience was far more nuanced. When they talked of *Heimat*, they borrowed a comprehensive and highly flexible cultural code, modern precisely because of its nostalgia, and developed from it a coherent set of ideals about how one might face the future, but recognise one's roots in a past (fictional or otherwise). While planners and governors worried that the city was on some level alienating, and that it was not a *Heimat*, they responded by arguing that they could create *Heimat* precisely here. Thus, their optimistic beliefs serve as a useful barometer to correct impressions of their so-called 'pessimism', and their practice in the design of institutions of the social state shows that they could use this discourse to unite the modern and the 'progressive' with the nostalgic and conservative. The strategy of mounting enormous exhibitions shows that they were not content to elaborate such ideas in the refined media which carried expert discourse, but that these bureaucrats, councillors and mayors were proactive evangelists for their moderate critiques and potential solutions. They were unwilling to leave such matters to guesswork and publicists, and while their critique of the modern metropolis was vigorous so, too, was their prescribed solution. Indeed, the elaboration of planning discourse and practice – far from unique to either Munich or Germany – meant that the link between problem and solution was constructed as an organic whole. By structuring the problem as a continuum running from alienating atomisation to reductive homogeneity, they could position themselves in the middle of that continuum, and thereby also the middle ground of the debate in general. Indeed, this metaphor of an unbridgeable divide between the individual and the mass, and the proposal of a non-revolutionary model of reconciliation, was a central trope in German cultural discourse in the early twentieth century. True, the NSDAP (Nazi Party) exploited this metaphor in their politics, while the SDP (Social Democratic Party) in their rhetoric (but not their action), and the KPD (Communist Party) in both word and deed, polarised the world into the individual and the collective. However, it was the universality and moderation of this reconciliatory theme which explains its appeal to the NSDAP, and the NSDAP's appeal to the public, rather than its radical extremism. Thus, the mainstream of German culture, represented by the Munich corporation, could be critical of modernity, and yet propose modern solutions to its problems: they could be progressive in their nostalgia.

Notes

1 George Mosse, *The Crisis of German Ideology: Intellectual Origins of the Third Reich* (New York, 1961); Fritz Stern, *The Politics of Cultural Despair: A Study in the Rise of Germanic Ideology* (Berkeley, CA, 1961), esp. pp. 27–34, 116–136, 153–182.
2 Arthur Herman, *The Idea of Decline in Western History* (New York, 1997).
3 Laqueur describes views of the coming century as focusing on modernism, sophistication and optimism on the one hand, and despair and foreboding on the other. Walter Laqueur, 'Fin-de-Siècle: Once More with Feeling', *Journal of Contemporary History* 1 (1996), pp. 5–47.
4 Dirk Schubert, 'Theodor Fritsch and the German (*völkische*) Version of the Garden City: The Garden City Invented Two Years before Ebenezer Howard', *Planning Perspectives* 19 (2004), pp. 3–35.
5 Wolfgang Voigt, 'The Garden City as Eugenic Utopia', *Planning Perspectives* 3 (1989), pp. 295–312.
6 David Matless, 'Nature, the Modern and the Mystic: Tales from Early Twentieth-Century Geography', *Transactions of the Institute of British Geographers* 3 (1991), pp. 272–286. Indeed, Matless considers this mysticism to be a key to the academic discipline of geography's modernity – whereas paradoxically, such mysticism in German historiography would be evidence of just the opposite.
7 Charles Masterman, 'Realities at Home', in Charles Masterman (ed.), *The Heart of Empire: Discussions of Problems of Modern City Life in England. With an Essay on Imperialism* (London, 1901), pp. 1–52 (pp. 7–8).
8 Volker Welter, *Biopolis: Patrick Geddes and the City of Life* (London, 2003).
9 Vidler, 'Agoraphobia', pp. 25–26.

10 This discussion will use the version in David Frisby, *Simmel on Culture: Selected Writings*, ed. with Mike Featherstone (London, 1997), pp. 174–185.

11 For a discussion of why Simmel has become so important in recent scholarship on space and the city, see Anthony Vidler, 'Technologies of Space/Spaces of Technology', *Journal of the Society of Architectural Historians* 3 (1999), pp. 482–486; Paul Nolte, 'Georg Simmels historische Anthropologie der Moderne: Rekonstruktion eines Forschungsprogramms', *Geschichte und Gesellschaft* 2 (1998), pp. 225–247.

12 Bryan Turner, 'Simmel, Rationalisation and the Sociology of Money', *Sociological Review* 1 (1986), pp. 93–114; Klaus Köhnke, 'Soziologie als Kulturwissenschaft: Georg Simmel und die Völkerpsychologie', *Archiv für Kulturgeschichte* 1 (1990), pp. 223–232. The 'rise' of Simmel has been largely due to the work in translation and analysis of David Frisby, perhaps most notably: *Fragments of Modernity: Theories of Modernity in the Works of Kracauer, Simmel and Benjamin* (Cambridge, 1985); *Simmel on Culture: Selected Writings*, ed. with Mike Featherstone (London, 1997); *Cityscapes of Modernity: Critical Explorations* (Cambridge, 2001).

13 See Andrew Lees, *Cities Perceived: Urban Society in European and American Thought, 1820–1940* (Manchester, 1985), pp. 105–247.

14 Joachim Radkau, 'Die wilhelminische Ära als nervöses Zeitalter, oder: die Nerven als Netz zwischen Tempo- und Körpergeschichte', *Geschichte und Gesellschaft* 2 (1994), pp. 211–241 and *Das Zeitalter der Nervosität*.

15 Esther da Costa Meyer, 'La Donna è Mobile', *Assemblage* 28 (1995), pp. 6–15; Anthony Vidler, 'Agoraphobia: Spatial Estrangement in Georg Simmel and Siegfried Kracauer', *New German Critique* 54 (1991), pp. 31–45; Tom Lutz, *American Nervousness, 1903: An Anecdotal History* (Ithaca, NY, 1991); Robert Ney, 'Degeneration, Neurasthenia and the Culture of Sport in Belle Epoque France', *Journal of Contemporary History* 1 (1982), pp. 51–68; Clark McPhail, *The Myth of the Maddening Crowd* (New York, 1981); Howard Kushner, 'Suicide, Gender and Fear of Modernity in Nineteenth Century Medical and Social Thought', *Journal of Social History* 3 (1991), pp. 461–491. For contemporary works, popular examples would be Tomàs Masaryk, *Suicide and the Meaning of Civilisation* (London, 1970 [Vienna, 1881]); Gustave le Bon, *The Crowd: A Study of the Popular Mind* (London, 1896); Max Nordau, *Degeneration* (English edn., New York, 1895).

16 Hilde Heynen, *Architecture and Modernity: A Critique* (London, 1999), p. 119.

17 For a discussion of the modernity of *Heimat* and mass media, see Adelheid von Saldern, '*Volk* and *Heimat* Culture in Radio Broadcasting During the Period of Transition from Weimar to Nazi Germany', *Journal of Modern History* 76 (2004), pp. 312–346.

18 An die hohe Kammer der Abgeordneten. Betreff: Bitte des Vereins für Verbesserung der Wohnungsverhältnisse in München (a. Verein) um Gewährung staatlicher Unterstützung, 5 January 1900. See also Vorschlag zur Beschaffung unkündbarer und unsteigbarer Wohnungen für Angestellte und Arbeiter in Münchener Großunternehmen, 19 January 1900, which appealed to businessmen to build housing because *Heimatgefühl* – a person's entire sense of belonging – would be good for labour relations and the economy of the city. SAM-WA-23.
19 Thomas Lekan, *Imagining the Nation in Nature: Landscape Preservation and German Identity, 1885–1945* (London, 2004), p. 125.
20 Edeltraud Klueting, 'Vorwort', in Edeltraud Klueting (ed.), *Antimodernismus und Reform: Beiträge zur Geschichte der deutschen Heimatbewegung* (Darmstadt, 1991), pp. vii–xii (p. vii).
21 Cited in Matei Calinescu, *Five Faces of Modernity*, p. 225.
22 Calinescu, *Five Faces of Modernity*, pp. 237–248.
23 David Gross, *The Past in Ruins: Tradition and the Critique of Modernity* (Amherst, MA, 1992).
24 Alon Confino, *The Nation as a Local Metaphor: Württemberg, Imperial Germany and National Memory, 1871–1918* (London, 1997), p. 97.
25 Celia Applegate, *A Nation of Provincials: The German Idea of Heimat* (Brkeley, CA, 1990).
26 Cited in Lees, *Cities Perceived*, pp. 162–163.
27 Armin Wegner, 'Gesang von den Straßen der Stadt', in Waltraud Wende (ed.), *Großstadtlyrik* (Stuttgart, 1999), p. 113. My translation. Wegner became a pacifist after seeing the Armenian Genocide with the German Army in the Middle East, and was declared 'Righteous Among the Nations' for his public opposition to National Socialism. He wrote best-selling travel books after the Great War about his journeys in the new USSR.
28 Graham Murphy, *Founders of the National Trust* (London, 2002); Leslie Cintron, *Preserving National Culture: The National Trust and the Framing of British National Heritage, 1895–2000* (unpublished doctoral dissertation, Harvard University, 2000); Roderick Nash, 'The American Invention of National Parks', *American Quarterly* 3 (1970), pp. 726–735; Mark Spence, *Dispossessing the Wilderness: Indian Removal and the Making of the National Parks* (Oxford, 2000).
29 K. Allison, 'The Provision of Allotment Gardens in East Yorkshire', *Northern History* 37 (2000), pp. 275–292.
30 Applegate, *A Nation of Provincials*, p. 63.
31 Cited in Frisby, *Cityscapes of Modernity*, p. 245.
32 Hermann Röhrs, 'Georg Kerschensteiner', *Prospects: The Quarterly Review of Comparative Education* 3–4 (1993), pp. 807–822; Irmgard Bock, 'Pädagogik und Schule: Stadtschulrat Kerschensteiner', in Friedrich Prinz and Marita Krauss (eds.), *Musenstadt mit Hinterhöfen: Die Prinzregentenzeit 1886–1912* (Munich, 1988), pp. 213–219.
33 Simmel, 'The Metropolis and Mental Life', p. 175.

34 Simmel, 'The Metropolis and Mental Life', p. 183.
35 Hans Grässel, 'Kultur und Schönheit des Bauens und Lebens', 1913, p. 13a. SAM-NLG-373.
36 Grässel, 'Kultur und Schönheit des Bauens und Lebens'.
37 Hans Grässel, 'Ästhetik des Schulhauses', 16 June 1915. SAM-NLG-367.
38 Grässel, 'Ästhetik des Schulhauses'.
39 Lothar Meilinger, *Das Münchener Waisenhaus: Eine Studie* (Munich, n.d.[c. 1905–1910], p. 34. SAM-HBA-727.
40 Meilinger, *Das Münchener Waisenhaus*, p. 34.
41 Hans Grässel, 'Ästhetik des Schulhauses'.
42 Barbara Miller Lane, *Architecture and Politics in Germany, 1918–1945* (Cambridge, MA, 1968), pp. 185–215.
43 Keith Lilley, 'On Display: Planning Exhibitions as Civil Propaganda or Public Consultation?', *Planning Perspectives* 3 (2003), pp. 3–8.
44 See, for example, Tag Gronberg, *Designs on Modernity: Exhibiting the City in 1920s Paris* (Manchester, 1998); Deborah Ryan, *Daily Mail Ideal Home Exhibition: The Ideal Home through the Twentieth Century* (London, 1997).
45 James Gilbert, *Perfect Cities: Chicago's Utopias of 1893* (London, 1991), p. 112.
46 Katja Zelljadt, 'Presenting and Consuming the Past: Old Berlin at the Industrial Exhibition of 1896', *Journal of Urban History* 3 (2005), pp. 306–333.
47 Gilbert, *Perfect Cities*, pp. 131–149.
48 Wilhelm Bertsch, 'Ausstellung München 1908. Programm Entwurf.', n.d. [before January 1907]. SAM-NLG-407.
49 Robert Rehlen, 'Die Anordnung der Ausstellung', *Ausstellung 'München 1908'*, 6 April 1908. SAM-NLG-408.
50 Hans Uebel, 'Der Sport auf der Ausstellung "München 1908"', *Ausstellung 'München 1908'*, 3 January 1908, p. 17. SAM-NLG-408.
51 Wilhelm Borscht, 'Festreden bei der Eröffnungsfeier der Ausstellung', *Ausstellung 'München 1908'*, 7 May 1908, p. 49. SAM-NLG-408.
52 Georg Kerschensteiner, 'Das Schulwesen Münchens in der Ausstellung', *Ausstellung 'München 1908'*, 7 May 1908, pp. 53–55. SAM-NLG-408.
53 'Der Erfolg der Ausstellung "München 1908"', *Münchner Neueste Nachrichten*, 30 January 1909. SAM-NLG-408.
54 Unknown newspaper, unknown date. SAM-NLG-408.
55 Karl Scharnagl, in *Amtlicher Katalog: Ausstellung 'München 1928: Heim und Technik'*, p. 42. SAM-A&M-648.
56 Scharnagl, in *Amtlicher Katalog: Ausstellung 'München 1928: Heim und Technik'*, p. 42.
57 Karl Mantel, in *Amtlicher Katalog: Ausstellung 'München 1928: Heim und Technik'*, p. 45. SAM-A&M-648. Emphasis in original.
58 This version of events comes from a syndicated story, 5 August 1928, which Jelinek (the exhibition's organiser) felt best represented the

reporting of the show; cited in the 'Schlußbericht. Ausstellung "München 1928: Heim und Technik"'. SAM-A&M-648.
59 See Scharnagl an das Referat XIII [Hochbauamt], 20 December 1926. SAM-KA-618/1.
60 Bund deutscher Architekten, Landesbezirk Bayern: An alle Mitglieder des Landesbezirkes, 22 December 1927. SAM-KA-618/2.
61 For further critical investigation of this film from the perspective of a critique of modernity or discourse on gender, see Michael Minden and Holger Bachman (eds.), *Fritz Lang's Metropolis: Cinematic Visions of Technology and Fear* (Rochester, NY, 2000); Thomas Elsaesser, *Metropolis* (London, 2000).
62 Frisby, *Cityscapes of Modernity*, p. 181. Emphasis in original.
63 Wolfgang Maderthaner and Lutz Musner, *Die Anarchie der Vorstadt: Das andere Wien um 1900* (Frankfurt, 1999) cited in Frisby, *Cityscapes of Modernity*, p. 221. See also Alan Mayne, *The Imagined Slum: Newspaper Representations in Three Cities, 1870–1914* (Leicester, 1993), and the fascinating recent collaborations between historians and archaeologists in Mayne and Murray, *The Archaeology of Urban Landscapes*.
64 For example, this is how Patrick Joyce encounters him in *The Rule of Freedom*.
65 See, for example, Werner Oechslin, *Otto Wagner, Adolf Loos and the Road to Modern Architecture* (Cambridge, 2002).
66 For example, as judge of Munich's *Stadterweiterungswettbewerb* in 1893.
67 Frisby, *Cityscapes of Modernity*, pp. 195–196.
68 Camillo Sitte, *Der Städtebau nach seinen künstlerischen Grundsätzen* (Vienna, 1972 [3rd edn., 1901]), p. 90.
69 Sitte, *Der Städtebau*, p. xix.
70 *Stadt-Erweiterungen in technischer, baupolizeilicher und wirtschaftlicher Beziehung* (Leipzig, 1876).
71 Sitte, *Der Städtebau*, p. 144.
72 Stefan Fisch, 'Neue Aspekte der Münchener Stadtplanung zur Zeit Theodor Fischers (1893–1901) im interurbanen Vergleich', and Wolfgang Hardtwig, 'Soziale Räume und politische Herrschaft: Leistungsverwaltung, Stadterweiterung und Architektur in München, 1870 bis 1914', in Wolfgang Hardtwig and Klaus Tenfelde (eds.), *Soziale Räume in der Urbanisierung: Studien zur Geschichte Münchens im Vergleich 1850 bis 1933* (Munich, 1990); Stefan Fisch, *Stadtplanung im 19. Jahrhundert: Das Beispiel München bis Ära Theodor Fischer* (Munich, 1988).
73 Fisch, *Stadtplanung im 19. Jahrhundert*, pp. 201–217.
74 Sitte, *Der Städtebau*, p. 144.
75 Sitzung des Wohnungsausschußes, 14 March 1928. SAM-WA-64.
76 Referat VII [Wohnungsreferat], 'Principles for Judging the Housing Question', in response to Scharnagl, 29 July 1930, letter requesting the

housing department to explain why the town had no working-class housing as had Vienna. Original in English. SAM-B&R-993.

77 Bericht über die Reise der Mitglieder der Stadtratskommission beim Wohnungsamt nach Nürnberg und Frankfurt-am-M vom 22.-24. November 1926. SAM-WA-63.

78 Franz-Josef Brüggemeier, 'Schlafgänger, Schnapskinos und schwerindustrielle Kolonie: Aspekte der Arbeiterwohnungsfrage im Ruhrgebiet vor dem Ersten Weltkrieg', in Jürgen Reulecke *et al.* (eds.), *Fabrik, Familie, Feierabend: Beiträge zur Sozialgeschichte des Alltags im Industriezeitalter* (Wuppertal, 1978), pp. 139–172.

79 Simmel, 'The Metropolis and Mental Life,' p. 181.

80 Bauamtmann Josef Jelinek, 'Die Vernunftehe Heim & Technik', in *Amtlicher Katalog: Ausstellung 'München 1928: Heim und Technik'*, p. 75.

81 Eve Blau, *The Architecture of Red Vienna* (London, 1999), p. 325.

82 Peter Rowe, *Modernity and Housing* (Cambridge, MA, 1993); Heynen, *Architecture and Modernity*; Mary Nolan, ' "Housework made Easy": The Taylorized Housewife in Weimar Germany's Rationalized Economy', *Feminist Studies* 3 (1990), pp. 549–578.

83 Bericht über die Reise der Mitglieder der Stadtratskommission beim Wohnungsamt nach Nürnberg und Frankfurt-am-M vom 22.-24. November 1926. SAM-WA-63.

84 Scharnagl an die Referate III [Finance] und VII [Housing], 23 April 1926; RR. Helmreich [Wohnungsreferent] an die sämtlichen Stadtratsfraktionen, 2 June 1926; Referat VII an die Stadtratsfraktion der Nazionalsozialistischen Arbeiterpartei, 12 June 1926. SAM-WA-64.

85 Karl Preis, *Die Beseitigung der Wohnungsnot in München: Denkschrift und Anträge des städt. Wohnungsreferenten vom 24. Dezember 1927* (Munich, 1927), pp. 79–80.

86 Preis, *Beseitigung der Wohnungsnot*, p. 95.

87 Generalbebatte um die 12.000 Wohnungen, Sitzung des Wohnungsausschußes, 14 March 1928, *Münchener Gemeinde-Zeitung*, 24 March 1928.

88 Bayerischer Architekten- und Ingenieurverband e.V. (ed.) (BAIVd), *München und seine Bauten nach 1912* (Munich, 1984), p. 86.

2
Großstadtfreude: joy in the metropolis

Chapter 1 showed that there were deep anxieties and discomforts elicited by the city in German-speaking Europe. It could be constructed as a site of placelessness, of anxiety, of psychic distress, home to little but ugliness and 'soul-rotting nervousness'. On one level, this is a potent critique of modernity, and would conform to the familiar view of German history – that there was a singular rejection of the modern world, and its agent, the metropolis. And, yet, few in the mainstream ever proposed leaving the city, destroying it, razing it to the ground. Discussion of the city by experts and laity was dominated by metaphors of reform, not revolution. Furthermore, they explored their critique of the city through thoroughly modern means – developing the knowledge and practice of planning; through schooling; through commodifying both past times and present places into *Heimat*. The mainstream of German urban discourse critiqued modernity, without ever proposing to abandon it. However, this moderate mainstream of administrators and politicians were far from overwhelmingly negative, and through their words and their deeds frequently exalted in the modern – an exaltation which is underrepresented in scholarly descriptions of cities in general, and German cities in particular. This chapter explores this sense of being urban, this sense of belonging in modern systems and modern processes. German experts and governors frequently expressed what I will call a *Großstadtfreude* – joy in the metropolis. It is crucial to understand and explore this positive side in order to correct the emphasis on the maladjustments to modernity in German culture.

People fêted the metropolis in several ways, and for several reasons. First, when planners and governors looked out at the horizons of their world, they saw not necessarily the rural *Heimat* which on occasions they claimed to admire. While they sometimes talked about mountains and forests, rivers and valleys, German administrators and urban governors increasingly saw other cities, and began to identify with them. A cultural shift took place in which experts acquired a universal, urban habit of thought and rejected the local and the particular. They imagined themselves in a community of similar urban, modern environments, and when faced with a task or a problem or an objective the instinctive response of the German official or urban politician was to reach out to his (and it almost invariably was his) brothers across the Reich and beyond. Thus they constructed themselves as members of a community of metropoles, all engaged in a modern project of improvement, however much they might talk of the peculiarities of their own city. Most came to talk with fluency about Hamburg, Munich, Berlin, Vienna, Frankfurt, Breslau and Prague. But they could also speak with some confidence about London, Birmingham, Lyon, Moscow, Budapest, Stockholm, Amsterdam, New York and Chicago. But this identity did not passively emerge: individual, nameable historical actors had to create it.

Secondly, this vision of themselves as part of a community of metropoles meant that city administrators and governors had to produce a language in which they could describe the areas around themselves – the 'not-city', the countryside. For it was in defining themselves against this 'other' that their very urban, modern nature was produced. It is too easy to forget that in this period, cities outside Britain and the Low Countries were often urban islands in a rural sea. Without widespread effective motorised transport and refrigeration, cities were still deeply and intimately dependent on the land around them for the provision of food. However, it is possible to detect the emergence of a sort of 'colonial' mentality among early twentieth-century administrators, in which the countryside shifted from being the source of goodness and health, and became viewed as a sort of redundant adornment or a functional unpleasantness. This process meant that the exact nature of the perimeters of cities had to be defined and explored, because this was the frontier territory, ripe for settlement and civilisation: the edge of the city was the interface between the civilised urban, and the empty 'other', ready for colonisation. Thus a major premise on which analysis of much early twentieth-century western culture is based is overturned: country good, city bad.

Finally, this chapter considers how values of rationalism, values which are so closely associated with modernity and modern forms of governmentality, were integrated into the symbolic hierarchy of signs and signifiers which constitutes the image of the city, as part of a passionate propaganda programme intended to convince 'ordinary

Germans' that their destiny lay in a modern technocracy. In particular, some people in early twentieth-century Germany felt a great sense of mission in finding ways for the buildings of science and administration, of rational expert knowledge and its bureaucratic agents, to be given form. Architecture was and is often described as a language, and the city as a text to be read.[1] This meant that new vocabularies would be necessary to communicate new ideas. For centuries, the edifices of the state and the church, and then the bourgeoisie, had dominated the structure of urban grammar: palaces, courts, operas, theatres, stock exchanges, art galleries. While bureaucratic administration was no less bourgeois than an opera house or less stately than a court, it was in a sense more insidious, because less congruent with the bourgeois ideology of individual freedom. Bureaucracy can offend the Liberal because it exists only to regulate and control. Its purpose is to do *for* or *to* the individual – indeed, state regulation is the clearest sign that the Liberal project is in some way failing, or needing correction. Bureaucratic logics, as Weber argued at the time and Foucault and Fukayama have argued more recently, are a widespread, extensive, burgeoning – even distinctive – feature of modern society, and they needed a way of giving themselves form and presence. In the USA, this question of finding an architectural form for administration was resolved with the skyscraper. Initially useless for either mass inhabitation (they were too expensive) or industrial production (for which horizontal spaces are needed), and certainly useless for things like the performance of opera or the worship of God, skyscrapers offered a clear urban presence for the only thing they were fit for: administration. But in Germany, the situation was different. Such bureaucratic functions in buildings had to assert themselves over cultural norms and existing cityscapes, and they often did this unapologetically, dynamically announcing their rational, bureaucratic intentions.

Liberal mentality and the community of *Großstädte*, 1890–1914

A variety of historiographical approaches have emphasised that over the last 250 years or so western societies have undergone a specific form of reordering, in which the principles by which knowledge is first generated, then applied, have undergone a major revolution. It would be unfair to caricature these approaches, or dismiss their differences, but rather than focusing on what separates them, it is important here to emphasise the themes which unite them. This is far from a comprehensive sketch – and nor is it meant to be, as (as will become clear) there is a large and easily accessible literature on all of these areas, but there are substantial points of agreement in many dominant characterisations of modernity. Marxians have described the rise of a specific social class which has analysed, categorised and sorted, and in the process of doing so has made itself rich and powerful. In sociology, powerful models of the shift towards a rational, ordering instinct have been developed. Max Weber emphasised the 'rise' of a bureaucracy, producing an endlessly reproducible, efficient, impersonal rule based on rational structures and expertise.[2] More recently, Jürgen Habermas has argued that the nature of power has changed twice in this period: first, during its relocation into a discursive, rational, masculine public sphere in the century after 1750. Then, from the mid-nineteenth century, this public sphere was crystallised ('refeudalised') into the institutions of the modern state.[3] Michel Foucault has charted the rise of an expert mentality which, like Habermas' model, is based around the rise of a certain form of discursive practice, in which the communicative act embodies the production and application of the knowledges by which the subject is regulated. While Habermas' public sphere is a more 'innocent' response to changing circumstances, Foucault emphasises the regulatory ambitions of the experts themselves.[4] Habermas is more likely to see the change as by-product of the irrelevance of handed-down systems of knowledge and power to modern problems, such as global trade, imperial administration, cholera prevention or the organisation of factory work. Bruno Latour, from a history of science perspective, has described a process whereby after the 'scientific revolution' of the seventeenth century, élites increasingly extended the scientific metaphor of 'the laws of things' to humanity. Thus they derived misplaced 'laws of man' with ever-increasing fixity; misplaced because they attempted to project the rigidity and moral neutrality of planets and atoms (laws of things) onto the flexibility and moral ambiguities of human existence (laws of man).[5] Zygmunt Bauman's reflexions on modernity largely concur, arguing that the specifically modern forms of human catastrophe embodied in the 'Final Solution' were the result of a misplaced – but inevitable – application of the laws of reason which underpin Habermas' modern discursive instinct.[6] Whereas Marxians have talked about the rise of a class, Weber, Habermas, Foucault, Latour and Bauman have talked about the acquisition of the apparatus of state power by subsections of this class – bureaucrats, public men, experts, social 'scientists', all bourgeois.

This consensus about the production and application of knowledge may imply the operation of some abstract historical rule or logic, of the sort typified by Spencerian 'progress', or Marxian historical materialism – but this is not the case. This rationality was borne by a personnel of real people, nameable individuals who had to find a way to relate to one another as such, and who had to overcome considerable physical and intellectuals obstacles to do so. Crucially, these people had to know how to identify themselves: they had to devise signs, symbols, habits and languages by which they could mark out an identity. The personnel charged with producing and applying this knowledge (a commission they may well have given themselves), was largely in the employ, or related to the activities of, urban governance. It was cities which commissioned the pedagogues and the social workers and the hygienists and the doctors and the cartographers which characterise so much of this rational apparatus (a fact which should call into greater question the readiness of historians to focus on national governments or 'national' discourse in 'national' fora). So it is among urban governors that we should look to try to see how they behaved as a group, how they gradually acquired the identity of governors, and the habits of government, in a specifically urban context.

In the very last years of the nineteenth century, and the first years of the twentieth, these urban experts began to organise themselves more formally into recognisable agents of state activity (what Habermas calls the 'refeudalisation of the public sphere'), and they defined their association with each other more openly and with a greater degree of institutional permanence. But this was not a smooth, obvious path to follow – although it may seem so from the overarching metanarrative interpretations of modernisation. A real difficulty for the people responsible for developing these processes was in relating to each other, and deciding to what extent they were involved in a universal, rather than a local, project. What does seem certain is that around 1900 in German-speaking Europe, a certain critical mass of these experts and governors cohered into more stable structures such as the Deutsche Städtetag (Conference of German Cities), and began to view themselves differently. As one American observer, Louis Robinson, commenting on the formation of the Deutsche Städtetag at the big 'City Exposition' in Dresden in 1903 summarised in 1908:

> The methods till lately employed by cities in working out their problems were highly individualistic. Each city did what was right in its own eyes – with the result that the problems remain still unsolved. But in recent years, co-operation among cities has come about, and the idea is

gaining ground that interchange of facts and experience is as indispensable in city affairs as in other lines of work.[7]

The negative effects of the isolation described here by this early sociologist, and the potential benefits of better cooperation, were made conspicuous in Germany in Hamburg, in the summer and autumn of 1892. A vicious outbreak of cholera – the last major outbreak in western Europe – took hold of the city, infecting 17,000 and killing half of them.[8] Richard Evans concludes that a major factor in producing the epidemic in Hamburg, and not elsewhere, was the *inexpert*, patrician nature of that city's government.[9] In short, Hamburg's administration was pre-modern, dominated not by experts predicating their rule on their knowledge, and nor by people who were involved with a party machinery, and therefore in some sense beholden (however imperfectly) to a wider (poorer) public. At the time of the cholera outbreak in Hamburg, the first Mayor of the city state had been a senator since 1855. Hamburg's government was inexpert, pre-modern and ineffective. As a result of this, thousands died, drawing into sharp contrast the difference between experiences in an idiosyncratic city and those in cities adopting a professionalised approach to managing their populations.

The production of this community of knowledge, this community of practice, was not, however, smooth and uncontested. No ineluctable historical logic was at play. So if the development of this distinctively metropolitan expert identity – supra-national, committed to the rationalising governmental process – is to be understood, the historian must engage with a detailed case study of who communicated with whom, why and to what effect. This investigation will help dissect some of the issues in the formation of the community of metropoles, and the foundation of a truly metropolitan, urban, modern identity. Perhaps a defining feature of a community is the capacity to identify itself and communicate in a common language. The most striking aspect of this gradual move towards a community of metropoles which impresses the historian from the archival record of *any* city in the western world in this period is the growing quantity of communication between cities, their governors and experts. Whenever one was faced with a problem, the expert's and governor's instinct was to turn his back on the local, and increasingly to enter into correspondence with other governors and experts in other cities, both inside and outside Germany – frequently, on a personal level. An example of this tendency in general to ally with distant urban solutions rather than local rural ones can be seen in the housing debate before and after the First World War. There was a sense in Germany in the 1890s – closely related to the sudden rise in the fortunes of the rhetorically violent SPD – that there was a deep problem in the ways that people were housed. This is explored more fully in Chapter 4 of this book. Here, the focus is on the ways one city's experts and governors set out establishing how they related to others', starting in the 1890s, with the tentative steps to formulate a specific 'housing question'.

In the 1890s, the 'housing question' became acutely important, because of the outbreak of cholera in Hamburg, an increasingly politically interested press, the rise of racial theories which emphasised the health and vitality of poorer citizens and the rise of both left- and right-wing populist parties in cities in German-speaking Europe which challenged the Liberal consensus on the *laissez faire* state. At the beginning of the 1890s, inspired by this interest in housing, the city of Munich's government tentatively began to ask that most stately of questions: 'What is to be done?' Asking, 'what is being done elsewhere?' was a first step in defining the problem, but also committed the city's experts to trying to understand their relationship to other experts and similar problems in other cities. Two brief early surveys were carried out by the Corporation. In these surveys, the activities of other German towns were examined, but at this stage the nature of the examinations was somewhat dry and statistical.[10] They interest primarily for their style, for the way they summarise the experience and significance of other city governments. Their style has the nature of a series of unpoliticised remarks written by a disinterested observer of a faintly visible 'urban horizon', with little expectation that much would come of them, and little sense that other cities should be viewed as much more than 'curiosities'. Thus we find out that:

> Bremen, which at this time has already built 258 workers' houses with a sale value of 950,000 M and 50 provisional barrack-flats [*Barrackwohnungen*], has been able to cope with sudden growth in demand [for housing], while Braunschweig has built nothing, but is prepared to lend money at 4%. In Frankfurt, they have built 25 buildings in a *Blocksistem* [sic] with 251 identical flats along with 248 other flats.[11]

The reports both continue in this tone, rattling off abstract nuggets of information, and it is difficult to imagine that anyone reading them might have been inspired to ally themselves with Bremen and its *Barrackenwohnungen* or Frankfurt and its *Blocksistem* [sic]. The tone and style of the reports reflect an interest in, but not at this stage an allegiance with or a sense of a community of, *Großstädte*. They also show a large degree of confusion among urban élites as to what the problem might be, and how it might be solved.

However, with the foundation of the Verein für die Verbesserung der Wohnungsverhältnisse in München (Association for the Improvement of Living Conditions in Munich, VVWM, of which more in Chapter 4) in 1899, a new phase began.[12] It was led by the Mayor of Munich, Wilhelm Borscht (a master baker, loosely allied to the Centre Party), and the Director of the Municipal Office of Statistics, Karl Singer. Municipal statistics offices began to be widespread in the Reich from 1890 onwards, and as one municipal statistician commented: 'the proper field of municipal statistics is housing statistics, especially the enumeration of tenements.'[13] The VVWM represents, therefore, the union of the expert knowledge and (quasi-)democratic political accountability so distinctive of modern government. Borscht and Singer seem to have been at the heart of a shift in focus over the next ten years away from a neutral, superficial interest in what other big cities were doing towards a more committed attitude, and a sense of interest, identity and allegiance. The campaign to found the VVWM was led by the head of the Municipal Office of Statistics, Karl Singer; his membership of an expert, scientific community interested in statistics and mathematics points to a crossover of a distinctly universalist set of academic discourses with recognition of the need and the possibility of social intervention. The language underpinning the establishment of the VVWM contrasts sharply with that from earlier in the decade. Mayor Borscht argued that the city was obliged by *'moderner Auffassung'* – a modern understanding of the world – to introduce urgent measures to deal with the 'in Großstäd*ten* bestehenden Mißständen' – problems existing in big cit*ies* (my emphasis) – and these words indicate that the inter-urban perspective and sense of allegiance were growing.[14] Crucially, the VVWM leadership did not see itself as concerned with 'a' city, but *the* city. The housing question was linked through a change in modern opinion to an obligation to understand a set of problems in the context of a key feature of modernity: the growth, proliferation and management of the metropolis.

When, in 1908, the city resolved to take a much more pro-active interest in the building of small flats, bureaucrats sent out quite a cursory questionnaire to German cities, comprising eight simple questions on one sheet of A4 paper, with spaces under each for other cities' answers. The replies were still highly varied, showing little of the inter-urban similarity in response and understanding of the problem which would become commonplace in the 1920s, but illustrating an eagerness on some cities' parts to work towards it. The twenty or so replies ranged from the embarrassingly blank, to the neutral, to the prolific. They ranged from long essays about the two flats for the Gasmeister of the Bamberg Gasworks to the City of Berlin, which wrote that it had only recently given a million Marks to small flat building, so it was too soon to reach any conclusions about housing provision,[15] to the wealthy city of Charlottenburg (institutionally independent, but in effect a suburb of Berlin), which had done nothing at all, and had to fill in an embarrassing set of blanks – *Nichts*; *Unbekannt*, etc. Other cities – Cologne and Nuremberg – sent detailed pictures and plans of the flats they had built, and proudly explained the features of each, detailing the contributions they made to the solution of the 'social question'.[16]

It is interesting to note that all sides in the housing debate increasingly used their awareness of other cities to bolster their cases, when trying to position themselves in Munich. Housing Director Schoener allied himself with French and German reformers and knew in detail the policies of a variety of German cities. Not only that, but he – like other architectural and housing reformers, such as Hermann Muthesius – had been to Britain (specifically to London, Birmingham and Manchester) to see what progress had been made there.[17] Equally, Liberal free marketeers and conservative anti-socialist opponents of municipal intervention in the housing field recognised, though sometimes agitated against, an 'inter-urban' expertise. It seems that they saw this universalising tendency as extending the reach of the interventionist state. Josef Humar, an opponent of *all* intervention in housing throughout the period and a significant figure in debates, even if only for his extremism, increasingly argued from a perspective of comparison and expertise from other cities, even when rejecting their solutions. Initially as president of the Munich Land- and Property-Owners' Association, and then subsequently also as town councillor from 1914 to 1933, Humar never failed to take positions *à propos* the housing question, the nature of poverty and the desires of the poor which bordered on the surreal. He argued frequently that the city government had been the dupe of sophisticated, work-shy fraudsters who were quite happy sharing twelve people or two families to a room because they had never known any better, and whose alleged homelessness was entirely the product of the gullibility of social reformers and anyone prepared to listen to those 'hirelings of the lazy, the SPD'. His favourite expression to infuriate his colleagues with regard to the housing crisis was the dismissive 'so-called'. He wrote that building from public means might well have taken place in *'ausserbayerischen Städten'* ('cities not in Bavaria'), but it was not appropriate here. Such building was not foreseen in the Bavarian rules governing municipal government, and so should not be adopted.[18]

And yet this contest between the local and the universal – which could be characterised as being between the pre-modern and the modern – was one which bureaucrats and experts vigorously engaged in. While in Chapter 1, the exhibition 'Munich 1908' was analysed to show its critique of modernity, the reasons for holding it reveal that, in fact, it was integral to this process of constructing a positive, urban identity. The impetus for the exhibition was rooted in two different impulses, and it is something of a 'chicken and egg' question to distinguish which came first. One aspect was the publicly stated desire to celebrate 750 years since the foundation of the city and to fête municipal achievements: this was all about local patriotism. There was another rationale, however, and that was to enter into a competition between cities which was perceived to be developing at the time. An early proposal for the exhibition spelt out that:

> A project should be brought to completion in 1908 [the Ausstellung 'München 1908'], a project which is intended to secure for our city her rightful place in the struggle with other cities, which from day-to-day becomes more serious and more difficult.[19]

There is a recognition of the new form of relationship between cities, and implicit in that is an accommodation with this idea of an emergent community, facing common problems and possibly finding common solutions. And this view of a peculiarly urban mission in which cities competed with each other, while all playing the same game in the same league, seems to have been shared by Mayor Borscht. In fact, he made this conception central to his speech opening the exhibition, beginning with the words:

> In the competition – as peaceful as it is strong and determined – between the big cities for the prize of the best possible fulfilment of their cultural mission, a new and significant phenomenon has emerged in the last decade . . .[:] *Ausstellungswesen* [holding exhibitions].[20]

While Borscht does not, as the previous author did, stress the novelty of inter-urban relationships as such, he does underline an emergent set of phenomena with which these 'big cities' operate. Here it is *Ausstellungswesen*, but his involvement in the debate about the housing crisis shows that he was aware of how these factors would act together to form a new whole.

This process continued after 1914, too – there was no 'rupture' into modernity in 1918, but just as the personnel of urban administration shows continuity, so do their ideas. If anything, rather than a nostalgic yearning for some notional pre-war compact between town and country, the sense of connection to other cities and alienation from any pre-modern, specifically rural association grew during the years 1914–23, largely focusing on the issue of food. Since the SPD rose to prominence in the 1890s, the issue of agricultural protectionism has been a central one in Germany for the working classes. Secret police archives from Hamburg show again and again that this was a vibrant topic for discussion in overheard conversations in working-class pubs before the war. Comments like this were typical features of socialist politics and working-class conversation, here recorded by an under-cover policeman, at the turn of the century:

> The 'hunger' question is the real problem right now, because the price rises which have taken over . . . change the whole perspective of things. Already since '78, where Bismarck decided for grain tariffs, the poorer people, so to speak, must go hungry, while the Junkers or the agrarians are nourished on the very fat of the workers.[21]

Large cities in this period were still deeply dependent on their surrounding countryside for the provision of foodstuffs, and in the hungry years of the war and after, 'only cities starved'.[22] The British blockade of the continent worked well and continued long after the ceasefire, exacerbating the effects of pre-war food tariffs. The inability of German cities (and their political agents in the Reichstag, the SPD and the Spartacists/Communists) to resist fully the agrarian interest in national political life immediately after the war led to both widespread starvation, and deep political turmoil.[23] In this turmoil, a rift opened up between starving cities and a countryside (which was, in fairness, frequently desperately short of man- and womanpower), which the Weimar administrations could never reconcile.[24] The sustained Allied naval blockade in 1919, combined with the decreasing capacity of German bureaucratic systems to administer food collection and fair distribution, led to many of the problems of the immediate post-war years. Even more than the thorny issue of agricultural tariffs before the war, the enormous, violent conflicts over provisions that erupted between cities and their hinterlands in Germany after 1918 helped define the future in specifically urban terms for so many.[25] Over the course of the war, the Army High Command and the Reich government badly managed food distribution, as well as the farming industry in general, such that by 1915 there were severe food shortages in German cities. Urbanites accused farmers of 'hamstering' food to secure higher prices, but when the Reichstag raised the price ceiling on potatoes, *still* supplies were not effectively restored. Secret police reports suggest that urbanites were convinced that the countryside and its forceful representatives in national government were betraying the war effort.[26]

Liberal mentality and the community of *Großstädte*, 1918–30

Belinda Davis draws attention to the fundamental re-orientation of German society produced by the war, from one in which political élites might appeal rhetorically to a primordial compact between city and land to one in which urbanites were increasingly confident about rejecting the rural, and saw themselves as compacted with more distant urbanites, rather than nearby country people. Concomitantly, after the war, urban experts travelled more, and identified themselves more and more clearly as urban. This could stretch to the point at which a Centrist town councillor (Liebergesell) in Munich in the 1920s, when contrasting Munich's tax contributions to the state of Bavaria with its returns, could shout out: 'That is an unbearable drain on the metropolis to the good of the open country!' It is worth quoting the German, too, for it contains a potent Anglicism, far more compelling than the English word 'drain': 'Das ist eine unerträgliche Auspowerung der Großstadt zugunsten des flachen Landes!' *Auspowerung* – out-powering – suggests depletion, but with an element of theft. His colleagues in the Council Chamber cheered him to the rafters.[27] The level of awareness of other cities among councillors and municipal employees, and the sense of connectedness to them, grew. In the housing debate in the 1920s, in the case of just one city, Munich, there were detailed reports of housing solutions gained during visits to Frankfurt, Nuremberg, Dresden, Chemnitz, Leipzig, Vienna, London, Amsterdam, Hamburg, Berlin, Frankfurt, Stuttgart, Cologne, Düsseldorf, Essen and other Ruhr cities.[28] Second Bürgermeister Küfner, responsible for economic development in the city for the years of the Weimar Republic and the early National Socialist period, presented economic reports throughout the period 1924–33 on his trips to Paris, Brussels, London, Amsterdam, Hamburg and Berlin.[29] The key development in the years after the war was that the exploration of the relationship between other cities and Munich became far more active. In the earlier period, although the municipality regularly sent representations to congresses and conferences, they did not automatically think of visiting other cities themselves, in person – or, at least, not in their capacity as governors or experts. Housing director Schoener's trip to London, Manchester and Birmingham in the early 1900s, or Hermann Muthesius' similar journey for the Prussian government, were something of an exception rather than the rule. Far more common had been the collation of information from elsewhere. But after the war, although there was an initial teething problem, municipal governors and experts proved eager travellers, while still keeping up the more passive, written correspondence with other cities.

That teething problem is worthy of some comment, because there was opposition to this interest in other cities after the Great War, showing how incompletely 'classical modernity' had been achieved, and the importance of personalities in producing modern instincts, identities and behaviours among governors. The faltering path towards a completely modern, universalising, expert governmentality was not easily or casually pursued and, as already stated, was not the result of the working-out of an abstract historical logic. It required rational actors to do things. Obstruction to the inter-urban model promoted by some in the administration came not from the right in Munich's council after the war, but the left. This is worth exploring, as it explodes any instinct to characterise the Republic's years into a progressive left or north, and a reactionary right or south. Ben Lieberman has already shown how a readiness to borrow money for social projects crossed party lines in municipal administrations in Prussia.[30] Thus we must down-grade the 'heroism' of the left in narrating the Weimar social project, and up-grade the centre and the centre-right's role in striving to produce a just society. In the post-revolutionary elections of 1919, Social Democratic parties of one form or another did very well across Germany, and captured the political mayoralty of Munich and the council with twenty-six of the sixty council seats. Fifteen seats went to the BVP (the Bayerische Volkspartei, successor to the moderate Catholic Centre Party) and eight to the liberal parties.[31] One might expect that the Roman Catholic BVP would interest itself most in a rejection of the essentially materialist underpinnings of a technocratic world view, but in fact it was the MSPD (Majority Social Democrats, the moderate left grouping, ten seats) and USPD (Independent Social Democrats, the radical left grouping, sixteen seats) which rejected the inter-regional, inter-urban and inter-national implications of envisioning the city as a universal set of modern phenomena, common to the whole industrialised western world. The BVP, on the other hand, proved keen to involve itself in this 'universalist' approach. The central feature of this alignment seems to have been personality and personal inclination. Joy in the city, joy in modernity, was not an easy party political issue.

In January 1920, the Director of Housing, Helmreich, wanted to take employees from the Housing Office and the Municipal Building Department to Augsburg, Nuremberg, Ulm, Frankfurt and Essen to see what solutions had been found to the problems there. They were particularly interested in 'the world-famous Ulm estate' – whose fame has not survived. SPD Mayor Schmid's reaction in the council meeting was this:

> I am completely against this. [The men involved] could look at plans and reports rather than travel around. It is just the same with the estate in Ulm. One can inform oneself about these things quite well through words and publications, pictures and drawings. I mean, making journeys now is hardly the most important thing. In any case, Senior Building Officer Rehlen has just been to Hamburg, Frankfurt and Charlottenburg [Berlin], and he should be able to fully instruct the others about what he has seen.[32]

Schmid's period of office is characterised by his opposition to, and obstruction of, almost everything imaginable, and despite the reunified SPD maintaining its largest-party status in 1924, the more ambitious and less confrontational BVP leader, Karl Scharnagl, became Mayor – with almost a palpable sigh of relief in the municipal administration. On this occasion, Schmid's attitude seemed to draw support from others. One Liberal (DDP) councillor, Strauß, immediately followed on:

> We should free ourselves from the example of other cities, and create things on our own initiative. The examples of other cities are by and large useless for us, because we have such different climatic conditions. One must create from the circumstances of place and area, and should not so lightly rely on templates.[33]

This is a firm rejection of the entire rational, universalising, modern project of social policy. This emphasis on deriving solutions from 'place and area' echoes the *Heimat* metaphor which Germans found so appealing, and Sitte's ideas about landscape and form. Second Bürgermeister Küfner, the 'a-political' Mayor, saw things very differently. Küfner's 'a-political' nature (he was appointed by the state as a civil servant, not elected as council leader) should not lead one to assume, however, that he was not programmatic and partisan. His vivacity would eventually meet its perfect ally in Mayor Scharnagl – and Küfner's sardonic wit and frequent humorous put-downs in the council chamber make reading debates taking place there more bearable. 'Travelling educates' ('*Reisen bildet*'), he stated tersely:

> Without it, one ages without maturing. Our experts should travel just as they should go to congresses, however problematic the results they bring back. The definitive issue of whether we are to remain on a high plateau is: speaking to others.[34]

Küfner's approach to the foreign and to the problematic was entirely differently cast to that of Mayor Schmid, and implicit in it is an understanding of the world expressed in terms of risk, not danger, and in terms of universalities, not localities. Not only that, but Küfner seems to be implying that the real reason for the objections to the travel plans were not pecuniary, but cultural; namely that challenging and problematic 'foreign' solutions might be imported back to Munich.

Later in the year, a similar proposition was again laid before the Council in a stormy, argumentative meeting, this time regarding the Congress of the German Association of Housing Departments in Berlin. The slightly surprising (in terms of conventional assumptions about 'rational' politics in Weimar Republic Germany) right–left divide over Munich's place in a community of either *Großstädte* or experts was fully played out here. The radical socialist USPD and the moderate socialist MSPD both thought that the national meeting was no place for either the Director of Housing, Helmreich, or anyone from the Municipal Building Department – maybe they feared that they would return, as Küfner warned and perhaps hoped, with challenging solutions, which might prove irresistible in their rationality. The conservative BVP and this time the Liberals argued they should be sent. Eventually, a compromise was reached, supported by all but the USPD, that one person – but not Helmreich – should travel outside Munich. Helmreich was outraged, and in an unusual piece of drama for a German bureaucrat, threatened to resign; he claimed it was short-sighted and narrow-minded of the city not to look elsewhere for solutions to shared problems. He promised, in a fit of pique, possibly sarcasm, certainly comedy, never to be so daft as ever to leave Munich again, a tone which drew Schmid's censure and 'merry uproar' from the councillors.[35]

Weiß (Liberal/DDP) suggested that maybe he and the others should go, as the cities all shared common problems – completely contradicting the DDP representative from the earlier meeting. The appropriately named Kämpfer ('fighter', USPD) shouted, 'Sure! If he can bring some flats back with him!' Scharnagl – later Mayor, but at this stage only a councillor – concluded for the BVP with their, and his, characteristic pragmatism:

> It is essential that our experts are well informed, not just about the conclusions reached in Berlin, but throughout the Reich and beyond – I only voice the concern that they do not bring back too many impressions from Berlin, and that they do not want to adapt our circumstances too closely to those of Berlin. But they should go.[36]

All of the worries about the modern metropolis which were discussed in Chapter 1 clearly inform Scharnagl's nervousness about the influence Berlin might have. He seems to be suggesting that the arch-metropolis, Berlin, had a peculiarly seductive property, and might insinuate itself into Helmreich's and the experts' consciousnesses, giving them the zeal of the convert and bringing Berlin's haste, nervousness and alienation back with them. He nevertheless insisted that there was a community of cities, that there were common problems faced by all urban governments and a common system of dealing with them – the rationalist, liberal intervention – to which he subscribed.

Urban selves and rural others: peripheries, edges and the colonial mentality

If the city was to define itself as 'urban', this meant that it had to decide what was '*un*urban' – urbanites had to specify a non-urban 'other' against which to contrast themselves. In short, this meant that experts and governors had to decide what the countryside was, what it was for and how it should be described and managed. Indeed, this debate among the middle-class cultural élites was a live one across Europe around 1900. As Nina Lübbren has shown, there was a huge migration of artists – both physically, and in terms of subject matter – from the big cities to so-called 'colonies' of artists beyond them. For these artists – and their urban consumers – the countryside represented honest people, true community, picturesque landscapes and national genius; in short, across Europe, many bourgeois art consumers constructed a sort of rural *Heimat*.[37] At precisely this time, planners in Britain began to suggest more systematically that the countryside was a very good place to put experimental communities known as 'Garden Cities'. While cities had been sprawling outwards into the country since their inception, and while model settlements such as New Lanark or Saltaire had often been placed outside them, the early advocates of the Garden City idea suggested that small, well-managed, systematically planned settlements should be established, separate from the city, but linked to it. In German, such low-density housing developments were called *Kolonien*, or colonies. These were 'satellite' cities (or really, picturesque, nostalgic housing estates) that represented, in Ebenezer Howard's bucolic imaginary, the 'city–country'. However, this metaphor of *mixing* town and country was not, it seems, as universally accepted as a linear presentation of the 'rise of the Garden City' might suggest.

A clearer example than Munich could not be wished for, because the issue of what the countryside should symbolise, what the countryside was *for*, was a hotly debated one, and one can see this in several clashes within the Municipal Building Department. As discussed in Chapter 1, in the mid-1890s Munich's experts and governors were involved in a massive planning exercise to develop one, over-arching city plan, encompassing the existing city, and a predicted growth outwards. Over the period in question, the municipality moved from a conception of the city as a geographically circumscribed entity, which would have to be contained if it was going to be understood or managed, to a point of view in which the city, and their role in shaping it, should be grown as far and as fast as possible. In short, they moved from a static to a dynamic model of the urban. This transformation will be dealt with in three parts: first, the sense of the city as a bordered entity, something to be limited and controlled, but with an empty, irrelevant void beyond it; secondly, the attempt to overcome that, and grow the city outwards; and, lastly, the attempt to order that growth around symbols of municipal authority to align the enlargement of the city around the modern functions of rational government.

The clearest symbol of the bordered conception of the city in the 1890s was perhaps the programme of ringing the city with *Pflaster-Zollhäuser* – toll-booths. As did many cities, the Munich municipality had the right to levy tolls on vehicles from outside the city using municipal streets. Hans Grässel started working for the City of Munich in 1890, and his first commission as architect-in-charge was to build a ring of toll-booths around the city starting in 1892. He would go on to build fourteen such booths, at all the main entrance points to the city, over the course of the 1890s, and even into the 1900s.[38] Clearly these structures were put up for a fairly specific *primary* purpose – the collection of money – but one should also recognise the mentality which underpinned them. To build a ring like this is to define a boundary, to mark the point of entry and thereby to contrast that which is without with that which is within. It is erecting a sort of fence which hems the city economically and visually, posits a permanent 'frontier territory' and fixes a stable boundary for the urban by placing buildings of some substance and permanence at that periphery.

This frontier mentality was certainly a conscious aspect of municipal policy, and had underpinned the city's acquisition of vast tracts of land around the city in order to regulate growth. Munich's Housing Director, Schoener, berated a meeting of the Housing Commission about how municipal policy had, in the past, been oriented towards retarding the growth of the city, to containing and limiting it. The physical walls of German cities were pulled down in the late eighteenth and early nineteenth centuries, but psychological walls remained. He pointed out that the city had acquired substantial amounts of land surrounding it in the fifteen years before 1908. This strategy was a common one for German municipal governments, and went hand-in-hand with their development of 'extension plans' in the 1890s. It had been done as a measure to contain the town in order to drive up the value and rentability of land in the town centre. It was a measure designed to distort the market in favour of the 10% of Munich citizens entitled to vote – namely, the middle-class supporters of the Liberal parties. Schoener went on to argue that the time had come to use this land for development. He challenged his colleagues with the following observation:

> I feel as if with this approach [using land ownership to control and stop development] we were stuck too firmly in the old conception of a city and city government with regard to land . . . in the corporation. The council chambers behave all too much as if they had bought to fulfil their own needs.[39]

He was right; they had. They had wanted to define and control the city, at an earlier stage, and surround it by a green belt. A second motive was the development of a valuable land portfolio. Yet at the same time that Grässel was building watchful huts at the border of the city, and Schoener was berating his colleagues for hemming the city in, a change was afoot. The town was enlarging itself; deliberately, self-consciously and methodically enlarging the urban, making the *Großstadt* ever *größer*.

The possible forms which this enlargement could take were radically altering. Up until the 1890s the enlargement of many European cities had been an essentially passive affair, from the state's perspective. Property speculators, industrialists, tram companies or the migrant poor in shanty towns would use land outside the city boundaries. Alternatively, small towns around large cities would grow until there was little or no green land between them and the municipality. In either case, when this occurred in continental Europe the state would incorporate the area into the municipality (in Britain and the USA, jurisdictional chaos still reigns). This process of incorporation was usually against the fierce opposition of the city concerned, which would then have to provide such areas with water, schools, gas, hospitals, poor law provision and the like – an expensive business when incorporating a shanty town of huts populated by those at the very edge of society.[40]

However, around 1890–95, a shift seems to have begun, in which incorporation in German cities was more pro-actively sought. This is crucial, because it shows that rather than seeking to limit, constrain or destroy the modern metropolis, people began to agitate for its enlargement, growth and expansion. This turns the conventional view of German culture's attitudes towards the metropolis on its head. A relatively mundane project like the construction of a municipal gasworks illustrates the importance of personal dynamics in the processes of change, as well as showing how an expansionist modernising city government might cross its borders in an attempt to impose modernity on the surrounding countryside.

In 1902 it was clear that the city's old gasworks on Thalkirchenerstraße near the city centre were no longer up to the job. Whereas the average production in the fifteen largest German cities per inhabitant was 75.4m^3 p.a., in Munich it was a mere 35.3m^3.[41] This was clearly a problem already, and would only get worse. Ries, director of the municipal gasworks, projected a growth in the population of Munich over the coming years of an unspecified amount and, maybe more importantly, demanded a gasworks 'in the new style' to cater for it. It should contribute to the existing *Stadtbild* (urban image, overall appearance of the city) and be 'organically bound to it' and the City Extension Plan, and at the same time would form a respectable focal point in the suburb he foresaw springing up around the works.[42] He anticipated that, although the plant was to be built on what was then a greenfield site, the city would naturally expand around it. I will return to this idea shortly, to discuss how the municipality organised its presence in these 'colonial' outposts.

More significant for the current theme was the creeping method of acquisition. In August 1906, the Corporation bought 17,392 ha about 1 km outside the city on the Dachauerstraße in Moosach for the gasworks. The problem was that, naturally, the parish of Moosach did not want a gasworks for a city of half a million people built on its land; they refused planning permission to the City of Munich. The city requested that the area in question be taken away from Moosach by the Bavarian government and given to it, so that its own planning regulations would apply, and this was done. An 'island' of Munich was created in Moosach. The Corporation duly granted itself permission to build its gasworks on someone else's doorstep. In 1912, the city requested the incorporation of the entire parish of Moosach, along with several others, and by the middle of 1913 this process was complete.[43] The city had stopped regarding enlargement as a danger and an expense, and come to view it as a necessity – especially if its modernising, industrialising project were to be brought to completion.

It is imperative to repersonalise these banal, everyday projects, because if we start looking at bureaucratic activities as stemming from the relationship of nameable, living, feeling human beings, rather than as simply the working through of the algorithm of modernisation, we can see exposed the ways in which this frontier territory was being re-imagined. Internal wrangling among bureaucrats about the nature of the buildings such as this gasworks are also illustrative, for it was in (to us, perhaps) banal projects like this that the peripheries of the city might be redefined, away from the clarity and fixity of the toll-booth ring and towards a colonising expansionism. In redefining the peripheries of the city, the nature of the city itself was called into question, and the relationship of the urban to the rural 'other' was recast. The key feature of the design of the buildings which the city government pitched outwards into the countryside was the pervasive idea that each should visually constitute the focal point of a new suburb not yet existing: it should be a kernel for settlement. The municipality would project itself into the centre of an as yet hypothetical urban enlargement. Two relatively typical municipal projects will serve as examples here: the gasworks just mentioned, and the school building projects. Planners and engineers worked together closely on the design for the new gasworks, sharing the assumption that they would attract settlement around them which would initially become the 'Gaswerkviertel' in the same way that the abattoir had unintentionally given rise to the Schlachthofviertel ('Abattoir quarter', a name the area still has today), and after that to an organic addition to the town.[44] Ries, the director of the gasworks, specified that 'the objective [is] more a reasonable architectonic set of circumstances, and other advantages,' and concluded:

> [T]he external forms of these factory buildings should be carried out in the utmost simplicity and clarity, and because of this we do not plan any great elaborateness in the architectonic details, as can be seen at many other cities' gasworks being built now. Of course, this in no way excludes any harmonisation [*Zusammenstimmung*] of the complex with the ideal of a friendly impression and an organic *Stadtbild* [city image].[45]

The intention seems to have been to create an ensemble with the potential visually to organise a new suburb as both something distinct from the main part of the city, and at the same time organically joined to it.

This industrial symbolism did not go uncontested, and nor did the idea that the area around the city was an uncivilised desert, needing colonisation. The whole complex was only 1km or so away from the western cemetery built between 1900 and 1904. A conflict erupted among the bureaucrats about whether this area should be visually characterised by the pre-modern symbols of the edge of the urban – the toll-house and the cemetery – or modern symbols of expansive urban modernisation. Grässel, who had designed the cemetery and toll-booth, was at two heated meetings called in the spring of 1904 to discuss whether the gasometers should be moved away from the cemetery or hidden by trees, arguing that they should not be visible from the cemetery.[46] Building Officer Bertsch took the gasworks directors' side, however, and his position as second in charge at the Office for Urban Extension and resident 'expert' at the Royal Building Commission seem to have carried the day. He agreed that the model of the project:

> seems to prove that the whole impression [*Gesamtbild*] of the establishment is a friendly one. Even the gasometers, with their lightly constructed, modern execution, make an interesting, and in no way un-beautiful, set of objects.[47]

In fact, Bertsch's proposal was to make the gasometers more visible by moving them towards the road, to refuse to hide them behind trees and attach a clock to the water-tower in the project, so that the industrial development would become *more*, not less, conspicuous in the area.[48] This solution was the one which was finally adopted. Thus, the city planted an outpost in the countryside outside it; then ensured that it would be visible through the clock and the absence of trees; and designed it to be a symbol of the city's administrative capabilities which would visually organise a projected new suburb. This contest, in which the genteel 'border' architecture of cemetery and toll-booth was pitched against the potent urban, industrial and technical symbol of the gasworks in a dispute about what the visual emphases of the expanding city should be, shows a clear commitment on the part of the most members of the Municipal Building Office to a growing city. Where Grässel proposed stressing the cemetery over the gasworks, the time-honoured symbol of the urban frontier over the industrial symbol of an expansive metropolis, Bertsch argued that the symbol of industry should be the organising element; whereas Grässel suggested hiding the gasometers with trees, Ries, Hollweck and Bertsch argued that their modern construction would make interesting buildings in their own right, and that they did not need to be hidden. Despite suffering a personal setback in this instance, even a relative aesthetic conservative like Grässel was not at all marginalised in the wider process of colonisation. Through his school buildings, he engaged complicitly in the impetus to grow the city outwards, which suggests that it was the superficial style of the colonial outpost's construction which bothered him, more than this method of proceeding in general.

Grässel's opinions about the role of schools as the organising visual element in a new or developing suburb show that he was in basic agreement with Ries and Bertsch about method, at least. He felt that schools were an important symbol of – and agent of – progress, and as such should be made as prominent as possible. In an essay of 1915, he stressed:

> The city should be very careful about how it builds schools, because, by and large, settlements will grow up around them. Once the city has laid gas, water and sewage pipes, the value of the land around will rise, and in the subsequent building, the school should be the orchestrating [*bildende*] point. Building regulations should be in place to control the inevitable development, because the most beautiful appearance of a school-house will be of no use to the city at all, if the surroundings are not harmonised with it.[49]

This theme of state buildings conditioning urban growth had already been picked up, with respect to Munich's famous school-building policy, by a national technical journal, *Das Schulhaus*. Discussing the school on Fürstenriederstraße, built by Grässel between 1901 and 1904, the journal described the placement of the school as being in open countryside.[50] As the *Schulhaus* article explained, the parish of

Laim had been incorporated into the municipality of Munich in 1900, as some of its area had been settled by industry on the Munich borders. However, the parish was a large one, and the whole area had been transferred to Munich's governance, including large stretches of agricultural land. Grässel was faced with a complicated situation. He was compelled by his ideology of '*Gliederung*' – the idea that every building should form a continuous link with the environment in which it stood, and which was explored with regard to the Implerstraße school in Chapter 1 – to reflect the rural nature of the site in the building. But as the *Schulhaus* article acknowledged, the nature of the site was dual:

> With regard to the layout of the site, far outside the periphery of the city, and the overwhelmingly rural character of the surroundings, a solution had to be found based on significantly different factors than are pertinent for the schools built in the city.
>
> Not only that, but the road on which the school lies is planned by the City of Munich to be a traffic artery. However, at the moment there is next to no traffic to speak of, and as the street has not yet been hemmed in by rows of buildings, it has not yet forfeited any of its rural character.
>
> Due to the absence of surrounding buildings, the architect [*Erbauer*] had to be sure that the work would be sufficient standing on its own, as much as later, when it will have to exert its influence on the *Stadtbild* [overall impression of the city] standing in the middle of the rows of buildings due to be dispatched to accompany it.[51]

One wonders why the city built this school at all, given there was no settlement around it to use it. The only satisfactory answer is that the municipality predicted a future demand, and built, as it were, to encourage and manage it, as Grässel described above. The Fürstenriederstraße school was a staging post for urban expansion, and, just like the gasworks, it was intended to place the municipality as visually and functionally central to that growth. First, the municipality would plan for and encourage enlargement; secondly, the Corporation would design itself into that extension, to become a visual still point in the turning world of urban expansion. Thirdly these staging posts were all potent institutional and architectural agents for key features of the modern state and modern society – not in any metaphorical way, but a literal one. Schools, gasworks, old people's homes, housing estates, tram depots and welfare offices do not *allude* to the key features of governmental modernity or urban administration; they *are* those features. The municipality's leaders and technocrats aligned themselves with the enlargement of the

Großstadt, and agitated for a dynamic municipal commitment to it, to be evidenced within it.

The dysfunctional countryside and the useful city

While the school and gasworks clearly illustrate the 'colonial' habit and show an expansive vision of the urban, modernising project, they do not indicate the ways in which contemporaries constructed the rural 'other'. Most literature assumes a dichotomy in German cultural discourse between what Zimmermann and Reulecke have characterised as 'City as Moloch, Country as Source of Strength'.[52] This simplistic contrast (and Zimmermann and Reulecke are not blind to its simplistic nature) can be challenged by examining not just the ways that the municipal authorities managed rural land acquisition in the spurt of industrialisation during the war, but in the ways that this management was related to the public through the metaphors deployed by journalists. Up until 1914, industrial functions had been woven into the city, but the large-scale factories developed on the outskirts of all German cities during the war were designed solely around the efficiency of production, and were often influenced by the ethos of Fordism. The war was not good for Munich, and hit its economy hard. Tourism stopped, beer consumption dropped, luxury goods – like furniture, gloves, hats and leather – were no longer purchased, so key sectors in the Munich economy suffered greatly. When the Reich government announced the establishment of a large munitions factory in the city, there was substantial excitement. The joy at the decision in May 1916 to build a Krupp ordnance works in the north of Munich was not, however, primarily an economic one. When the Krupp concern announced its intentions, it provoked a flurry of activity on the part of the municipality, as they bought up the land around the works. They did this for several reasons. First, their impulse to control was aroused. Secondly, they saw the potential to expand the city and they wanted to seize it. Thirdly, they wanted to condition this expansion.

When Krupp announced they would buy land to the north of the city, the municipality's immediate response was to buy land there, too. The city bought its plots strategically (and many newspaper reports confirm this strategic consciousness[53]), so that the city's land divided the Krupp land, which would compel Krupp to negotiate with the Corporation in the use of the area. It also allowed the municipality to develop an early industrial estate (at a similar time to the development of the first industrial estates in Britain, at Trafford Park in Manchester and Wembley Park in London). To encourage such development there, the municipal government announced the immediate commencement of the construction of express tram links to the sites, and the provision of housing for the first foremen who were coming from the Ruhr. The press response to this developing industry was ecstatic. There was not a single negative reaction. But what is more interesting are the metaphors and style of argument used about the countryside – the world beyond the city limits. Munich's largest circulation daily, the *Münchner Neueste Nachrichten*, led on the front page with a description of the transformation from the rural and the idyllic to the industrial and urban. The article, entitled 'A Tour Round the Munich Krupp area of the Future', started by describing a bounded city; the Jewish cemetery by Grässel, and his toll-house – two potent symbols of urban frontiers. Beyond them lay 'an idyllic fantasy, open fields, lush greenery, all a long way from the war, where we can enjoy the poetry of the country lane'.[54] But if one carries on to Alt Freimann, the article exalted:

> you stand in the crucible of the future world of Munich [*im Brennpunkt des Münchener Zukunftslandes*], which is suddenly, along with the name Krupp, on everyone's lips. Now you stand in the Munich-Freimann Industrial Estate![55]

The author went on to emphasise the healthy contrast between the developments which were taking place there – the roads and railways which were being laid out – with the private garden suburb which had been built adjacent to this land before the war. From these houses (described as a *Gartenkolonie* – a garden *colony*), there was a view which would have been the same in an eighteenth-century landscape, and lists all the Elysian details. It laid especial emphasis on the derelict pig farm, which had gone bankrupt before the war. It concludes:

> This is the land that the City of Munich has bought to secure the future development of the city. Here it will sow a special seed, from which we anticipate a distant, rich harvest, rich enough perhaps to transform the entire structure of our city from the very bottom up.[56]

The overall tone in this article is that the countryside is pretty, but redundant. The municipality, through its town planning policies, would colonise it and make it useful.

In a later article, one which Hans Grässel cut out, underlined, glued in his scrap-book and surrounded with (unfortunately) illegible shorthand notes, one journalist pointed out another type of restructuring which was hoped for from the plant and the municipal land purchases:

Alongside the economic significance to Munich of the industrial plans for the land around Freimann, there is a greater, but perhaps slower, influence we can expect, namely on the architectural formation and reformation of the city.[57]

The article celebrated the booming industry of the north of Munich, mentioning the Rapp Motorenwerke, which was doubling its workforce, and was about to change its name to the one we are more familiar with: BMW. Furthermore, the *Münchner Neueste Nachrichten* offered a prognosis for the future, and placed an industrial vision at the heart of it:

Furthermore, in the course of following decades, this development of the north should lead to a not too nerve-wracking revision [*nicht zu ängstlichen Umgestaltung*] of the *Stadtbild*, with Munich moving towards the ideal image of the city, which would have been so easy to organise earlier, but is now exceptionally difficult, and will never again be fully attainable.[58]

So it seems that over-arching metaphorical structure of the discussion of this industrial colony in the countryside was that the development, by including industry in the *Stadtbild*, brought the city closer to an urban ideal, that the lack of such a visual and economic presence in the fabric of the Bavarian metropolis was a failure of some sort.[59] This way of envisioning the city seems to be a significant statement of affection or acceptance of the phenomena of modernity – in this case, the manufacture of *Millionenartikel*, mass-produced goods.[60] The presentation of the countryside as an unproductive void beyond the urban, and the focus on driving the city outwards and focusing growth on symbols of the modern, rational, governmental project seriously undermine the capacity for historians to rely on a 'rural = good, urban = bad' dichotomy with which to understand German culture.

Modern signs, modern citizens: technological symbolism in the city

As has just been seen, with schools, gasworks and factories, experts and governors were keen to exaggerate the visual impact of modern structures and functions before and during the war – a wish which did not diminish after it. This consistent desire to highlight the technological, the bureaucratic and the industrial shows a group of Germans who seem to have been completely opposed to the idea that cities and modernity were 'bad' – just the reverse. They celebrated them. As has also been seen, the municipality seems to have shared a metaphor with the mainstream journalistic idiom of the time, that modern projects like this were the right direction for Germany to be going in. This begs questions about the ways 'ordinary' Germans responded to these conspicuous projects, and whether modernisers like these were able to use these powerful physical tranformations of the urban environment to persuade and convince. The evidence suggests that they were.

A key project which demonstrates the capacity of these municipal experts to transform public discourse in this way, which emphasises the leadership rather than responsiveness of the expert class, would be the Technisches Rathaus, or 'Technical Town Hall', and the gas and electricity administration centres either side of it. The enormous administrative–technical complex was constructed in the second part of the 1920s, although it had been designed and planned in 1918–19. It was not just architectural Modernism which this project (and other ones like it, such as the enormous 'high-rise' hospital for sexually transmitted diseases on Thalkirchenerstraße) hoped to project onto the city, however, and a brief discussion of these highly prominent plans should reveal just how ideologically laden these buildings were. More importantly, to examine them is to examine the council's faith in *Leistungsverwaltung* – literally, 'the management of achievements' but, more prosaically, the provision of modern services – and to show how it attempted to make this mediocre architectural Modernism function as a shorthand for that success. The importance here lies not so much in the building of the Technical Town Hall itself, but in charting a change in the ways journalists described it, and characterised the public's response to it, for this would seem to show that the building (or, rather, complex of buildings) succeeded in placing bureaucracy and administration and service provision at the heart of a positive urban consciousness and identity.

The Technisches Rathaus complex, comprising the Technisches Hochhaus, the Elektrizitätsverwaltung and the Gas Board, sought to elevate municipal government to the dominant feature of the urban horizon, and make the Corporation the only architectural feature of the skyline which could compete with the church. But it sought to do more than that; the idea of a specifically Technical Town Hall detaches the political (and traditional) dimensions of the urban government from the technical (and novel) ones. From this ensemble, the Corporation's electricity, gas, water, engineering and building services would be directed. In short, the Technical Town Hall glorified neutral, apolitical, universalising technology and aligned the municipality with it. As Figure 2.1 shows, the high-rise (*Hochhaus*) does not impress now for what might be called its Modernism. In part, this is because of the development of a canon of modern architecture which has privileged those architects not working predominantly in brick. However, as Walter Müller-Wulckow's influential studies in the late 1920s show, to contemporaries, working with brick was a perfectly 'Modernist' solution, just as white or coloured plaster scrim could be used to disguise a multitude of historicist sins.[61] Not only does the historiography of European Modernism neglect to show brick building as essential to the Modernist project as fully as they might, it tends to privilege the plastered buildings of particular architects over their brick work – just as it privileges flat roofs over pitched. The plastered walls of Weißenhof (a commercial failure, and arguably on balance a negative contribution to the 'cheap housing' question) are always shown, while the neighbouring housing project by a trade union housing association in brick (a successful solution to the 'cheap housing' question) is ignored.[62] Even a seminal Modernist text intended to define the canon of Modernism, *Der Sieg des neuen Baustils* by Walter Curt Behrendt (1928), shows more buildings relying on visible bricks than not, but subsequent connoiseurial literature has proved reluctant to redress the balance.[63]

Modernist or not, the Technisches Rathaus complex certainly represented a bold and committed statement of engagement with modernity at the heart of the old city. As such, the building should be seen as part of a redevelopment of the Unterer Anger, an area of the mediaeval city centre which had traditionally been the corn exchange and produce market. The grain halls were demolished at the end of the war and a competition was held to build an office structure capable of uniting all the technical and service elements of the city in one building. The project was the pet of the city's second Mayor, the a-political Hans Küfner. He was a well-travelled man, and a technocrat *par excellence*, running most of the technical aspects of the municipality. His influence is probably discernible in the choice of project winner – the designs by Munich municipal Bauamtmann Leitensdorfer, who had previously been involved in the development of municipal hydro-electric power stations on the River Isar. These projects – the plan was a three-stage development, not one single one – were designed in 1919, and put into immediate effect. It is worth pausing for a moment to reflect on what the Munich Corporation was actually pledging itself to in 1919: a flat-fronted, entirely unadorned, plaster-faced white building, fitted out

2.1 The *Technisches Rathaus* – Technical Town Hall, 1920s.
The Technical Town Hall – Munich's first 'skyscraper'. Designed in the last months of the war, it impressed contemporaries as a bold experiment in modern building.

2.2 The Munich *Elektrizitätsverwaltung* – the Electricity Board, 1920s. The Electricity Board HQ attracted huge criticism at the beginning of its construction during the inflation. However, the Technical Town Hall at the end of the block seems to have rescued the project in the eyes of contemporary commentators.

entirely with 'normed' fixtures and components, ending in what was to be Germany's first *Hochhaus*, built with curtain walls suspended on a reinforced concrete frame.

The Electricity Board headquarters, shown in Figure 2.2, had some considerable impact. It was begun in 1920, put on hold in 1922 and the first part of the project to be completed in 1926. The initial response to the whole ensemble was varied, but generally opinion was hostile before the tower block was completed, and favourable after. As the electricity headquarters was nearing completion in the summer of 1926, the *Münchner Neueste Nachrichten* praised a 'significant and courageous modesty' in the building, and said that it would 'surely constitute a *städtebauliche* focal point'. It noted in passing the uniformity of the windows and the internal fittings, and then went on gently to praise the building:

Joy in the metropolis

Whoever can free themselves from the long-cultivated habituation to decorated architectural styles, and who really takes on board the Munich spirit of building [*Münchener Baugeist*] as it was before the beginning of the building of the reign of the first King Ludwig [r. 1825–48] will find here, in new materials, masses and functions, something of the old Munich spiritual quest, without 'Olde Worlde' touches, in the sense of regularity and unity.[64]

The reference to Munich building before Ludwig I implies an appreciation of the neo-classical, rather than the more playful gothic styles deployed by the 'builder king'. However, before the completion of the entire project, support was not universal. The *Allgemeine Zeitung* led with the screaming headline '223 identical windows in one façade!' as the competition was decided just two months after the armistice, and went on to establish the general character of criticism for Modernist building in the next seven (if not seventy) years. The contemptuous subheadline was: 'A piece of Munich architecture. Insipidness cannot be white-washed away! Poor Blumenstraße. And a tower block still to come?'[65] The parameters of international criticisms of Modernism were firmly staked out: 'This building will be boring, factory-like, devoted to over-functionalism [*Nur-Nützlichkeit*], and painfully bleak.'[66] The *Völkischer Beobachter* – not in the late 1920s a conservative newspaper in cultural terms, and representing the more radical, left-wing elements of the NSDAP – wrote of the building's official opening in 1927:

> One could not really claim that the new headquarters of the Munich municipal electricity works . . . makes what one might call an elevating impression. The famous lack of decoration – which, according to Bürgermeister Dr. Küfner, corresponds to the modern demands of strict *Sachlichkeit* – did not need to be so odiously and exaggeratedly brought to the eye, just to create a giant barracks with six floors to disgrace the entire area for the next hundred years.[67]

Many other journals agreed.

However, by the time the tower block was nearing completion two years later, these views had entirely disappeared. The fourteen-storey concrete frame which towered over the entire city skeleton-like until its walls were filled in attracted substantial comment and many visitors, and when the tower was completed both national and local press were ecstatic. The *Völkischer Beobachter* – just two years after its initial complaints about the project – led with the headline: 'A Tower Block in the Munich Style!' It went on to say that the whole plan of articulating the two lower elements through the tower was 'incontrovertibly the greatest of inspirations on the part of the architect'.[68] All the Munich and Bavarian newspapers had pull-out picture specials covering the new tower, and so did significant national ones – many Berlin papers, the *Kölnische Zeitung*, the national edition of the *Völkischer Beobachter*, the *Frankfurter Allgemeine* and the *Welt am Sonntag*, and it was featured in national and even international trade journals.[69] The *Vossische Zeitung* had a picture special entitled, 'The Battle of the Skyscraper', detailing the various projects recently brought to completion in Germany using tower blocks. Munich's is one of the least Modernist (in the art-historical sense of a stripped-down, whitewashed experiment in mass and right-angles to achieve its aesthetic qualities) – but, as already mentioned, it was planned in the last few months of 1918, and so did not have a familiar vocabulary of Heroic Modernism to draw on. However, it was singled out for especial praise by the newspaper in comparison to the other tower blocks, because of its sense of contribution to and continuity with the rest of the *Stadtbild*. The caption read, 'The Technical Town Hall in Munich, whose link to the older buildings to which it is joined can only be called a complete success', whereas the far more 'Heroically Modernist' Newspaper Tower in Frankfurt was described as 'interesting', but 'lacking any meaningful link with its surroundings'.[70] Martin Wagner, a celebrated Modernist architect famous for his Berlin housing estates, gave a speech in Munich in 1930 which dealt with the tower block – and praising Munich as the model to which all aspired. Wagner concluded that he was not fundamentally opposed to tower blocks as such, but that architects were far too keen and uncritical about them. They caused planning (*städtebauliche*) problems, they drove up land prices and caused difficulties for car parking and traffic – however, in Munich it was successful, as 'only in Munich was the tower block in the right hands: public hands'.[71]

Opposition to the proposed tower did not just come from the press; some records survive of opposition from the people in the area which would be affected. The State Planning Authority invited objections, and received four (which survive). Carl Gerber, a printing and publishing company with a works in the vicinity of the proposed tower, complained:

> In our opinion, the new construction in the currently planned height constitutes a damaging blow to the beauty of this part of city, without the city, or the general public, obtaining any advantage therefrom. The imitation of American conditions at every opportunity seems to us totally inappropriate for Munich, which has, up to now,

so praiseworthily striven for the preservation and creation of a good, unified *Stadtbild* [overall impression of the city].[72]

This was the only one of the four recorded criticisms which the Municipal Building Office chose to answer in words rather than statistics – perhaps because it was the only one which involved ethical and aesthetic criticisms. The Municipal Building Office answered firmly:

> It should not go un-remarked that there exists a manifest prejudice in this question, which will not face the facts: the idea that the tower is an imitation of American circumstances does not match with the truth that the plan comes from a time [1918–19] in which we knew nothing of American tower-block ideas, and pursues the objective of nothing more than, firstly, the elevation and promotion of the administration building of the City according to ancient German tradition, and, secondly, the building of a landmark in this significant portion of 'Old Munich', which has become completely smudged, vague, meaningless and incomprehensible. [The Unterer Anger] will become, through the construction of the tower, greatly elevated; the tower will be a landmark of its significance far and wide, and develops and symbolises the new orientation of the City of Munich.[73]

This 'new orientation' was undoubtedly technical, and the Corporation's technocrats had some substantial success in overcoming this 'manifest prejudice'.

This near-Damascene conversion of the Münchener to the tower block did not escape newspaper comment either. The official *Bayerische Staatszeitung* wrote:

> Well, the Berliners have at last managed to build a tower block themselves, and they rant and rave about how everyone should go and see it, and they praise its architect, Bruno Paul. And us Münchener? The municipal building department has been ensconced on the 14th floor of our tower block for well over a year! At the time there were plenty of critics. Not one Bürger was proud. They say we Münchener do not like new fangled things, but we got used to it, and now we love it – it is our house on the Unterer Anger. Now the Münchener sees the joy of the Berliner at his tower, and says, 'Ja, mei. Dös ha'm wir scho lang!' ['Yeah, yeah, yeah! We've had one of those for ages!'][74]

Nationally, the *Welt am Sonntag* also noticed the conversion, and like the Bavarian paper, caricatured the supposed insularity of the Bavarian as in fact being more of myth than a reality, something of a comedic affectation.[75] Two men talk in a skit about their new '*Häuserl*' (cute little house), one of whom pretends not to like it, 'but in reality, he's quite fond of the little *Häuserl*, with all its functional simplicity. "In America . . .

'Oh, shut up with your America. You're talking like a man without a brain. It isn't American – it's Bavarian!'

– 'Well, did we really need it?'

– 'If I didn't know you so well, I'd have said you were a complete cretin. The city is growing, the population expanding; everything's getting bigger, so the municipal administration is growing too – which you know full well.'"[76]

Indeed, the Münchener did seem to know full well what the reality of the modern *Großstadt* was, and accepted it accordingly once they had been taught what to expect and how to understand it by the Corporation. Thus, this programme of activity by the Corporation was not some mere esoteric debate over styles or planning strategy, with little or no relevance to the citizen. It seems to have been an important agent in teaching the citizenry to engage with the state's modernising projects in a positive and supportive way.

Conclusion

It seems clear that although underlying discomforts about the *Großstadt* and modernity existed, the partnership between the metropolis, its governors and its experts was one of affection and trust. Even when they built to control and modify the effects of the urban on the city dweller – to end alienation, de-individuation and fragmentation – they still supposed an urban future and modern techniques of influence and intervention. They built this supposition into the city through an eager participation in a mode of understanding of the phenomena they sought to manage, in that they took part, alternately passively and actively, in the establishment of a framework for describing society, culture and the city which appealed to a universal set of experiences, positioned firmly in the economic, social and geographic form of the metropolis. They promoted this supposition through the attempts to re-form the orientation of Munich from the rural to the urban, promoting the settlement of heavy industry in the city and developing rural land into industrial estates. They nurtured this supposition through growing the city outwards, pro-actively increasing its size and scope, and by conditioning this growth through organising it around symbols of municipal life and government. They developed this supposition after the war by searching for, and finding,

Joy in the metropolis 101

potent signifiers of technocracy to push into the skyline, thereby competing visually with the church spires which had traditionally been the distinctive feature of city horizons, not just in Munich, but in many cities across Europe.

All of this shows a culture underpinned by a mentality which was fundamentally at home with the city, which regarded it as a given, and which promoted it rather than tolerated it. It seemed the city's governors and experts resolved to stick by modernity and a cautious architectural modernism, and that – as the experience with the Technisches Rathaus showed – by doing so, they brought the citizenry with them. It could well be that this was a common approach in other cities throughout the Reich, and also in Britain and America. If so, we need to challenge any generalised assumptions of antagonism towards, or anxiety about, the modern metropolis in western culture in the early twentieth century.

Notes

1 Georgia Clarke and Paul Crossley, *Architecture and Language: Constructing Identity in European Architecture, 1000–1650* (London, 2000); David Cowling, *Building the Text: Architecture as Metaphor in Late Mediaeval and Early Modern France* (Oxford, 1998); John Summerson, *The Classical Language of Architecture* (London, 1964); Charles Jencks, *The Language of Post-Modern Architecture* (6th edn., London, 1991); Mark Gottdiener and Alexandros Lagopoulos (eds.), *The City and the Sign: An Introduction to Urban Semiotics* (New York, 1986).
2 Weber's historical–rational narrative is perhaps most clearly developed in *Economy and Society* (New York, 1968 [1904]).
3 Jürgen Habermas, *The Structural Transformation of the Public Sphere: An Inquiry into a Category of Bourgeois Society* (Cambridge, 1989).
4 For example, in *History of Sexuality, Vol. I* (London, 1979); *Discipline and Punish: The Birth of the Prison* (London, 1977).
5 Latour, *We Have Never Been Modern*.
6 Bauman, *Modernity and the Holocaust*.
7 Louis Robinson, 'The German Städtetag', *Annals of the American Academy of Political and Social Science* 31 (1908), pp. 169–172 (p. 169).
8 Richard Evans, *Death in Hamburg: Society and Politics in the Cholera Years, 1830–1910* (London, 1987), p. 295.
9 Evans, *Death in Hamburg*, pp. 1–27, 285–326.
10 Bericht an das Comité zur Errichtung von Arbeiter- und billigen Beamten-Wohnungen, 29 December 1890, and Bericht zur Frage der Arbeiterwohnungen, April 1891. SAM-WA-23.

11 Bericht zur Frage der Arbeiterwohnungen, April 1891.
12 Antrag, betreffend die Wohnungsfrage in München, 12 July 1899. SAM-WA-23.
13 O. Landsberg, 'Conferences of German Municipal Statisticians', *Publications of the American Statistical Association* 12 (1911), pp. 661–664. For a narrative of the rise of the importance of statistical knowledge in German governmental thinking, see J. Adam Tooze, *Statistics and the German State, 1900–1945: The Making of Modern Economic Knowledge* (Cambridge, 2001).
14 Besprechung über die Förderung des Baus kleiner Wohnungen, 30 January 1899. SAM-WA-23.
15 Magistrat der Königlichen Haupt- und Residenzstadt Berlin to the Magistrat der Königlichen Haupt- und Residenzstadt München, 15 May 1908. SAM-WA-23.
16 Ober-Bürgermeister, Cöln [sic] to the Magistrat der Königlichen Haupt- und Residenzstadt München, 16 June 1908; Stadtmagistrat Nürnberg to the Magistrat der Königlichen Haupt- und Residenzstadt München, 12 May 1908. SAM-WA-23.
17 Sitzung der städtischen Wohnungskommission, 4 November 1908, p. 13. SAM-WA-23.
18 Grund- and Besitzer-Verein München an die hohen Kollegien der Königlichen Haupt- und Residenzstadt München. Betreff: Antrag zur Erbauung von Kleinwohnungen durch die Stadtgemeinde München und Verwendung gemeindlicher Mittel zu diesem Zwecke, 13 June 1908. SAM-WA-23.
19 Anon., '1. Lesung. "Aufruf!" – als Entwurf aufzufassen'. SAM-NLG-407.
20 'Festreden bei der Eröffnungsfeier der Ausstellung', *Ausstellung 'München 1908'*, 7, May 1908, pp. 49–50. SAM-NLG-408.
21 Vigilanzbericht by Graumann, 10.9.1898, in Richard Evans, *Kneipengespräche im Kaiserreich: Stimmungsberichte der Hamburger Politischen Polizei, 1892–1914* (Hamburg, 1989), p. 101.
22 Hermann Beckstein, *Städtische Interressenpolitik: Organisation und Politik der Städtetage in Bayern, Preussen und im Deutschen Reich, 1896–1923* (Düsseldorf, 1991).
23 Dieter Gessner, 'Agrarian Protectionism in the Weimar Republic', *Journal of Contemporary History* 12 (1977), pp. 759–778.
24 Robert Moeller, *German Peasants and Agrarian Politics, 1914–1924: The Rhineland and Westphalia* (Chapel Hill, NC, 1986); Avner Offer, *The First World War: An Agrarian Interpretation* (Oxford, 1990); Suda Bane and Ralph Lutz (eds.), *The Blockade of Germany After the Armistice, 1918–19: Selected Documents* (Stanford, CA, 1942).
25 Belinda Davis, *Home Fires Burning: Food, Politics, and Everyday Life in World War One Berlin* (London, 2000), pp. 48–56.
26 Davis, *Home Fires Burning*, pp. 67–75.
27 Sitzung des Wohnungsausschußes, 14 March 1928. SAM-WA-64.

28 Bericht über die Reise der Mitglieder der Stadtratskommission beim Wohnungsamt nach Nürnberg und Frankfurt a.m. vom 22.-24. November 1926; Bericht über die Dienstreise nach Dresden, Chemnitz, Leipzig und Halle vom 13.–17. September 1925. SAM-WA-63; Preis, *Die Beseitigung der Wohnungsnot*, pp. 79–80.

29 Pressebesprechung am Mittwoch, 13.II.24 nachm. 3h über Grundlagen f. Münchens wirtsch. Zukunft; 'Eine Erklärung des Bürgermeisters Küfner', *Münchener Zeitung*, 306, 8 November 1927; exchange of correspondence between BM Scharnagl, BM Küfner, *Münchner Neueste Nachrichten*, *München-Augsburger Abendzeitung*, November 1927. SAM-B&R-1638.

30 Lieberman, *From Recovery to Catastrophe*.

31 Peter Steinborn, *Grundlagen und Grundzüge Münchener Kommunalpolitik in den Jahren der Weimarer Republik: Zur Geschichte der bayerischen Landeshauptstadt im 20. Jahrhundert* (Munich, 1968), p. 551.

32 Minutes of Verwaltungsausschuß, 8 January 1920. SAM-RSP-693/4.

33 Minutes of Verwaltungsausschuß, 8 January 1920. SAM-RSP-693/4.

34 Minutes of Verwaltungsausschuß, 8 January 1920. SAM-RSP-693/4.

35 This debate comes from the Minutes of the Verwaltungsausschuß, Betreff. Tagung der Vereinigung deutscher Wohnungsämter, 20 June 1920. SAM-RSP-693/4.

36 Minutes of Verwaltungsausschuß, 17 June 1920. SAM-RSP-693/4.

37 Nina Lübbren, *Rural Artists' Colonies in Europe, 1870–1910* (Manchester, 2001).

38 Edelgard Voglmaier, *Hans Grässel: Architekt und städtischer Baubeamter in München* (unpublished doctoral dissertation, Technische Universität München, 1992), p. 24.

39 Sitzung der weiteren städtischen Wohnungskommission, 4 November 1908. SAM-WA-23.

40 Dagmar Bäuml-Stosiek, 'Großstadtwachstum und Eingemeindungen: Städtische Siedlungspolitik zwischen Vorsicht und Vorausschau', in Friedrich Prinz and Marita Krauss (eds.), *Musenstadt mit Hinterhöfen: Die Prinzregentenzeit 1886–1912* (Munich, 1988, pp. 60–68) (p. 64). For an excellent English-language introduction to the process in one city in the 1920s, see McElligott, *Contested City*, pp. 95–124.

41 Programm für den Neubau eines Gaswerkes in München, 1903. SAM-GW-278.

42 Ries, Direktor der städtischen Gasanstalt to the Stadtbauamt and Stadterweiterungsbüro, 19 April 1904. SAM-GW-278.

43 Max Megele, *Baugeschichtlicher Atlas der Landeshauptstadt München* (Munich, 1951), p. 47. Megele shows in painstaking detail how this process was repeated with schools, hydro-electric power stations on the Isar and the Schwabing hospital.

44 Direktion der städt. Gasanstalt, 'Städtische Gasanstalt München. Gaswerk bei Moosach', 31 December 1903; Bauamtmann Bertsch to Stadtbaudirektor Schwiening, 8 February 1904. SAM-GW-278.

45 Ries and Hollweck [Director and Chief Technician of the Municipal Gas Company], städtische Gasanstalt to Referat Xa [Stadtbauamt], 17 June 1903. SAM-GW-278.
46 Städt. Gasanstalt, Zeichnung C, No 2, 'Städtische Gasanstalt München. Gasbehälter nach Osten gelegt', December 1903; Sitzung vom 11. Febr., signed Schwiening, Bertsch; Grässel, Bertsch and Schwiening to the Direktion der städt. Gasanstalt, 26 April 1904; Bertsch to Schwiening [*Stadtbaudirektor*], 8 February 1904. SAM-GW-278.
47 Ries and Hollweck to Referat Xa [Hochbauamt] and Verwaltungsreferat Lipp [*Verwaltungsausschuß*], 8 June 1904. SAM-GW-278.
48 Bertsch to Schwiening [*Stadtbaudirektor*], 8 February 1904. SAM-GW-278.
49 Grässel, 'Ästhetik des Schulhauses', pp. 4–5.
50 'Ein neues Münchener Schulhaus', *Das Schulhaus*, 7. Jg, nr. 11 [n.d.], pp. 403–414. SAM-NLG-367; BAIVn, *München und seine Bauten*, p. 617.
51 'Ein neues Münchener Schulhaus', pp. 403–414 (pp. 404–405).
52 Zimmermann and Reulecke (eds.), *Die Stadt als Moloch?*
53 See the many cuttings in the file, 'Krupp'sche Grundstückankäufe'. SAM-NLG-400.
54 'Ein Rundgang im künftigen Münchner Krupp-Gebiet', *Münchner Neueste Nachrichten*, 20 May 1916. SAM-NLG-400.
55 'Ein Rundgang im künftigen Münchner Krupp-Gebiet'.
56 'Ein Rundgang im künftigen Münchner Krupp-Gebiet'.
57 'Das Krupp-Project und das Münchener Stadtbild', *Münchner Neueste Nachrichten*, 10 June 1916. SAM-NLG-400.
58 'Das Krupp-Project und das Münchener Stadtbild'.
59 There were many articles pursuing a similar theme: 'Krupp und die Stadt München', *Münchner Neueste Nachrichten*, 17 May 1916; 'Die Krupp'sche Geschütz- und Munitionsfabrik in München', *Münchener Zeitung*, 17 May 1916; 'Die bayerischen Geschußwerke bei München', *Münchner Neueste Nachrichten*, 20 October 1916; 'Die erste Arbeiteransiedlung des Kruppwerkes', *Münchner Neueste Nachrichten*, 4 April 1917; 'Von der Bauhütte des Münchener Kruppwerkes', unknown paper, 12 May 1917; 'Vom Neuland bei Freimann', *Münchner Neueste Nachrichten*, 15 May 1917; 'Baukunst und Großindustrie', *Münchner Neueste Nachrichten*, 10 November 1917. SAM-NLG-400.
60 Munich's industry was not especially underdeveloped relative to other capitals, such as Paris and London, but it focused on quality goods – even in the heavy industrial sectors; aircraft engines, scientific instruments, glass and lenses, quality printing and steam locomotives dominated, to the exclusion of genuine 'mass' products. Nothing, apart from litres of beer, was previously manufactured by the million in Munich.
61 Walter Müller-Wulckow, 'Deutsche Baukunst der Gegenwart' series: *Bauten der Arbeit und des Verkehrs* (Berlin, 1929); *Bauten der*

Gemeinschaft (Berlin, 1929); *Wohnbauten und Siedlungen* (Berlin, 1929); *Die deutsche Wohnung* (Berlin, 1932).
62 Richard Pommer and Christian Otto, *Weißenhof 1927 and the Modern Movement in Architecture* (London: 1991), throughout.
63 Walter Curt Behrendt, *Der Sieg des neuen Baustils* (Stuttgart, 1927).
64 *Münchner Neueste Nachrichten*, 6 June 1926. SAM-HBA-502. Ludwig I was known as the '*Baukönig*' (building king), planning (among many other things) the Königsplatz, the university (which he brought to Munich in 1826), the immense, eight-lane Leopoldstraße, the Feldherrenhalle, the Ruhmeshalle and enormous 'Bavaria' overlooking the Wiese, the Siegestor, the ministries between the Residenz and the Maximilianaeum, the Botanic gardens and the Ludwigsvorstadt. He and his son, Maximilian II, and their preferred architects von Klenze and Gärtner, were responsible for much of the ring surrounding the mediaeval core of the town. Preferred styles were a very austere Greek classicism, brightly painted Venetian gothic and High Renaissance.
65 *Allgemeine Zeitung*, 27 January 1919. SAM-HBA-502.
66 *Allgemeine Zeitung*, 27 January 1919. SAM-HBA-502.
67 *Völkischer Beobachter*, 17 April 1927. SAM-HBA-502.
68 *Völkischer Beobachter*, 27–28 October 1929. SAM-HBA-502.
69 This is a small selection from the huge file of press cuttings on the collection of buildings in SAM-HBA-502.
70 'Der Kampf um den Wolkenkratzer', *Vossischer Zeitung*, n.d. SAM-HBA-502.
71 'Moderne Städtebau', *Münchener Zeitung*, 27 January 1930. SAM-HBA-502.
72 Buchdruckerei und Verlagsgesellschaft Carl Gerber to the Lokalbaukommission, 1 June 1927. SAM-HBA-489.
73 Stadtbauamt to the Lokalbaukommission, n.d. [c. end of June 1927]. SAM-HBA-489.
74 'Unser Hochhaus', *Bayerische Staatszeitung*, 20 July 1930. SAM-HBA-502.
75 This is a highly accurate perception. At the risk of anachronism, the 'Laptop and Lederhosen' rhetoric of the current Bavarian government sums up this deep commitment to technology with a slightly 'Olde Worlde' gloss.
76 'Das Mammuthhaus', *Welt am Sonntag*, 3 November 1929. SAM-HBA-502. The comedy German (or rather, Bajuwarisches) original is:

– 'Schneid ab mit Amerika, sag i dir. Du redst daher, wia a Mo ohne Kopf. Is net amerikanisch – is Bajuwarisch.
– Hätt's jetza dös eigentli braucht?
– Wenn i di net a so guat a kenna tat, nacha tat i sagn, du bist a Depp. D'Stadt wachst, d'Leut wern mehra, alles wird grösser, d'Verwaltung wachst natürli aa und nacha woaßt as scho.'

3

The interior world of modernity

The layout of a city can affect many aspects of a person's behaviour, and of the appearance and character of a place. But if one wants to manipulate the actions and experience of a person through total environmental control, then one needs to intervene in the microspaces in which the rituals and practices of everyday life are framed and carried out. Thus when the state came to intervene in medicine, education and social care, when it took on the responsibility for housing, it obtained with it not only a possibility, but a duty to structure the environments in which the *objects* of this ordering process could be enclosed. However, contemporaries struggled to find a way to legitimise and organise their interventions in the interiors of buildings, and produce a satisfactory language in which to describe their objectives. It would mean challenging that axiom of liberal political theory: that the authority of the state should diminish, as a space becomes less public and more private. But what might be called the 'impulse to control' was strong in what administrators, social reformers and municipal politicians were doing – whether designing hospitals or social housing projects. And whereas at the beginning of the period in question, the turn of the century, governors and experts relied on the layout and appearance of buildings to achieve their effects, believing the mind to be particularly susceptible to the effects of light and colour, by the 1920s planning discourse had not only matured and grown, but had also acquired a more effective control over the levers of the state apparatus, such that the interiors of not only 'state' buildings (like hospitals and schools) could be openly discussed, but those of 'private' buildings (most crucially, the home) were also open to scrutiny.

These two factors – the developing intellectual confidence and ambitions of planners, combined with their increased capacity to act as executive agents of the state – meant that by the 1920s, planners were not ordering environments to *suggest* lifestyles, atmospheres and patterns of activity to citizens. Instead, they were using spatial forms to *compel* certain types of behaviour on a micro-level. This process took place not just in Germany, but in Britain, France and the USA as well, and stemmed from the move from the conception of urban design as a set of technical problems, to a more 'totalising' planning discourse which emerged in the 1890s, as discussed towards the end of Chapter 1. By and large, in the liberal economies of the nineteenth-century industrialising world, the state (as representative of the public interest) had little control over the internal spaces, functions and uses of buildings. While the state could meticulously set out the geometries of street alignment, and prescribe heights, widths, depths and fire prevention measures in buildings, it had remarkably little say over what buildings were used for, except in proscribing certain 'noxious' or 'nuisance activities'. In the late nineteenth century, within 100ft of each other, one might easily find alcohol sales and leisure space (and probably a lodging house), chemical preparation, pottery and furnaces, the preparation and storage of cadavers, the education of children and the storage and sale of perishable fresh food. Above each of these would also have been residential accommodation. Such patterns could be found in most European liberal economies of the mid-to-late nineteenth century. Continental European cities could seem superficially well regulated, with their orderly building façades and even building heights and depths, and well-regulated use of materials to prevent fire and disease. But, in practice, most functions had to be highly integrated, due to pragmatic limitations on cheap transport, so behind the well-organised façades, rabbit warrens of varied activities and functions wove complex patterns. In particular, tram and bus travel was largely the preserve of the rich until the Great War, so housing, industrial production and all the interstitial functions of sustaining and provisioning urban life had to be close together, if not fully integrated. In particular, workers had to live close to where they worked, and their provisioning had to be close by as well. Thus, industry, housing, leisure and food provision were all, by necessity, closely integrated in all European cities. Describing the huge AEG factories in Berlin Moabit in the 1900s, Alan Waterhouse has characterised the situation thus:

> In Moabit, by 1906, 1,600 men were engaged in the assembly of turbines in a single hall. Given the pathetic state of transit facilities, a location close to their enormous labour pool, albeit crowded into the tenements of Moabit and Wedding, was essential to AEG operation. So constraining were the mechanical relations and excessive land rent

that the new factories, despite their great areas of glass, could be little more than huge multi-storey sheds, overpowering in their bulk and urban intrusiveness.[1]

Woven in among the sheds were the dwellings and functions of urban life. Asserting spatial order in these life-worlds and material environments was a difficult task for the modernising state to accomplish.

It is the attempt to bring order to this chaos through the restructuring of urban experience that this chapter addresses: not of the city as a whole but the ways that contemporaries produced spaces cut off from this unmanageable mish-mash of experience and function. While descriptions of 'outdoors' in the city often focus on its cacophonous, chaotic nature, 'indoors' is a place where order and calm can be produced and communicated.

While many planners despaired of truly imposing one, coherent order on an extant city, they were more confident about using the interiors of buildings (over which they did have total control) to produce a smaller reforming environment. This chapter deals with a process of increasing intellectual confidence – but also a process by which material, physical spaces came to be used more vigorously to assert and enforce policy decisions. In the period before the Great War, planners had to recognise that their capacity to regulate the inner lives of buildings – namely, the parts where most social interaction takes place – was limited to those buildings produced for the helping projects of the state. Planning discourse in this period is littered with the desire to take rudimentary anti-pollution laws and health regulations further, to develop from them a more ambitious set of goals about using spatial regulation to intervene in urbanites' emotional, psychological, family, private, work and leisure life. However, experts were also frequently unable to secure the full collaboration of the liberal state in doing this.

But they *did* have access to a variety of environments in which the citizen and the state would encounter each other, typically as part of a rational 'helping' project. Such environments would include schools, care homes and hospitals. Because they were constructed by city governments, city governments and their armies of experts could intervene more directly in their spatial organisation – where the nation state would typically not intervene at all. Each of these places – school, hospital, care home – implicitly constructs the individual as being in need of help, and of being in some way disordered. Correspondingly, the task presenting itself to planners, designers and politicians was how they might best produce an environment which enabled help to take place efficiently – and, in particular, which minimised resistance to that help when it had been offered, and which was conducive to restoring order in either the social or individual body.

The chapter thus begins with an examination of how contemporaries at the turn of the century in Germany constructed the uncooperative, truculent citizen, and responded to his or her irrational resistance to help by reforming the interiors of those buildings which framed the interface of beneficent state and vulnerable citizens. Orphanages, old people's homes and hospitals are places where no-one aspires to be and yet, if the politics of social reform and intervention were to succeed they had to be environments in which people accepted that they might have to go. For example, much about the design of hospitals shared features in common with the design of prisons; indeed, hospitals were viewed as prisons in many respects, places of enforced isolation from society, for the good of society. In the case of old people's homes, many contemporaries viewed them similarly, and they were typically built (if they were built at all) on barrack-like or dormitory principles. This meant that old people often refused to go to them. By reconfiguring the interiors of these spaces, contemporaries hoped that they would become places which the citizen might seek out and enter voluntarily. Thus their impersonal, institutional aspects were hidden away and an idea of 'personality' was promoted in their design. This 'personality' would mediate between the human individual and the impersonal uniformity of the state.

The second half of the chapter looks at the space which, before the Great War, was considered the most resistant to penetration by the expert gaze of the state: the interior of the home. After the war, constructing safe and healthy housing for the population was a matter of utmost political urgency – the search for an effective housing policy is the subject of Chapter 4. But this new-found urgency meant that in the Weimar Republic journalists, clergymen, trade unionists, politicians, experts and so on were compelled to assess the purposes and functions of domestic space. Given that the state was now charged with producing domestic space for the first time, people had to define for what purpose, and to what end, this instrument would be deployed. When planners came to discuss that most elemental of domestic spaces, the kitchen, with all its 'home and hearth' qualities of nurture, warmth, nourishment, social interaction, labour and femininity, a violent debate erupted over what sort of woman this new space would construct; for few but the most peripheral radicals disputed that, to some degree, a woman's place was in the kitchen. Would she be modern, rational and individual? Or would she be traditional, elemental and social? By exploring the two dominant kitchen designs of the 1920s, the second half of the chapter examines these questions, and shows how space might be used to coerce women into cooperating with the answers to these question which contemporaries developed.

The social state and the ungrateful citizen

In many strands of cultural commentary in German-speaking Europe at the turn of the last century, one persistent feature can be identified. There was in human life a terrible divide between the head and the heart, between the rational life of the individual and his or her emotional and spiritual life. In the field of government and the effective administration of the state, this had led to a dispute between the rational state and the emotional individual. Contemporaries in many contexts – from lifestyle reform, to art, to politics, to cinema – struggled to define a model of reconciliation of both citizen and state. They searched for ways to facilitate the reconciliation. Contemporaries struggled to define an individual who could be induced to be sufficiently rational, so that he or she might be 'improved' and freed from disease, poverty and ignorance; and a state which might be sufficiently 'spiritual' so that it might be enchanted with warmth, compassion and an organic bond with those for whose benefit it existed. One of the primary means alighted upon to facilitate this rapprochement was space. Urban space and the interior spaces of buildings were believed to offer a primary means of intervening in people's lives, and transforming their experience of the world.

In Germany in the early twentieth century, one of the ways that contemporaries suggested this potentially devastating divide might be overcome was by constructing a sort of analogy between the individual human personality and the individual building of the state's interventionist projects. If buildings could also have a personality, experts might construct a more direct and intimate relationship with the citizen. While architects acknowledged that when the citizen encountered the state in a building, he or she was of a 'type' (poor, sick, ignorant, infirm), as was the building (care home, hospital, school, orphanage), some also argued that the human was a 'type *plus*'. The individual may well encounter the state as a patient, but the individual even as 'type' possessed an additional unique dimension, an irreducible, authentic humanity or soul which was often excluded from the institutional architecture of the hospital or the school. The 'impersonal' hospital and the 'personal' person were, therefore, fundamentally oppositional. Thus, if they could characterise the individual (his or her class, gender, religion, or 'type' notwithstanding) as having a 'personality', and model a building as also simultaneously having individuality and character, then the interaction between the building and the individual could be related in the terms of a sort of 'man-to-man' chat, rather than as the meeting of the forces of cold, rational, inhuman logic on the one hand, and a vulnerable, emotional individual on the other.

This anxiety about conflict and reconciliation was a pervasive one in Europe generally, and Germany specifically, in the years before the war. Conflict between classes, between rich and poor, between city and country, between religion and the secular, between technology and nature, between men and women were frequent themes in popular journalism, novels, melodramas and social and political discourse. And yet contemporaries struggled to describe a process by which this reconciliation could take place, apart from the violent convulsions proposed by those on the Marxist left. The nation, humanity, class, race or the *Heimat* might all function as vehicles of this reconciliation. Planners across Germany showed, in their architectural and spatial politics, a repeated interest in fostering a notional 'personality' or 'character' in both the practical administration of their building departments, and in the final products. They wanted to emphasise the unique personality of planners, rather than their agency for the rational state; and they wanted to produce 'characterful' buildings. They did so while also trying to look, Janus-like, towards a future society perfected by the application of a universal, social-science discourse. Therefore, while trying to focus on personality and the individual, they sought to integrate the impersonal advantages which an approach to social administration based on statistics, planning and expertise might bring.

One can see why these two forceful directions were so hard to reconcile in the twentieth century. To be effective in achieving large amounts of change among a population of millions in a short period of time (by, say, teaching them all to read, or curing them all of tuberculosis), projects of social intervention must generalise, must deal with the average, the typical. And yet, the actual object of change is the individual: by definition, in Judaeo-Christian cultures, utterly unique and sacred in this uniqueness, revealing in it their direct relationship with God. In the emphasis on personality and character, contemporaries attempted to capture the genius of what Ferdinand Tönnies in 1889 dichotomised as *Gemeinschaft* and *Gesellschaft*. *Gemeinschaft* was the organic community of personal, purposeless bonds of affection supposedly banished forever by the modern world of money, contracts, associations and science. Tönnies contrasted this with *Gesellschaft*, the modern form of society, in which human relationships were constructed anonymously and legalistically (typified by the rise of the contract), and constituted only for the achievement of goals – be they pecuniary profit, clean water, improvement of pay of coalminers, or the promotion of the 'national interest'. The discovery of a unifying genius which might offer the advantages of both *Gemeinschaft* and *Gesellschaft* was the 'holy grail' of many social, political and cultural critics in Germany in the first half of the twentieth century, whether communist Modernists, liberal Nationalists or National Socialists. In attempting to master the scientific aspects of city government – clean water, hygienic sewerage, effective education, the control of sexually transmitted diseases – they sought to identify and emphasise the achievements of *Gesellschaft*: the technological, capitalist, rational modern society. The constant mission of Germany's expert class was to demonstrate to themselves (and perhaps even to the world, in their drive for *Kultur*) that the great early twentieth-century quest for reconciliation between head and heart was possible. They sought to bring to the products of rational, 'social-scientific' projects a certain transcendental quality, and thereby rescue the individual metropolitan (the German word is *Großstadtmensch*, which means 'big city person') from the threatening, universalising forces of the modern world which belittled them. By doing so, they hoped to render the intended objects of those forces – the poor, the disordered – malleable collaborators in the projects of their own improvement.

However, it seemed to many in Germany in the first thirty years of the twentieth century that the more the modern state did for its citizens, the more the citizens felt distant from it, and from each other. This process of estrangement caused some perplexity throughout ruling circles in Germany, and measures were taken to bring an end to it. The Prussian and Austro-Hungarian governments devised a course for their civil servants in 1911 which was intended to show them how to fill this void, using the positive example of Munich. One participant on the course, a Prussian civil servant, described the goal of the course as tackling the spiritual discontent of the time, which was such that:

in our time of the highest technical achievements, of refined luxury and the greatest possible material wealth, that is to say, a time which appears to offer, like no other has done before, a happy and carefree life, a deep swathe of disaffection is clearly visible, that our deepest yearning finds no consolation in this time; in short, we have been made aware, as perhaps no generation has been before, that man shall not live by bread alone. He wants more from life than from day-to-day to receive all his bodily needs; the individual must again be made to feel one with the great connectivities of existence, and harmony must rule again between head and heart, reason and emotion, body and soul. That is the fundamental principle of this course.[2]

He went on to elaborate that the state was primarily responsible for ensuring that this void was filled, arguing as a good German Hegelian that it would protect its people, and that it was the embodiment of their ideals. The state 'arches over its people like the protective vaults of a cathedral, so that each and every one of them can erect his altar undisturbed', and should help its citizens achieve 'the most beautiful possibilities for fulfilling the universal striving towards personality'.[3] The impersonal state should assist the individual in the production and sustenance of a 'personality'.

However, something was not right in this equation, something remained mystifying. These stately activities and this stately provision were not producing the desired effect. Klihm, the Prussian civil servant cited above, described the facilities which the city of Munich had built, ending with the truly impressive Müller'sches Volksbad, a palatial Jugendstil (the German name for Art Nouveau) swimming pool complex, with fountains, steam rooms and painted domed ceilings, built in the heart of Munich and popular haunt of both the bathing public and Wittelsbach princes and princesses alike. Yet despite facilities like these across Germany, despite the provision of culture, leisure, education and the like, the population was disaffected:

> What is not done today by the state and municipalities for the welfare of the people [*Volkswohl*] and their health? More than ever before! It must ultimately be the fault of the people itself, when, despite the best of conditions, it cannot find any joy or satisfaction in life.[4]

It seems he was not talking about Munich people or Bavarians either, for he had nothing but praise for them and their *Gemut* – their spirit, soul or disposition. He suggested that the organisers of the tour must have had a training in drama, for when the 130 or so civil servants alighted at the Hauptbahnhof in Munich, there they saw (or heard, to follow Klihm's metaphor) a stunning city informed in every detail by 'the *Leitmotiv* of a tremendous symphony of personality, which struck us as soon as the beat of the city had started'.[5]

Other participants in the course concurred, arguing that Bavaria had not neutralised the SPD itself – the SPD occupied one or both of the city's Reichstag delegates, elected through universal suffrage, throughout the period, and other cities in Bavaria were absolute Red strongholds. Instead, it had neutralised the most threatening aspects of social democracy, perhaps the most coherent political voice of this disaffection, and of this cleft between providential state and ungrateful citizen. One Berliner civil servant on the tour commented on the fact that Bavaria had developed a 'royal Bavarian social democracy', characterised by Vollmar and Müller, rather than the Berlin troika of Stadthagen, Lebedour and Rosa Luxemburg.[6] The colours of Bavarian socialism were blue and white, not red – i.e. it was a national form of socialism, and therefore more organic and less confrontational. In the next breath, he went on to sum up the architecture and design of the city: 'And then we saw the effects of a modern system of building [*einer modernen Bauordnung*] stretched out over the whole city, a proud monument with no posturing.'[7] While this commentator did not explicitly say that the buildings and planning of the city were responsible for the fundamentally non-confrontational nature of Bavarian social democracy, he associated them in his description of the urban landscape and the political landscape.

Recognition, then, of both the problem that a city governments might be trying to solve – the alienation at the heart of modern society – and of their success in doing so. Hans Grässel, one of Munich's most prominent architectural civil servants, collected stories about this sort of political and social disaffection, reinforcing the impression that there was a conscious connection between them and the built environment in the solutions of the city of Munich. Newspaper clippings about it litter the 400 or so files left in the municipal archives documenting almost every detail of this man's adult life. One newspaper clipping he took from the *Münchner Neueste Nachrichten* in 1912, one of the most influential papers in Germany, records the paper's outrage at the way certain aspects of modern culture encouraged this alienation, and in turn the SPD. In a front-page article, the paper (Munich's, and Bavaria's, largest) attacked the Centre Party Ministerpräsident (Premier) of Bavaria, Georg von Hertling (the first 'political' prime minister of Bavaria, from the Centre Party), for a wilful naïveté in the face of the rise of social democracy, and the disaffection which it implied:

You would have to laugh, if it was not so sad, when we read about things like this [disaffection and alienation] while statesmen, professors and philanthropists rip their hair out trying to work out how on earth to explain the immense growth of social democracy, and how we can most effectively cure this 'sickness' – to use the words of Herr v. Hertling. Herr v. Hertling and his ilk recognise only the symptoms of the sickness, which do not have their origins in the hovels of the proletariat alone, but in the fancy palaces of Monaco, Aix-les-Bains and so on, or in the wildly luxurious fittings of the latest ocean liner.[8]

Grässel underlined the conclusions of the editorial in a red crayon: disaffection and alienation lay in the 'effortless fulfilment of wishes', and von Hertling should acknowledge the 'great and terrible secret' that the cause of social democracy did not lie in the proletariat, but 'in the hearts of very many of the best men which the *Volk* possesses'.[9]

From principles and arguments like these, a new class of experts worked to integrate the technical administration of planning based on hygiene and traffic with the more holistic, totalising one, based on aesthetics and a model of lifestyle reform. Alongside colleagues in countless other large cities in Germany, people like Grässel developed visual and spatial solutions which they thought would challenge the 'effortless fulfilment of wishes', and alter the nature and interpretation of social services, thereby transforming the way in which the modern, alienated urbanite would experience the brave new world in which they lived. It seems that he, and the governing classes he represented, felt that for all that the novel institutions of the social state which city governments built so enthusiastically in this period were created *for* the citizens of the town, it was difficult to convince the *Bürger* (if the analyses above are credible) that it was done in any sense *by* them and not *to* them. They felt external to these processes, and alienated from them. Whether the fault lay, as the Prussian civil servant argued, in the people themselves or, as the Bavarian civil servant implied through his selective underlining, in the habits of their rulers, both argued that changes to the environment in which the citizen lived, moved, worked and played could improve the situation. To paraphrase and summarise Grässel's arguments taken from his writings as a whole, the building was a place of encounter between the citizen (an individual), the social state (impersonal modern authority) and rational scientific and social-scientific processes (impersonal modern discourse) – the product of the mid- and late-nineteenth-century 'discovery' of statistics on health, mortality, income and the like. These three things could come together only in a space – there are, as Edward Soja argues, no a-spatial historical processes.[10]

Thus the building presented an opportunity. As such a place of encounter, the building could reconcile the three. It could humanise and individualise the state and the achievements of modern society and science. It could provide a point of access or exchange for the individual and personal with the universal, statistical and impersonal. The physical, built environment could be used, it was thought, as a transformative agent, making Germans into happy, cooperative citizens who embraced modernity and modernisation. The hundreds of articles on psychology, perception and cognition, both academic and popular, which litter Grässel's papers, and the many references he made to them in his work, underline the ways in which early psychology – whether in its Pavlovian or Freudian forms – contributed to these debates on environmental determinism. Whether the buildings functioned quite as benignly or thoroughly as their designers intended, they certainly could transform the ways lives were perceived to be lived. This section examines how some of those preoccupations were realised in institutional buildings, all in the period between 1895 and 1914, returning to the theme of interior organisation and design.

Urban governments showed an interest across the board in infusing their projects with personality and character, especially in the period before the First World War. They tentatively extended their social provision, enlarging the remit of the orphanage as they 'discovered' child abuse, developing new hospitals to look after (or isolate) the sick and began to care for a population which was, for the first time, surviving in large numbers into old age. Here, I will focus on a new orphanage, an old people's home and a hospital. All three building types had to find ways to address a group of people who were in a highly paradoxical situation: on the one hand, they were in need, and the modern state wanted to help them. However, they had also either lost their homes or their health and whatever independence they had had, and were compelled to adapt to an unwished-for institutional existence. This meant that the social state, at the moment of its greatest generosity, could also be greatly resented.

Producing a home for homeless children
The orphanage, largely destroyed in the Second World War, attempted to do just this. It was opened in 1900 at the opposite end of the Nymphenburg canal from the royal Wittelsbach summer

residence of Schloß Nymphenburg in a rapidly growing new suburb, and was part of a complex of buildings that the city government had commissioned in the vicinity, the other two being the Heiliggeistspital – the Holy Ghost Old People's Home – and a school. Grässel's aim was to develop an interior and exterior which would encourage the orphans to develop a sense of belonging, and which would banish any institutional character. The original interior no longer survives, but the effect of the whole building was summed up in a leading German architectural journal of the time, the *Deutsche Bauzeitung*, in an issue entirely devoted to the structure:

> It is indeed a noble thought to give sunny days to children denied a father or a mother, at least during their stay in the institution [*Anstalt*], instead of robbing them for ever of the magic of cosy homeliness through accommodating them in barrack-like rooms. It must be said, such an urban conception [or, 'such a municipal conception' – *eine solche städtische Auffassung*] corresponds to real artistic and real human sensibility. The feeling of pure joy which clearly enthused the creator [*Verfasser*] of the institution does the same to every visitor.[11]

The techniques that Grässel used here were the same as he had in many of his buildings, and constantly impressed contemporaries into thinking the city had spent a lot more on its projects than it in fact had. He would paint the walls of all the major circulation spaces (hallways, staircases, entrance halls) with frescos; the rest of the walls he would paint in reasonably bright (but not strong) colours, typically grey, yellow, or green. A stripe of geometric designs or organic swirls would be painted at dado-rail height, and the doors would also receive some treatment, either a false marbling or a geometric formation. For furnishings, he would buy sturdy, but mass-produced and cheap, items, and paint them with folk designs of flowers and bright colours. All this would be done by out-of-work or newly qualified artists (of which there was an abundance in Munich, as the centre of the Central European art world), who could be employed cheaply. The frescos could be of various subjects: wildlife scenes; the countryside; themes from the history of Bavaria; religious imagery; or fairy tales and popular folk stories. The intention was to make the interior of these institutional buildings homely, warm and welcoming, thereby giving them a place in the citizen's heart.

It was not just the architectural press that noted Grässel's, and the city government's, success in this area. A populist Roman Catholic devotional pamphlet of the time, the *Seraphischer Kinderfreund* (the

'Seraphic Children's Friend'), ran a regular column called 'Brother Marianus' Social Chit-Chat'.[12] As a whole, the weekly journal, costing 10 Pfennigs, was dedicated to a sort of twee, pious appreciation of children and their angelic nature, and a general exposition of the Roman Catholic view of the world. Its standpoint (judging from this one issue) was conservative in many ways – most conspicuously in religious matters – but it also espoused a reformist and sometimes radical conservatism of the type often to be found in the politics of the more leftist wing of the Centre Party and the Catholic trade unions. This particular article starts off, 'Whoever wants to see a little bit of the social question resolved should go and stand on the Schloß Nymphenburg canal', and argues that there, if the viewer looks both ways, he or she will see the reconciliation of wealth with poverty, the royal palace with the municipal orphanage. The theme of the social question was handled, for this paper, more in terms of reconciliation and peace-making than conflict and tension; this approach was bound to appeal to Grässel, and Grässel's approach was bound to appeal to them. The paper (or 'Bruder Marianus') wrote:

> We must praise the Munich municipal councillors and governors, and their Building Director, Hans Grässel, and say: 'You have created for the poor children a home the likes of which is not to be seen anywhere else in the world.'[13]

'Marianus' said that he had travelled widely through Germany, Austria and France, and had not seen the like for friendliness and warmth in design, yet it was all done 'in artistic accord with the progress of modern art and technology'. A contemporary pamphlet about the building also praised the sobriety and simplicity of the building – its *Schlichtheit* – but went on to say that this sobriety was not a cold, institutional one:

> In the rooms, halls and corridors, the architect [*Erbauer*] constantly tried to avoid all cold, barrack-like blandness [*kasernenmäßige Nüchternheit*]. All of the spaces in the building should be a dear *Heimat* to their young inhabitants, and as such, they should remain in their memories for the rest of their lives.[14]

By being such, 'the young lad is shown the goodness and solidity that the craftsman can achieve, and the girl will become conscious of what a clean, orderly, light and friendly home should look like'.[15] Social divisions and social problems could be overcome, contemporaries hypothesised, by the determined way the city government manipulated the environments of its most deprived citizens.

Spatial organisation and the preservation of personality in old age
At the opposite end of the 'care spectrum', the city government invested substantial amounts of money in old people's homes, building four major ones between 1900 and 1927, all of which were designed by Grässel. Just one will serve as an example here, the Heiliggeistspital. It was built on the Dom Pedro Platz, behind the orphanage, and was begun in 1904 and opened in May 1907. The building was designed for 600 poor elderly people, and impressed contemporaries primarily for its facilities and interior design. They marvelled at the central heating, the beautiful (electric) lighting, the quantity of running hot water, the kitchen facilities, the fire protection measures, the lifts and the internal telephones. The building was the subject of many postcards at the time. One description of the building from its opening described the frescos in the entrance hall and staircase: up the staircase were painted angels symbolising the human virtues essential to the completion of the building – social care, hard work, good governance. They lead up to the centre of the painting, and across the ceiling of the entrance vestibule was a painting of a model of the project. Above the model hovered the Holy Ghost – a misty light shining across the sky. The anonymous author of a document of unknown purpose (the author was not Grässel, for it was sent to him for comments) concluded with an astounding analysis of this image: 'One could almost imagine that here [in the Holy Ghost] the deliberations of both council chambers are symbolised.' The hyperbole aside, the interior arrangement of the building is important, because it demonstrates the alignment of the city government with the ideology of the personal and the character-full (*charaktervoll*), using the mechanisms and possibilities offered by subscribing to the activities of the impersonal, social state to restore, or at least venerate and acknowledge, personality and individuality. It also demonstrates that this alignment could take effect only when material space was altered to enable it to do so.

The interior organisation of the building – of any building – was something which was extensively debated by the council, because this determined both its functional success and its cost. The city council opted for internal solutions in this building (and in the Schwabing hospital, which will be looked at next) which substantially increased the cost of the project, but which also allowed what they called 'personality' and 'character' to flourish throughout. Thereby they could challenge the anonymity, the disjointedness and discontinuities of modern life in general, and of the modern metropolis in particular, while still behaving 'modernistically', and integrating the citizen into the processes of modernisation. For example, one newspaper drew attention to the fact that this building demonstrated a totally new conception of organising care for the poor, in that they would no longer be separated by sex – i.e. by type. The city had taken the expensive measure of making most of the rooms twin rooms, getting away from the ward or dormitory customs traditionally followed in old people's homes in other cities right across Europe. Naturally, this was expensive, but it allowed the city to challenge the usual practice 'which often separates half or a whole lifetime of joy and sorrow because of bureaucratic reasons'.[16] Married couples, brothers and sisters and even friends would be allowed to stay together. Here the elderly would find privacy and dignity, and it also enabled them to bring one or two of their own possessions with them, which traditional dormitory solutions did not do. The whole impression was '*charaktervoll*' – full of character. Another newspaper remarked that mostly the elderly resented going into homes because they were impersonal and institutional, but this one 'will not have the effect of alienating them, and making them mistrustful of the people who were providing for them'.[17] It seems that contemporaries recognised both the city government's ambitions to forge some sort of accord between the individual, modernity and the modern metropolis, and also its success in fulfilling them by devising symbolic and spatial schemes which responded to a rhetoric of reconciliation.

Commenting on another, later, old people's home, this strategy of devising accommodation was described in greater detail by Grässel. He said that to give value and dignity to old age was the difficult part of a commission like this, as institutions usually had a 'barrack-like form', and that old people's homes were sometimes seen as places for the old to go to die off. He said that the city government had always impressed upon him the belief that it did not view such elderly people as 'burdensome poor', and that this viewpoint had caused much tension and conflict between the poor and those who sought to govern them. The city government was the real force behind the overall ideology of the building, and had contributed to the smallest details: 'these rooms will be the witnesses for hundreds of years', he explained, 'which will speak of the high conception of the mission on the part of Munich Council'.[18] It was they who had, right until the late 1920s, insisted that old people's homes should be built in styles and materials which the residents would understand and with which they would feel at home. He concluded that all his institutional buildings (*Anstalten*) should be understood in terms of reconciliation and unity:

So, when you are asked, as usual, in what style a new municipal institution has been built, do not answer, in a baroque style or a renaissance style, but in a Munich style, which is characterised by speaking clearly, in the exterior as well as interior, not just the language of reason, function and usefulness, but also that of the heart and *Gemüt* [spirit, soul, disposition], and thereby becomes attractive.[19]

The head and the heart were reconciled: that central theme of early twentieth-century discourse was here managed in the built environment. This attempt to allow the heart, the *Gemut*, personality and character to permeate the buildings the city built was conspicuous not just in Grässel's residential buildings of (especially) the years before the First World War, but also in others – unemployment offices, welfare offices, delousing stations and bathhouses, and hospitals.

Healing spaces, confined places
The hospital was perhaps the closest encounter which most people had then with 'pure' science. While hospitals at that time were not the shrines to scientific investigation which they have subsequently become, they were the sites of cold, rational interventions in people's lives: archetypal symbols of modernity in two senses. First, they were modern because they were scientific, rational, investigative and observational. Secondly, their modernity lay in their bureaucratic, secular social provision, the product of a new form of state and governmental organisation. They could quite easily be highly resented interventions, and while the municipal government would receive nothing but praise for building humane psychiatric institutions, paediatric units, maternity hospitals and rural tuberculosis sanatoria, the politics of normal hospital construction were more problematic. Before the First World War, hospitals were conceived of primarily as places of enforced isolation and containment. This is evidenced in the usual plan of the buildings: late nineteenth- and early twentieth-century hospitals have a wide, patrollable perimeter, with a high fence or wall. Hospitals, in an age before antibiotics, could not cure disease, they could only contain it, and try to ensure that the poor were warm enough, clean enough and well-fed enough to withstand it. As one of the leading contemporary architectural journals commented, the broad, grassed perimeter and the high fence of the Schwabing Hospital was designed 'to prevent a forbidden traffic with the outside world'.[20] Even by the mid-1920s, the average stay in the Schwabing Hospital in North Munich was forty-four days,[21] and in a period of limited or non-existent social security, this could easily take a poorer, or even a moderately well-off, family into utter

destitution. It was no wonder that people resisted going into hospitals and that the police had responsibility for ensuring that when someone had a contagious disease, he or she would be taken to the requisite institution. Sometimes the pattern would be that neighbours, fearing contamination themselves, would inform the police of people secretly kept at home, who would remove them with force if necessary to the hospital, for their – or everybody else's – own good.

The process by which the interior of a hospital might be organised was complex, but in this period contagion and infection was still not fully understood, so it was remarkably flexible.[22] Thus there was not an obvious spatial or aesthetic set of principles by which this intervention in people's lives could be organised. The government of Munich had identified the need for a new, large hospital in 1898–99, and set about visiting other cities in Germany to view their installations.[23] Senior Building Officer Eggers was responsible for the first round of designs, but died shortly before their completion. The city's medical professionals, other administrators and politicians cannot have been overly impressed with his proposals, as they were immediately and completely dropped on his death and the project started entirely anew by Building Officer Richard Schachner, who would go on to become one of Munich's most daring and inventive architects. His plans were approved on 1 July 1904.[24] The principles which underpinned the design of the building were explained in a report the Council produced in May of that year.

As one would expect in a report of this nature, the aesthetic considerations did not take prime position. First, the report established the need for a new, large hospital for the rapidly growing city with its dynamically expanding and changing social composition, and new responsibilities brought about by the 'new culture'. It then outlined the practical requirements of such a building, and discussed whether to use a pavilion or a corridor system to best suppress contagion. Penultimately, it pinpointed the defects of the Links der Isar and Rechts der Isar hospitals which would have to be remedied if Munich was to develop a high-profile, modern health-care system: psychiatry, alcoholism, pathology, gynaecology, venereal disease and paediatrics were all outlined as areas of weakness in the city's extant health services. Lastly in the forty-page report came 'Fundamental Principles for the Architectural Formation of the Buildings', the considerations about how the building would have to look; although last in order of priority in the report, it is perhaps a measure of its importance that it was included at all.[25]

The committee of aldermen, town councillors and doctors required that the building's form should spring from its functions, and that all decoration in the old style should be avoided; that is to say, they demanded a piece of modern architecture:

> Completely apart from financial considerations, artistic reasons and the functional purpose of the building demand that there should be no bays, turrets and the like, which are not required for functional reasons. On the same grounds, all gables, fancy decoration, overly high roofs etc. must be rejected.
>
> It is intended that the entire hospital facility including grounds, which will fulfil all the requirements of the most up-to-date technologies and be built in the most modern building techniques available, should be, in both its interior and exterior, completely modern in the best sense of the word. There will be no room for the application of no-longer-justifiable architectural motifs from earlier stylistic periods, or the application of frilly bits and bobs.[26]

The building fulfilled its aesthetic brief absolutely. Schachner succeeded in creating a work of outstanding clarity and simplicity, which impresses for these qualities nearly 100 years after it was designed. Yet the committee clearly worried that this drive to be 'modern' would create a 'cold' environment – and coldness has always been one of the accusations thrown at modern architecture (the accusations against the Electricity Board Headquarters were discussed in Chapter 2). It was a charge levelled at the designs for the hospital by Councillor Stiersdorfer, who seemed intent on making trouble not just about the design of the hospital, but about any other features he could possibly criticise.[27] In response to this, the planning committee specified that lively colours should be used throughout 'to banish the notorious hospital or barracks character from the complex'. The individual rooms 'should not have the icy cold character of most hospitals, simply warehouses for the sick . . . [They are] boring, repulsive and depressing':

> A hospital should not be the site or symbol of terror or horror for a suffering humanity, but a place of refuge, sought out gladly by our people, a sanatorium for body and soul. Therefore the traditional practice of dull colours and institutional corridors will be avoided, and the consultation rooms will not – as they usually are – be built like greenhouses and fitted out as disconsolate glass boxes, but the fitting out of these rooms will be in a homely character. . . . We must, in this sense of the whole thing, take a step nearer [*Man muss nur in diesem Sinne der ganzen Sache etwas naeher treten*].[28]

They neglected to specify to what or whom they must step nearer, but it seems they probably meant the citizen–patient, anxiously and probably unwillingly confronted by modern science and the modern state in this building. To what extent did the municipality succeed in creating this new, 'anti-institutional' ambience in its hospital? They succeeded to a great degree, if contemporary assessments are to be believed.

The leading contemporary architecture journal, *Deutsche Bauzeitung*, had a two-part special on the project in the autumn of 1906, showing in detail the model and the building plans. They commented that the hospital had been divided up into individual buildings, in each of which approximately 150 sick could be tended. Within the buildings themselves, large wards had been rejected, partly on hygienic grounds, but mostly on humanitarian ones. This ensured that 'the individuality of the individual patient can be allowed far more scope than in most hospitals in other big cities'.[29] They went on to argue that the interior of the building had banished the 'frosty coldness which plagues most modern hospital buildings'. The rooms were light and airy, but:

> friendly, airy, light rooms in the sense an artist might mean it, not according to the meanings that doctors might have, which seem all too often to be encountered in modern hospitals. They measure lightness according to the square-metre area of the windows, airiness according to the quantity of cubic metres encompassed, and friendliness according to how light the paint is.[30]

Clearly this trade journal felt that the city had been successful in reconciling science and social intervention with the more personable qualities of friendliness and personality, both in terms of the way space was partitioned, and the way it looked. This was a quality which the city had developed as a whole, as one visiting Berlin civil servant noted:

> This city seems to be like a weightlifter's barbell, with the two weights of beer and art joined together through the joining bar of personality and *Gemütlichkeit* [heartiness, cosiness, friendliness, warmth].[31]

The same author described seeing the Schwabing Hospital as the highlight of the whole tour of Bavaria which he undertook for the Prussian government, regarding it as the 'most strongly impressive sight there is to see in the city', offering a quality of architecture – and therefore care – not to be found in Berlin, even in the new Birchow Hospital. He described with a witty anecdote how he had felt humbled before this particular movement of the 'symphony of personality'. The hospital director explained that patients in Munich's hospitals were provided with beer (as Bavarian regiments in the Bundeswehr still are):

> One wit exclaimed, 'What, even the drunkards? Do they get beer too?' The director almost jumped out of his skin, and said, 'Drunkards? We don't have any of them here.' Then he explained passionately that the patients were not allowed any spirits, and there was no delirium. He did have a few alcoholics on his wards, but he thought one could be fairly sure of one thing – 'North Germans'. Once again a slight knowing smile crept across our faces, and one stood corrected as a '*Schnapspreuß*' [hard-liquor-drinking Prussian] before this Eldorado of solidity and individuality.[32]

In the period before 1914, then, it seems that the city government attempted, through its architectural patronage, to bring warmth and personality to cold and impersonal processes by reducing the scale and changing the appearance of the spaces in which they took place. Whereas Chapters 1 and 2 suggested that the fortunes of the city-as-idea are usable to diagnose a position *vis-à-vis* modernity, this chapter and Chapter 4 show how important space was to producing change, and how contemporary Germans might walk a path between *Angst* and *Freude*. They demonstrate that the city of Munich was in the mainstream of the modernist attempt to infuse the modern – technology, cities, bureaucracy, expertise – with more transcendental values – warmth, emotional attachment, spiritual meaning – and thereby eliminate the conflicts of modern, bureaucratic, capitalist society. In short, the city governors wanted both to exploit and embrace modernity, and control and 'cure' it. In doing so, it was hoped that the citizen could be helped to be 'modern' in all the best senses of the word: rational, but not alienated; individual, but not atomised; social, but not homogeneous.

In the period before the war, the period in which Germans were being compelled to come to terms with modernity in its social, economic, cultural and governmental forms, it would seem on the basis of the Munich city government's analysis and actions that there was no delusional analysis of modernity. There was no uncritical yearning for a past that never was, and nor was there a naïve fêting of future possibilities which could not be realised. Far from exhibiting any pathological response to modernity, the city government seemed intent on using the new types of spatial and social organisations called forth by modernity – hospitals, care homes and the like – to guide the individual German into modernisation with balance and support. In the post-war period, in which it has been suggested that a more fundamental rejection of modernity and modernisation in German society occurred,[33] it will be important to determine whether the Corporation could sustain this middle ground, and whether it could carry its citizenry with it. It is to the new form of commission so characteristic of urban design and social manipulation in the 1920s, social housing, to which I will now turn, focusing on the room deepest in the private home: the kitchen.

Domestic space and the modern citizen

As is well known, at the end of the First World War Germany fell into a prolonged period of chaos and disorder. When this found a coherent political voice, whether through socialism, communism, nationalism or Catholicism, it made it clear that social calm and political stability would be predicated on the capacity of the state to provide healthy, affordable housing in well-functioning cities – a theme which is examined in Chapter 4. However, this left urban experts and governors across the new republic confronted by an imperative to specify and resolve a problem which frequently had a nebulous definition. In part emboldened by this volatility, violence and disorder, this expert class of governors and planners in German cities proposed a way of reforming the city and the citizen, by producing and applying a certain sort of knowledge about *interior* space, which would in turn create rational, orderly subjects to inhabit it.

This expert class responded to the demands underpinning urban political unrest by positing a new way of designing and living in homes. In doing so, they borrowed heavily from the discourse of 'scientific management' derived from US consumer goods industries. Up until that point much 'women's work' had not been susceptible to this management discourse, because it took place in the secret, obscure spaces of the home, outside the gaze (and often interest) of governors and experts. The imperative to produce housing exposed the domestic space of working-class families to public scrutiny, allowing male experts to prize open the socio-spatial domestic arrangements of a class which had, in the past, often been closed as tightly as a clam. Whereas the design of hospitals and schools and other public buildings was a recognised part of governmental activity, focusing on the interiors of homes was rhetorically explicitly constructed as being outside the realm of public discourse. By questioning the domestic interior's status as exclusively private, a 'state-free space', and recasting it as a site of labour and production, experts rightly recognised the enormous burden of domestic management which women carried, often alongside paid work outside the home. The dual nature of domestic spaces – as spaces of labour and work, on the one hand, and familial sociability and leisure, on the other – led to a contest among planners, governors, publicists, feminists and 'experts' in Germany and the USA about how best the rational state might intervene in them, in order to produce the ideal home, the ideal city and the ideal citizen.

In German housing and planning policy, this contest crystallised around a discussion of what sort of female subject these improving projects of the helping, rational state would define. While some experts characterised the woman at home as worker, a productive citizen of the social state, other experts emplotted her life as maternal and social. In the former model, the woman-at-home was to be scrutinised and organised in order to make her domestic labour efficient; in the latter, the woman was explicitly cast as invulnerable to rational scrutiny, and responsible for the organisation of her home herself. Crucially, rather than simply narrate and emplot women's lives in advice literature, journals, visits by social workers or hygiene campaigns, however, both sets of experts set out to *enforce* their vision through the use of space. In particular, this section will focus on the room most associated with women's domestic labour: the kitchen. It will deal with the conflicting models for kitchen design offered by the city planners of Frankfurt and Munich in the 1920s, examining their links to the American models to which they were responding.

In examining these two competing spatial models of how the state might modernise its citizens in the domestic sphere, two arguments are pursued. First, physical space has been an under-recognised, under-analysed category in historical investigation. In particular, the role of *physical* spaces and *physical* barriers in *enforcing* social relationships and behaviours has been under-examined in favour of discussing the symbolic values of spaces, and these symbols' capacity to *suggest* social relationships and behaviours. Such symbolic value is of enormous importance, and has been examined to great profit by historians, but it is insufficient for understanding the force-relations inherent in spatial organisation.[34] Thus the interior spaces of a prison do not *suggest* imprisonment, by being the repositories of symbols of imprisonment. The spaces of a prison *produce* imprisonment; being locked in a prison cell is not metaphorically, but literally, constraining. Whereas before the war interior spaces were designed to suggest or imply responses in the citizenry, after 1918 interior space was used more directly as a coercive agent.

Secondly, a habit of historical enquiry must be called into question which, when dealing with buildings, focuses on ones which belong to a canon. This canon does not even have to include 'real' buildings and spaces; more architectural–critical ink has been spilled over the unbuilt Panoptikon than all the spaces in all the prisons in the world. In the twentieth-century German context, this has meant focusing again and again on the 'rise' of Modernism, one of the key features of architectural analysis highlighted in the Introduction. This Modernism has been cast as the bold spirit of the true, liberal, creative Germany, the daring adventurers of the humane social experiment that was Weimar, thwarted by the inhuman barbarity and stylistic *Kitsch* of National Socialism.[35]

However, overwhelmingly most architecture and design in 1920s Germany was *not* Modernist. By habitually focusing on the exceptional, the rare and the experimental, architectural and design historians have overlooked the vast majority of spaces and environments which shaped the day-to-day lives of not just German citizens but of *all* humans. From our births in mediocre hospitals, through our education in average schools, to our family lives in unexceptional houses, our rites of passage are shaped by the banal, the inherited, the conventional. Although innovation happens, and while it can be important, we should not allow ourselves to be distracted by it at the expense of other more important and persistent phenomena. Furthermore, architecture and design historians have focused on the rhetoric of the ambitions and aspirations of the producers of designs and spaces, frequently privileging architects' and experts' own hopes for a particular space over and above the actual effects which such a space might inevitably exert on its users.[36]

So, in short, while historians of the symbolic meanings ascribed to space have successfully focused on the banal, they have not dealt with the physical and the material. Those who have dealt with the physical and material have too readily confined themselves to narrating the 'rise' of something they particularly prize: Modernism. In doing so, they have overlooked the lived realities of both the buildings they describe and the overwhelming number of unhistoricised buildings and spaces with which they rarely engage at all. Of the two models analysed in the second half of this chapter, one sits inside the Modernist canon, and one outside it. The kitchens designed by the city of Frankfurt were placed in housing estates which exist comfortably in the Modernist narrative, and so have received some – albeit limited – scholarly attention (Figure 3.1). The counter-model proposed by the city of Munich (Figure 3.2) has never, to my knowledge,

3.1 The Frankfurt Kitchen, c. 1926. The traditional kitchen for poor families was usually a room (sometimes the only room) with a stove. This one has running water, storage, fitted appliances and food preparation areas – and a wall, separating it from the rest of the flat.

3.2 The Munich Kitchen, c. 1927. The Munich Kitchen aimed to make housewives' work easier through rational planning, but prevent them being isolated from the social life of the family, by ensuring that their work and social lives were spatially united. It was also a lot cheaper, and more space efficient.

received any attention anywhere, although ultimately it was used very frequently in German social housing projects. The two models differ spatially in one crucial way. The Frankfurt planners, designers and experts abandoned the traditional German working-class arrangement of combining the social space of the family and the work-place of women together into the *Wohnküche* ('living room-cum-kitchen'). Instead, they divided the woman's work-space from the woman's domestic social and leisure space with a wall (Figure 3.1). Munich's experts tried to borrow what they perceived as advantageous in discussions of efficiency, but they challenged the idea that women in their domestic social and work lives were in any way legitimate subjects of rational scrutiny. Instead, they used domestic space to enforce a union between the work and social life of the woman-at-home (Figure 3.2). They preserved the union between work-space and social-space. It is these competing modernities which must be explored. To do this, the American parameters and paradigms which influenced Frankfurt's projects need to be established, because it was those parameters and paradigms which other experts – just as modern – wanted to disrupt and subvert.

Woman as producer and consumer: the American heritage
Two key decisions took place in Frankfurt which made such a radical reform of the working-class kitchen possible: first, the appointment by an ambitious, socialist Mayor, Ludwig Landmann, of Ernst May as chief city architect and planner, charged with developing a high-volume, low-cost housing strategy. His first major act in office was the second key decision: he hired Margarete Schütte-Lihotzky, whom he had in his earlier career poached from Vienna City Council, where she had designed an all-in-one kitchen and bathroom, in which a worktop folded down over the bath-tub.[37]

May was fascinated by scientific management's productivity benefits, and its capacity to free up 'leisure time' for workers, and instituted conveyor-belt production facilities of standardised building components.[38] What transformed debate on women's spaces was the publication of a book by an American self-styled feminist, Christine Frederick. In 1919, she published *Household Engineering: Scientific Management in the Home*.[39] The translator into German was Irene Witte, the woman who, along with Erna Meyer, introduced the American ideology of the fitted kitchen to Schütte-Lihotzky – and countless other Germans – and who planted the idea in Schütte-Lihotzky's head that women in their domestic lives might be subject to the same sort of rational scrutiny usually reserved for optimising capitalist productivity.[40] Schütte-Lihotzky equated this rationalisation with liberation, and this allowed what was an essentially very highly regulated and deterministic set of manipulations of women's lives and space to be couched in heroic rhetoric. Lore Kramer has identified a crossover between the work of Christine Frederick and a longer tradition of American, patrician middle-class feminism dating back to Catharine Beecher in the mid-nineteenth century.[41]

Beecher is credited with being at the intellectual and ideological core of the trend known as 'the cult of domesticity'.[42] Beecher is remarkable not just for her formulations of what it meant to be a woman and the rights and obligations it implied, but for her linkage of these to what it meant to be a housewife in an ill-planned kitchen, placing women's work and women's space at the heart of any understanding of women's social existence.[43] Her formulations of what a kitchen should be were intimately bound up with her attempts to establish a discourse of home economics, the female, domestic and private version of that great nineteenth-century male, public theme of political economy. Beecher saw in housework the most terrible, confining drudgery for women and sought to find relief for it, and Beecher's rhetoric of boredom, oppression and fatigue rings through all of Frederick's and Schütte-Lihotzky's writings.

Beecher's two great works on this area showed that in kitchens where men worked – favourite examples being the Mississippi paddle steamer and the mobile military camp kitchen – the organisation was rational, the kitchen was small and the equipment was to hand. But in kitchens where women worked as servants or as housewives the equipment was spaced so that the sink might quite possibly be in a different room to the stove, and the preparation areas of food tended to be a long way from storage, cooking and waste-disposal areas. In brief, kitchens designed by men for women were irrational and maximised work thereby imprisoning women, while kitchens designed by men for men were highly rational and did not burden them. Based on the ship's galley kitchen, she came up with the 'workshop kitchen', the first conception of the domestic fitted kitchen, planned and installed in one step.[44] Beecher's campaigning had considerable impact in the USA, not least due to her followers' exploitation of the World's Fairs in Chicago in 1893, and St Louis in 1904, to showcase her kitchen plans.

As Mary Nolan has demonstrated, this American 'rational' approach to work had already had some impact on German industrial production in the 1900s, but became more generally popular in the immediate aftermath of the Great War.[45] These practices were underpinned by an entire economic mode of thought and social operation, dominated by frequently mutually antagonistic 'gurus', Frederick Taylor, Henry Ford and Frank and Lillian Gilbreth. They sought to break down every action into its component parts, denying any continuity whatsoever to the most mundane of actions, dividing labour into its irreducible synchronous elements – called 'therbligs' (or 'Gilbreth' backwards).[46] At the same time that the housing debate was raging in Germany, this 'time and motion' discourse united with a new set of technologies to produce the ultimate flattening of time into space. The experiential time of human life, lived out in cycles of growth and seasons, was transformed into a set of spatial measurements and manipulable data. This new system of economic and industrial analysis did not just devalue time. According to Kern's famous thesis, time and space became conflated, and experiential, human, life-cycle time was banished.[47]

An example of such a new technology permitting the ever greater blurring of the space–time distinction was the chronocyclegraph, a gadget invented by Frank and Lillian Gilbreth in 1918. It worked to deploy new technologies to increase this collapse–conflation of the space–time distinction. Its functioning is described and illustrated by a 1940 book on the subject:

> It is possible to record the path of motion of an operator in three dimensions by attaching a small electric light bulb to the fingers, hand or any other part of the body, and photographing, with a stereoscopic camera, the path of light as it moves through space. [With the introduction of variably flashing lights and time-lapse stereoscopic photography] it is possible to measure accurately time, speed, acceleration and retardation, and to show the path of motion in three dimensions.[48]

The individual's time and space were thus mapped onto a grid, where the operations could be transformed into a series of time–space statistics (matrices) and subjected to intense expert scrutiny. As Lillian Gilbreth wrote in *The Homemaker and Her Job*: 'We divide a process into operations, and these operations into cycles of motions, and these cycles of motions into elements of motions.'[49] The key feature of these motions is that they become synchronic or recombinant. They can be rearranged in any order to suit the productive needs of capitalism, and lose their affinities with the way that humans experience time as a unique, flowing series of events and experiences. In effect, one arrives at a situation of a stack of synchronic moments, the order of which is relevant only to the imperatives of capital optimisation, rather than a row of unbroken diachronic experience for the person involved in manufacture. Labour is not only divided between members of society, but the divided labour of individuals has itself been scrutinised and redivided in the service of capitalist modes of production.

When Witte translated *Household Engineering: Scientific Management in the Home* in 1922, this twelve-part self-improvement course in how to be an efficient, productive housewife quickly became the bible of *avant-garde* German architects – May and Schütte-Lihotzky in particular. In the book Frederick, as Beecher had

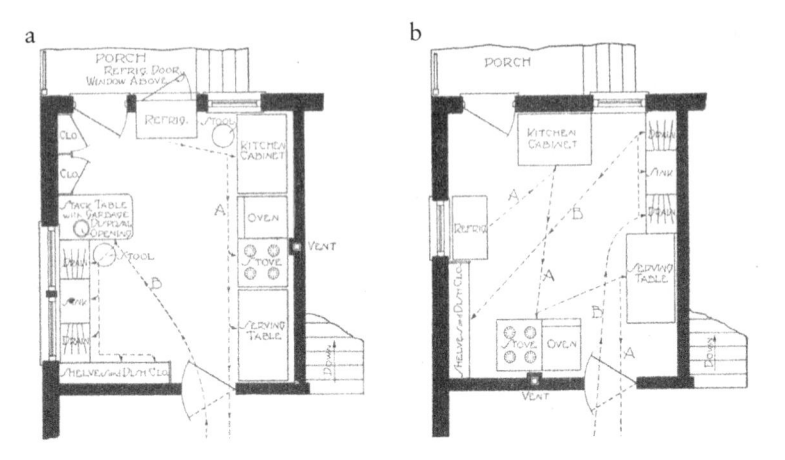

3.3 Christine Frederick's 'efficient' and 'inefficient' kitchens, 1919. By subjecting the labour of the housewife to a scrutiny usually reserved for labour in capitalist enterprises, Frederick attempted to 'design out' aspects of the kitchen space which might cause women more work and inconvenience.

done before her, suggested a way out of the 'treadmill' of domestic chores. Her solution, like Beecher's, was spatial: the end of the traditional *Wohnküche*, the usual arrangement in poorer homes which fused the social space of the dining and living area with the productive one of the cooking and food preparation area. Frederick described the near suicide-inducing drudgery of housework, and how the threat of this might make them fear to enter – and hope to leave – the domestic sphere which was rightfully theirs. She viewed this as a threat to all civilisation, and particularly the 'American way of life', its highest form.[50]

The key was the division of the home into a kitchen, where work was done, and the rest of the house, which was for the enjoyment of that new commodity, leisure (Figures 3.3a, 3.3b).[51] Frederick provided a worked-out model of how the rational kitchen could introduce the woman to scientific management, and Figure 3.3b shows how this would function to reduce the walking time a woman would do in the course of her work. The model for the newly divided kitchen was to be the man's world of industry: 'The bench of the mechanic can serve as a model for the kitchen . . . The kitchen must follow this workshop ideal.'[52] Just as the man left the home to go to his workshop, so the woman must leave it to go to hers, making her efficient, and also rewarding her with the dignity of a work-place without allowing her to leave the home. Her production-based rhetoric appealed to the communists May and Lihotzky, and they eagerly set about trying to transform Frederick's theories into social reality, using space to enforce this distinction, as can be seen in Figure 3.1.

Liberating women, segregating women: Frankfurt
Yet May and Schütte-Lihotzky's understanding of Frederick was faulty. Despite the fact that in Frederick the woman is (almost) never referred to as anything but the worker, despite the fact that the whole rhetorical emphasis is on liberation and production, on the housewife becoming 'a productive citizen of the State, not a social debtor',[53] the real clue to what Frederick was arguing lay in one subsection of one chapter – but it was a theme to which she would return and dedicate the rest of her professional life. Frederick was a conservative trying to 'rescue' the women's movement in the USA from the anti-communist hysteria about a 'Red Web' plotting to destroy American cities from within, which threatened to obliterate it in the early 1920s.[54] Whereas the book is dominated as a whole by talk of the woman as worker, as urban, as productive – all words guaranteed to draw in the most *avant garde*, Heroic Modernist architects – there is a brief section called 'The Housekeeper as Trained Consumer', in which Frederick argued:

> Never before in the history of the family have the burdens of purchasing been placed so heavily on woman's shoulders. This is because today the modern woman is *chiefly a consumer*, and *not a producer* . . . *To become a trained consumer is therefore one of the most important demands* made on the housekeeper today . . . Also it may be said here, *that every woman should be a trained consumer, whether she has a family* (i.e. husband or children) *or not*.[55]

In this astute analysis she revealed her true colours, ones which would have appalled May and Schütte-Lihotzky. Frederick did not actually conceive of the woman in the kitchen as a unit of production, but of consumption, marking out the transition between the industrial and monopolistic phase of capitalism. Her major work of 1929, *Selling Mrs. Consumer*, was dedicated to Herbert Hoover, 'do-nothing' president of America's slump years, and the work was targeted at advertisers and marketing managers.[56] It sketched the psyche of the woman as Frederick saw it, replete with theories of suggestibility, passivity and inferiority complexes. Re-reading *Household Engineering* in the light of this work, and Dolores Hayden's analysis of it, transforms the

1920 book from a self-help course into an advertising catalogue. Indeed, both Frederick and Lillian Gilbreth made their fortunes in the 1920s through promoting certain products in their books and magazine articles while feigning scientific detachment. Frederick summed up in 1929:

> Consumptionism . . . is the greatest idea that America has to give to the world; the idea that workmen and the masses be looked on not simply as workers or producers but as *consumers*.[57]

May and Schütte-Lihotzky would have been outraged, but their misreading of Frederick went deeper than their glossing over that one subsection, or their obliviousness to the lists of approved brand names. Where German planners read production, and saw the liberation of women from pre-modern family structures, Frederick actually argued for something quite different. Frederick wanted her planned kitchen to be a bare shell – a space the woman planned herself, compelling her to perform and invest in the role of housewife, and so she might fill it with products she had bought. She never envisioned it as a ready-made socially provided unit, over which she had no say. It was to be a repository of, and assistant to, consumer capitalism, not the symbol of socialised production and the social state. If a municipality installed the whole thing, there would be no room to buy the gadgets – electrical gadgets, in particular – on which she felt the whole future of the American economy, and actually therefore all of civilisation, rested. These ideas underpinned debate about social housing in Germany – sometimes without being explicitly acknowledged.

With both socialist and capitalist inflections, this rhetorical model was widely propagated in Germany in the 1920s. However, the Frankfurt Kitchen did not reign as supremely as the literature might imply; there were other spatial models which proved more capable of satisfying the rationalising impulse, while enforcing very different familial arrangements. Metaphors of science and liberation permeated women's magazines, newspapers, trade journals and the popular press, and were frequently deployed in order to legitimise the radical rearrangements of women's lives. And yet many working-class women resisted this model of liberation with vigour. While wealthier working-class Germans aspired to have a parlour for 'best' (the '*gute Stube*'), most could not afford it. Investigations in 1927 indicated 4.24 people per dwelling in Munich, with 29.3% of the city population living in one- or two-room dwellings, and a further 22.6% living in three rooms.[58] Munich was entirely typical.

The 'problem' of the parlour, therefore, cannot have been very real among Germany's poor. And yet the parlour for 'best' loomed large in the writings of countless household reformers like Schütte-Lihotzky, Meyer and Witte, because it symbolised to them the aesthetic vulgarity of the working classes. Building 'tasteful' furniture into the home was a way of stopping working-class women moving 'crass' furniture in.[59]

But here was a problem. The attempt to force women to behave in a certain way undermined the liberationist credentials of the Frankfurt model, and the aesthetic underpinning of Schütte-Lihotzky's arguments begins to make this spatial segregation seem more and more like an act of aggression on working-class women than an act of liberation. Contemporary critiques of the Frankfurt Kitchen were diverse, but the end effect of each was to tend towards the Munich solution. Adelheid von Saldern has shown that working-class women in Germany perceived the rational household *not* as a series of aesthetic decisions and ergonomic calculations, but as a household which practised birth-control.[60] Christina Benninghaus also confirms that the back-breaking nature of women's and girls' domestic work was often perceived to be of value in itself, demonstrating love and dedication to the family.[61] Just how much some experts got it wrong has been well explored by Karen Hagemann in her oral history projects. Whereas 'experts' privileged what they considered to be rational arrangements of space, women themselves used complicated spatial and visual arrangements as a way of asserting their status among neighbours. A house which was 'homely' (namely, full of knick-knacks, curtains, rugs, pictures, plants, furniture and the like, all requiring dusting, cleaning and polishing) staked a claim to be considered *bürgerlich*, or middle class, and thereby offered the housewife greater stature in her *Hof* (courtyard). A house which was difficult to manage, yet which was managed well, demonstrated that the woman was not a sloven, and that she did not have to work outside it. Sometimes, those who did work outside or who took work in disguised this fact from others and their husbands through elaborate housekeeping rituals, thereby allowing them to maintain control over their secret earnings.[62]

Liberating women, socialising women: Munich
This rationalising model was far from all-conquering, either in the 1920s, or since – despite Schütte-Lihotzky's assurance in the 1980s or 1990s, when she was writing her memoirs, that 'today this is still surely the most desirable way to organise life in mass-housing'.[63]

Many were dissatisfied with both of these discourses. Whether a consumer or a producer, the woman in the Frederick–Schütte–Lihotzky model is conceived of in the framework of a Marxian, materialist dialectic, or a consumerist–capitalist one. Munich, like Frankfurt, was committed to a massive housing programme. However, whereas May and the Frankfurt city government saw the 'open plains' of the aesthetic and productive post-revolutionary order as the antidote to social unrest and cultural malaise – and a (quasi-)scientific paradigm as the best way of achieving it – the Munich city government rejected, fundamentally, any idea that the worker, or the woman-as-worker, were commodities or instruments. Munich's governors and urban planners could not reconcile themselves to expensive experimentation in the means of production, relying instead on the pre-existing corporate capitalist structures of the German construction industry for the material aspect of the building programme. They rejected the May system of socialised pre-fabricated building partly because it was too expensive, but largely because it constructed women as productive units, needing rational scrutiny.

In contrast to the Frankfurt Kitchen, the Munich Kitchen was joined onto the living room, but at the same time offered many of the facilities of the fitted variety. This kitchen is in fact not really a kitchen at all. In German it is called a *Kochnische*, or a 'cooking niche'. It is an extension of the living room, and there is no barrier between the social world of eating and family life and labour world of food preparation and household administration. This feature, seen in Figure 3.2 in a mass-housing project, is to be found in all of Munich's social housing projects of the late 1920s. It was no less determinist, no less resolute in its enforcement of certain social arrangements than the Frankfurt arrangement, but it was predicated on a model of working-class womanhood which ascribed greater agency to women in the management of their lives.

The Munich Kitchen offered several advantages, both practical and ideological; most notably it was cheaper and smaller. But it also allowed the city to challenge the commodification of women as productive units by making a spatial elucidation of their central spiritual, social place in the home, a spiritual significance which demanded spatial organisation. Lastly, it also overcame the resistance to resettlement, frequently seen in projects in Frankfurt, as it allowed a flexibility of space great enough to enable families to accommodate what little kitchen furniture they might own, if they wished. Residents of May's Frankfurt estates commented on this to a study party of the Munich Corporation, and in Munich's designs every effort was made to emphasise the housewife's own capacity to organise her domestic space, within parameters established by the city government.[64] When the Munich party went to Frankfurt, they made a request to interview housewives there, a request which May did not fulfil. So some of the party seem to have interviewed the women behind May's back. This was a remarkable thing for experts to do at this time, and heightens their claim to be more responsive to women's own wishes. These women had a long list of charges that this kind of housing had diminished their freedoms, and when it came to kitchens singled out that they could not talk to their families or friends while working; nor could they bring their furniture with them from their old flats. Munich's Socialist Housing Director Preis argued:

> The leading role in small flats must be given to the *Wohnküche*, the opposite of the opinion put forward elsewhere, which argues from health and other grounds that the Frankfurt kitchen is to be preferred, a view rejected in Munich. In opposition the Münchener argues that it is in the character of the German whenever possible to be in company.[65]

One could hardly argue that this was an especially German characteristic. Given the deep rhetorical significance of efficiency, of engineering the 'new woman' and of American production paradigms and feminist discourses, the problem for Schütte-Lihotzky's opponents was what vision — economic, spatial, gender — of modernity should be put in its place.

To answer this, the historian can point to the huge exhibition organised by the municipality of Munich to promote its housing policies, and which should be seen as an adjunct to its housing programme — an exhibition which was discussed in Chapter 1. The *Ausstellung 'Heim und Technik'* — 'Home and Technology' Exhibition — set out to promote the city's new mass-housing policy not only among its own councillors and citizens, but also to the wider world, through a challenge to Stuttgart's Werkbund exhibition of the year before. It was planned in chronological parallel to the unfolding of the large-scale housing plans of the '12,000-Programme' in 1927–28. Unlike Stuttgart's primacy of aesthetics and exteriors (and comfortable place in the narrative of the rise of Heroic Modernism), the Munich exhibition explicitly intended to formulate clearly how a flat should function internally, and has been ignored by historians. Its aim was to define what the modern dwelling and the modern woman's relationship to technology, science and industry should be.

The exhibition was organised with walkways above and through thirty apartment interiors, including five designed for the 'new' single woman. Overall, it was a huge financial and media success. The exhibition was organised by the Municipal Building Department and, in planning it, key figures in the council stated their views on women's place in the world, and how the home should define it. There were, it is true, appeals to a sort of 'elemental' home and an essentialist view of women, but they were always accompanied by an attempt to integrate that vision into an idea of the modern, the new era, the new human being which Modernists were so keen on engineering. In short, they liked the idea of engineering futures, but disliked the models which Frankfurt, and the focus on rational scrutiny behind it, implied. The city explicitly rejected International Movement paradigms, such as Le Corbusier's famous dictum that a home was a machine for living, asserting:

> The so-called modern building method will be for us, therefore, not so much a stylistic as a practical question . . . The impact of the [council's] buildings . . . will not stem from the idea of the 'machine for living', but from the demands of developing a sense of belonging and family.[66]

One of Munich's two Mayors, Karl Scharnagl, wrote on the opening page of the exhibition catalogue:

> Home and technology – two words which encompass two fundamentally different worlds. Fundamentally different in the meaning of their very nature, in their significance for each and every one of us, in the effects which they have on human society. But they are also synonymous in this sense: they reach out to every modern person, they grasp him, and force him to take a position . . . What technology can achieve in the completion of the home must be constantly shown to us, and most especially to women, the very soul of the home. The City of Munich is fully aware of this, and is currently engaging itself in the tricky task of showing how to use technology for the completion of the home, and at the same time do justice to the diverse relationships inherent in the social organisation of this city.[67]

Scharnagl seemed to recognise that home and technology might be constructed as binary opposites – as, perhaps, tradition versus modernity, the warm versus the cold, the comforting versus the threatening, the living room versus, rather than integrated with, the kitchen. He also suggested – as did Frederick – that the residential unit is a place of encounter for the woman between what Frederick called 'unfeminine' technology on one side,[68] and the 'traditional' home (whatever that might be) on the other. As such, he felt it worthy of particularly close governmental supervision. This was an encounter which was not to take place unchaperoned; space would be that chaperone. The city had an obligation, in the Mayor's analysis, to make sure that woman remained the soul of the home. This was reflected spatially in the Munich Kitchen, in the efforts of the Council to place the soul at the heart of the body, rather than topographically removed. The city's plans acknowledged the ambition of governmental intervention to secure this goal but, unlike the 'functionalist' approach, admitted a level of diversity not permitted in the Frankfurt model. This appeal to reflecting and empowering social diversity was a consistent feature of all of Scharnagl's speeches and writings on the built environment, and diverged sharply from the classic Heroic Modernist idiom. Whereas May and other Modernists predicated their vision on typification – building for *'the'* worker, *'the'* mother – Munich city council deliberately and explicitly built homes for different types of workers existing in different social contexts in the different parts of the city.[69]

One might question whether Munich's mass-housing programmes genuinely accommodated this desire to control the city, and at the same time appeal to its social diversity. On balance, however, Bauamtmann Joseph Jelinek, who organised the 'Home and Technology' exhibition for the City of Munich, and was himself a municipal architect, best summed up the overall attitude. He described a *Vernunftehe*, a 'marriage of reason', between home and technology. He started by arguing that technological progress and rational planning in housing might mean the end of slavery for women – just as Catharine Beecher, Christine Frederick, Ernst May and Margarete Schütte-Lihotzky had done – but he also asserted, as did Beecher and Frederick, that 'the strongest cradle of the soul [*Gemütes*] is the home. The woman is its protector.'[70] She could not be commodified or instrumentalised in a modern sense; her labour was not divisible. The elemental mother would be freed by technology, and by the Fordist, capitalist, rational planning paradigm, to stand watch over the home as a whole organism, not to be separated from it. Jelinek appealed to a sense of freedom; he announced through the introduction of science and technology into the home the emancipation of women, and trumpeted the end of their slavery – but then backtracked significantly:

> The housewife still has a lot to do – potatoes will never peel and boil themselves. We have not come that far – and we never will, and we never want to. *Because it is the joy of the housewife to create in the*

> *home, to organise her home herself, to make it homely and cosy . . .* The housewife loves to have flowers at the window, not just because they are beautiful, because they decorate the home, but because she is related to their female nature. In the life of flowers, natural laws reign. The world of technology is also ruled by natural laws. Both, then, flowers and technology, have the same basics. In the flower, however, lies something else, something outside the laws of nature, something unattainable, a something which will always defy definition, call it life force, soul, spirit, feeling or what you will. And it is this something which is related to the nature of woman, this something which distinguishes flower and woman from the grandest and smartest gadgets which technology has produced. [71]

It should perhaps be pointed out that the affinity of women and flowers may well not have been a reference to the decorative value of women, but the strongly grammatically feminine nature of 'flowers' in German. The planning of the exhibition at every level often deployed a rhetoric of 'the woman as creator'. For Jelinek, the woman was firmly contextualised as an elemental, inscrutable figure, whose social role was indivisible just like the linearity of time which underpinned human experience. She was rational, in that (like flowers) she followed natural laws, but these laws should remain unstated, untested. She could not be conceptually separated from the social life of the home, and this conceptual proximity between work and social roles could be structured, and even enforced, by spatial means. At the same time, however, technology and capitalist analytical structures – cold modernity, perhaps – might assist her in her mission to protect the domestic world. A well-planned *Kochnische* would also save her time and energy, allowing her to devote herself more completely to her social roles. She is, in Scharnagl's analysis, the soul of the home, and in Jelinek's vision she is the fulcrum of a material world of technology and science on the one hand, and an un-nameable, irreducible realm of deep meaning and significance on the other.

Conclusion

The great modernist quest for some sort of unity between head and heart, rational and elemental, is played out here, in the kitchen, the consulting room and the orphanage. The burgers of Munich seem to have been committed to finding a reconciliation, rather than new ways of expressing and enforcing a demarcation. Indeed, the German word for appeasement or reconciliation, *Versöhnung*, runs through almost all the journalism and debate of this period, not just in Munich, but across the Reich. Through resisting or reformulating the 'scientific' or institutional model, they hoped to find a synthesis which would reconcile the modernity of rational planning and social provision with the positive features of what they assumed to be a pre-modern, elemental society, characterised, they felt, by the social–familial role of the woman, and one in which the vulnerable and weak would recognise their need, and pro-actively collaborate in eliminating it. It was to be a rationally planned, technologically competent traditionalism, if that is not too great a paradox. It was a modern solution, and space was its coercive agent.

In Munich, the citizen was spatially defined as primarily social and familial, human and individual, not productive and functional, or typical and uniform. In the kitchen, the female citizen's work environment was inseparable from her social role as a mother and a friend to visitors, and was not to be described symbolically in terms of industrial paradigms, whether in the consumptionist discourses of corporate America (Frederick), or the productivist ones of Soviet Russia (May). Munich City Council wanted to define the best of the factory, and put it into the service of an idealised, elemental home and an essentialist view of woman, just as they hoped to define the best of the hospital, and put it into the service of an idealised, unique personality. The personal and social roles of women as mothers and family-members was privileged over their more impersonal ones as domestic managers, while allowing the economic, spatial and cooking advantages of rational planning to be fully exploited. The fusion of living and cooking space, which Munich did not invent but which they invested with modern, social, helping rhetoric, in fact transpired to be the more popular model in modern housing. In the case of hospitals, orphanages and old people's homes, the citizen was constructed as an individual, each with the story of a lifetime to tell, and who would resist – perhaps even, reasonably resist – attempts to make his or her experience of need fit a statistical, typifying and universalising model of social change. To this end, the city government went to considerable expense, redesigning old people's homes and producing innovative and costly solutions in order to emphasise the humanity of the projects and to orientate them towards the personality of the individuals they were supposed to serve, rather than the impersonality of the state which provided them.

Like Beecher, Frederick, May and Schütte-Lihotzky, Munich City Council's leaders, planners and architects were informed by their preconceptions of the nature of a built cultural artefact, the determining possibilities of space, their basic assumptions about what it meant to be a poor woman, parentless child, sick citizen or old person and their underlying assumptions about advanced capitalist modes of production and the division of labour. But it appears that the committed revolutionary communism of May and Schütte-Lihotzky, which placed Frankfurt at one architectural extreme, and the folksy nostalgia of the quasi-rural settlements favoured by those both on the far-right and liberal left either side of the Great War, always remained to many councillors and experts in many cities implausible and unrealistic solutions to the difficulties posed by modern social and cultural organisation. Crucially, one can arrive at this picture only once historians begin to accept, and therefore to research, the coercive (and not suggestive) nature of space and emphasise, and therefore investigate, the often peripheral (and not mainstream) nature of Modernism.

Notes

1 Alan Waterhouse, *Boundaries of the City: The Architecture of Western Urbanism* (London, 1993), pp. 286–287.
2 Hans Klihm, 'Erinnerungen an die Studienreise der Berliner staatswissenschaftlichen Vereinigung nach Oberbayern und Schwaben (1)', *Trierischer Zeitung*, 17 June 1911. SAM-NLG-360.
3 Klihm, 'Erinnerungen an die Studienreise der Berliner staatswissenschaftlichen Vereinigung nach Oberbayern und Schwaben (1)'.
4 Hans Klihm, 'Erinnerungen an die Studienreise der Berliner staatswissenschaftlichen Vereinigung nach Oberbayern und Schwaben (2)', *Trierischer Zeitung*, 19 June 1911. SAM-NLG-360.
5 Klihm, 'Erinnerungen an die Studienreise der Berliner staatswissenschaftlichen Vereinigung nach Oberbayern und Schwaben (1)'.
6 Radical socialists who went on to found the USPD – the anti-war, hard-left branch of the SPD – and the proto-communist Spartacist League.
7 'Durch Oberbayern und Schwaben. Studienfahrt der Vereinigung für staatswissenschaftliche Fortbildung. 2) München', *Tägliche Rundschau* (Berlin), 20 June 1911. SAM-NLG-360.
8 'Memento!', *Münchner Neueste Nachrichten*, 25 April 1912. SAM-NLG-374.
9 'Memento!', *Münchner Neueste Nachrichten*, 25 April 1912.
10 Edward Soja, *Post-modern Geographies: The Reassertion of Space in Critical Social Theory* (London, 1989).
11 'Das städtische Waisenhaus zu München', *Deutsche Bauzeitung*, 23 December 1903. SAM-HBA-727.
12 'Soziale Plauderei des Bruder Marianus'.

The interior world of modernity 145

13 'Ein altes Schloß und ein modernes Waisenhaus', *Seraphischer Kinderfreund*, April 1901. SAM-HBA-727.
14 Lothar Meilinger, *Das Münchener Waisenhaus* (n.p. [Munich], n.d. [c. 1902–4]). SAM-HBA-727.
15 Meilinger, *Das Münchener Waisenhaus*.
16 Unknown newspaper, 20 May 1907. SAM-NLG-51.
17 Unknown newspaper, unknown date. SAM-NLG-51.
18 Stadtbaudirektor Hans Grässel, 'Besichtigung des neuen städtischen Altersheims an der Waldfriedhofstraße in München, Montag den 16. April 1928'. SAM-NLG-60.
19 Stadtbaudirektor Hans Grässel, 'Besichtigung des neuen städtischen Altersheims an der Waldfriedhofstraße in München, Montag den 16; April 1928'.
20 'Das Krankenhaus Schwabing München', *Deutsche Bauzeitung*, 6 October 1906.
21 'Das Krankenhaus Schwabing', *Münchner Neueste Nachrichten*, 11 May 1926. SAM-ZA-KH-KHS.
22 Jeremy Taylor, *The Architect and the Pavilion Hospital: Dialogue and Design Creativity in England, 1850–1914* (Leicester, 1997).
23 Direktion des städtischen Krankenhauses München-Schwabing, 'Das städtische Krankenhaus München-Schwabing', n.d. [1910 or after]. SAM-NLG-399.
24 Direktion des städtischen Krankenhauses München-Schwabing, 'Das städtische Krankenhaus München-Schwabing', n.d. [1910 or after]. SAM-NLG-399.
25 'Grundsaetze für die architektonische Ausgestaltung der Gebaeude', Bericht der mit der Vorberatung des Projektes der Erbauung eines III. grossen Krankenhausbaues im Norden der Stadt betrauten Kommission, May 1904. SAM-KH-44.
26 Bericht der mit der Vorberatung des Projektes der Erbauung eines III. grossen Krankenhausbaues im Norden der Stadt betrauten Kommission, May 1904, p. 39. SAM-KH-44. See exchange of letters Stadtbaudirektor Schwiening, Magistrat der Königlichen Haupt- und Residenzstadt München; Stadtbaudirektor Schwiening, Gemeindebevollmächtigte Stiersdorfer, March 1908–October 1910. SAM-KHS-15/1.
27 See exchange of letters Stadtbaudirektor Schwiening, Magistrat der Königlichen Haupt- und Residenzstadt München; Stadtbaudirektor Schwiening, Gemeindebevollmächtigte Stiersdorfer, March 1908–October 1910.
28 There is a possible alternative translation, which depends on interpreting 'der ganzen Sache' as a dative, not a genitive: 'We must, in this sense, take a step nearer to the whole thing.' Bericht der mit der Vorberatung des Projektes der Erbauung eines III. grossen Krankenhausbaues im Norden der Stadt betrauten Kommission, May 1904, p. 40. SAM-KH-44.
29 'Das Krankenhaus Schwabing München', *Deutsche Bauzeitung*, 22 September 1906.

30 'Das Krankenhaus Schwabing München', *Deutsche Bauzeitung*, 6 October 1906.
31 'Durch Oberbayern und Schwaben. Studienfahrt der Vereinigung für staatswissenschaftliche Fortbildung. 2) München', *Tägliche Rundschau* (Berlin), 20 June 1911.
32 'Durch Oberbayern und Schwaben. Studienfahrt der Vereinigung für staatswissenschaftliche Fortbildung. 3) Streifzüge durch die Isarstadt', *Tägliche Rundschau* (Berlin), 22 June 1911. SAM-NLG-360.
33 Peukert, *The Weimar Republic*, throughout.
34 For example, Sharon Marcus' discussion of novels and the lobbies of apartment buildings, *Apartment Stories: City and Home in Nineteenth Century Paris and London* (Berkeley, CA, 1999); Lynda Nead's use of songs to analyse a pleasure garden, *Victorian Babylon: People, Streets and Images in Nineteenth-Century London* (London, 2000).
35 Heynen, *Architecture and Modernity*; Peter Rowe, *Modernity and Housing* (Cambridge, MA, 1993); Peter Gay, *Weimar Culture: The Outsider as Insider* (London, 1974); John Willett, *The New Sobriety: Art and Politics in the Weimar Period* (London, 1978); Peukert, *The Weimar Republic*.
36 For example, in Thomas Markus' *Buildings and Power: Freedom and Control in the Origins of Modern Building Types* (London, 1993), plans of both 'real' and 'ideal' buildings are shown. However, 'real' and 'ideal' are often ascribed equal importance, and producers' rhetoric surrounding the plans is privileged at the expense of how they must have intervened in people's lives.
37 Blau, *The Architecture of Red Vienna*, pp. 182–187.
38 May was far from the only 'hero' of Modernist architecture to be so; the word 'Taylorism' appears in all of Le Corbusier's works of the 1920s and 1930s. Mary McLeod, 'Architecture or Revolution: Taylorism, Technocracy and Social Change', *Art Journal* 2 (1983), pp. 132–147.
39 Christine Frederick, *Household Engineering: Scientific Management in the Home* (London, 1920 [Chicago, 1919]); first German edn., *Die rationelle Haushaltsführung: Betriebswissenschaftliche Studien*, trans. Irene Witte (Berlin, 1922).
40 Gerd Kuhn, *Wohnkultur und kommunale Wohnungspolitik in Frankfurt am Main, 1880–1930: Auf dem Wege zu einer pluralen Gesellschaft der Individuen* (Bonn, 1998), pp. 142–176; Margarete Schütte-Lihotzky, *Warum ich Architektin wurde* (Salzburg, 2004), p. 153; Mary Nolan, ' "Housework Made Easy" ', pp. 549–577; Rita Pokorny, *Die Rationalisierungsexpertin Irene M. Witte (1894–1976): Biografie einer Grenzgängerin* (unpublished doctoral dissertation, Technische Unversität Berlin, 2003), pp. 80–88.
41 Lore Kramer, 'Rationalisierung des Haushaltes und Frauenfrage – Die Frankfurter Küche und Zeitgenössische Kritik', in Heinrich Klotz (ed.), *Ernst May und das neue Frankfurt, 1925–1930* (Berlin, 1986), pp. 77–84.

42 A trend first outlined by Barbara Welter in the 1960s. Barbara Welter, 'The Cult of True Womanhood', *American Quarterly* 18 (1966), pp. 151–174; she enlarges her thesis in *Dimity Convictions: The American Woman in the Nineteenth Century* (Athens, OH, 1976), pp. 21–41.

43 Catharine Beecher, *A Treatise on Domestic Economy for the Use of Young Ladies at Home and at School* (New York, 1989 [Boston, 1841]), pp. 121–134, 268–298 and esp. 366–370, 'On the Importance of a Convenient Kitchen'; Catharine Beecher and Harriet Beecher Stowe, *The American Woman's Home, or, Principles of Domestic Science* (New York, 1869).

44 See Valerie Gill, 'Catharine Beecher and Charlotte Perkins Gilman: Architects of Female Power', *Journal of American Culture* 2 (1998), pp. 17–24; Dolores Hayden, *The Grand Domestic Revolution: A History of Feminist Designs for American Homes, Neighborhoods, and Cities* (London, 1981), esp. pp. 55–63.

45 Mary Nolan, *Visions of Modernity: American Business and the Modernisation of Germany* (Oxford, 1994).

46 Literature promoting this phenomenon is easily to be found in the public libraries of industrial towns in Britain. A good introduction to the basic principles can be found in Frank Gilbreth and Lillian Gilbreth, *Applied Motion Study: A Collection of Papers on the Efficient Method to Industrial Preparedness* (New York, 1917). Lillian's application of them to the home are analysed in Laurel Graham, 'Domesticating Efficiency: Lillian Gilbreth's Scientific Management of Homemakers, 1924–1930', *Signs: Journal of Women in Culture and Society* 3 (1999), pp. 633–675.

47 Stephen Kern, *The Culture of Time and Space, 1880–1919* (Cambridge, MA, 1983).

48 Ralph Barnes, *Motion and Time Study* (2nd edn., New York, 1940), p. 15.

49 *The Homemaker and Her Job* (New York, 1929), cited in David Gross, 'Space, Time and Modern Culture', *Telos*, 50 (1981–82), pp. 59–78.

50 Frederick, *Household Engineering*, p. 7.

51 Frederick, *Household Engineering*, p. 19.

52 Frederick, *Household Engineering*, p. 34.

53 Frederick, *Household Engineering*, p. 381.

54 For a good analysis of this phenomenon, see Hayden, *The Grand Domestic Revolution*, pp. 280–289.

55 Frederick, *Household Engineering*, pp. 316–17. Italics in original.

56 Hayden, *The Grand Domestic Revolution*, pp. 281–287; Janice Rutherford, *Selling Mrs. Consumer: Christine Frederick and the Rise of Household Efficiency* (Athens, GA, 2003), pp. 121–135, 146–157.

57 Cited in Hayden, *The Grand Domestic Revolution*, p. 286. My italics.

58 Preis, *Beseitigung der Wohnungsnot*, p. 12.

59 Adelheid von Saldern, 'Social Rationalisation of Living and Housework in Germany and the United States in the 1920s', *History of the Family* 2 (1997), pp. 73–97 (pp. 81–83).

60 Saldern, 'Social Rationalisation', pp. 87–89.
61 Christina Benninghaus, 'Mothers' Toil and Daughters' Leisure: Working-Class Girls and Time in 1920s Germany', *History Workshop Journal* 50 (2000), pp. 45–72.
62 Karen Hagemann, *Frauenalltag und Männerpolitik: Alltagsleben und gesellschaftliches Handeln von Arbeiterfrauen in der Weimarer Republik* (Bonn, 1990), esp. pp. 106–114 on household reform; 'Von "guten" und "schlechten" Hausfrauen: Möglichkeiten und Grenzen der Rationalisierung im großstädtischen Arbeiterhaushalt der Weimarer Republik', *Historische Mitteilungen der Ranke Gesellschaft* 8 (1995) pp. 65–84.
63 Schütte-Lihotzky, *Warum ich Architektin wurde*, p. 147.
64 Bericht über die Reise der Mitglieder der Stadtratskommission beim Wohnungsamt nach Nürnberg und Frankfurt a.M. vom 22.-24. November 1926. Stadtarchiv München [SAM]-Wohnungsamt [WA]-63; Jahresbericht des Vorstandes der Gemeinnützigen Wohnungsfürsorge AG München, 1928, p. 8. SAM-Bürgermeister und Rat [B&R]-1458.
65 Preis, *Beseitigung der Wohnungsnot in München*, p. 14.
66 GeWoFAG, *Die Siedlungen der Gemeinnützigen Wohnungsfürsorge AG München* (Munich, 1928), p. 6.
67 Karl Scharnagl, 'Geleitwort', in *Amtlicher Katalog: Ausstellung 'München 1928: Heim und Technik'* (Munich, 1928), p. 13.
68 Frederick, *Household Engineering*, p. 84.
69 This position was most fully elaborated in Referat VII [Wohnungsreferat], Principles for Judging the Housing Question [in English], 1930. SAM-B&R-993.
70 Josef Jelinek, 'Die Vernunftehe Heim & Technik', in *Amtlicher Katalog: Ausstellung 'München 1928: Heim und Technik'*, p. 75.
71 Jelinek, 'Die Vernunftehe Heim & Technik', p. 75. My italics.

4

The production of space and the execution of social policy

The deployments of space in care homes, hospitals and dwellings in Chapter 3 showed how potent a tool space can be for the interventionist bureaucrat, enabling him (and it was almost always a 'him') to transform the experiences of the elderly or a family, by bringing together and dividing. This chapter moves from the *micro*-example of interior space to investigate the ways in which the capacity to manipulate space is intimately linked with all social policy. It explores more closely the ways the whole improving, helping, interventionist project of the twentieth-century state might actually be predicated on its capacity to define and manipulate the technologies of space.

The primary technology deployed in the control of space is building, and the main discourses in which that technology is debated are (in this context) architectural and urban design. This chapter aims to show that when there were changes in thinking about social and economic policy the early twentieth-century state often found that these could not be acted upon unless there were also changes in the way that architecture was thought about and produced. In this context, architecture becomes a dynamic technological intervention in human affairs, as transformative a historical agent as the railway, the machine gun or penicillin.

This chapter focuses on one conspicuous intersection of social policy and spatial reform: housing. Housing is a particularly potent example, as it was one of the central areas of social policy intervention in the western state between c. 1900 and 1975, and because the discussion of it to date has been severely one-sided. 'Housing' is both a space and a policy. However, the spatial aspect of the policy – the actual dwelling which must be produced – in some histories functions as illustration rather than explanation, such that much writing on housing and cities contains little in the way of architectural evidence, or analysis of how structures worked to change the lives of those using them.[1] This chapter will challenge the unwillingness to regard design as a historical 'fact' or cause, in the way that, say, laws or speeches are regarded as facts and causes by historians.

It is necessary first to clarify the way the word 'architecture' is used here. Usually, architecture is to building what literature is to writing. But just as most of what we read is not 'literature' in its formal sense, the same goes for most of the building the citizen experiences. From our origins in banal hospitals, through our education in mundane schools, adolescence in typified housing, journeys to work along unremarkable roads, looking at unexceptional shop fronts, to our eventual demise in yet another (or perhaps the same) banal hospital, our lives are conditioned by the structures which almost never appear in academic analysis. 'Architecture' needs to be broadened to include all building. Panayotis Tournikiotis has surveyed the way historians discuss ordinary, mundane building, and concluded that, in short, they have not: historians *qua* historians have largely avoided investigating architecture altogether.[2] On the rare occasions when historians do touch on architecture, they privilege the words of architects over the buildings they produce and the lives that take place inside them. Introducing her study of German architecture in the early twentieth century, Kathleen James-Chakraborty shows that the historiography of architecture privileges architects over buildings, and not even in architects' architectural activities: it is the words architects produce, rather than the spaces, which produce most comment and fascination.[3] Borrowing heavily from the connoiseurial tradition of art history, historians in general focus on a small number of iconic, famous buildings, and/or they place more emphasis on what architects wrote than what they built. This chapter sets out to challenge this. Using the example of housing, it will argue that, very often, the capacity of the state to pursue effective policy was as much to do with design as it was with finance, electoral change or political disorder.

It is not conventional in most historical investigation to argue that the capacity to manipulate space effectively is linked fundamentally to the capacity to execute policy. Thus, there are several strands that the chapter is trying to bring together in its analysis of housing and policy. The chapter opens by identifying why the language and problems of aesthetics and design were so important to social policy discourse from the 1890s onwards. The next section addresses the transformation of the political and architectural issue of housing from being a vaguely formulated 'question' in the 1890s, to being a 'policy' in the 1920s. Central here is how the 'home' was conceived of, described and investigated, because one cannot formulate a policy on something which one does not understand (or claim to understand). This shift from question to answer sets up the hypothesis that the social question of housing can be seen in fact as an architectural question. It was not solely problems of *laissez faire* liberal political ideology or public financing which made social housing such a difficult issue to resolve, but one of poverty of design alternatives. Thus it is important to understand the problems in contemporary design of homes which impeded the execution of policy, even when the money and political will were there. The question part of the 'housing question' really was that: an open ended enquiry, the results of which would be uncertain.

The last two sections of the chapter examine that intersection in the architectural and stylistic policies of Munich City Council's housing activities before and after the First World War, showing how important it is that we shift the location of significant architectural innovation away from the 'singular genius' which drives the narratives of Modernism and art history, and towards the less glamorous, but more productive, world of design innovation within the deeply unglamorous world of municipal corporations. For it was among their employees that the accretive changes which allowed aesthetic discourses to acquire their moral regulatory power developed, and it was solutions devised here which underpinned effective housing policy for the following fifty years.

The politics of aesthetics

The language of design and the language of social policy frequently blended in the early twentieth century, but this aestheticisation of political discourse was in no way 'superficial' or 'ethereal' – and for two important reasons. The first reason why aesthetic idioms were so dominant in the late nineteenth and early twentieth centuries was entirely practical. Probably the most important element of the so-called 'social question' in this period across Europe was the 'housing question', and yet contemporaries were puzzled by the fact that there was little or no shortage in volume of housing in the early twentieth century. However, the *form* which housing took meant that it was unsuitable for poor people. Thus, the solution to the problem lay not in increasing supply of housing – indeed, the housing market was failing so spectacularly because of its supply-side bias. Rectifying the problems meant changing the design of housing, so that the priorities of the supply side matched up more realistically to the financial capacity of the potential consumers or users of housing. While there were many obstacles to the creation of this match – legal, political, financial – a central problem was the absence of design, and therefore aesthetic, alternatives to the *status quo*. Put simply, social order, public health and stable family life was frequently endangered because contemporaries could not (or would not) devise an suitable environment in which they might flourish. Thus it gradually became apparent around 1900 that the design of housing was the problem, not the supply.

Secondly, at the beginning of the twentieth century, when Europeans wanted to discuss social reform, they often located its discussion in languages of art and aesthetics. This was not because they were approaching the problem superficially, but because for conservatives and liberals, and even non-Marxist socialists like Ruskin and Morris, metaphors of class and economics were felt to be dangerous and dehumanising. Indeed, discussing the world in terms of class was felt to be pandering to precisely the social divisiveness so many contemporaries wished to overcome. Relying on the explanatory power of economics was seen as yielding to exactly that a-spiritual world view which they wished to supplant. Patrick Joyce has argued that this process of aestheticisation was integral to the entire liberal project of ordering and regulating the city in the late nineteenth century, concluding that:

> given the scruples about direct political intervention that appear to have marked liberalism, the aesthetic took on a particular significance as a mode of indirect governance, and functioned in an analogous manner to engineering or sanitary solutions by presenting intervention as no intervention at all.[4]

When Engels addressed cities and spaces (as he frequently did), he invariably pointed out how superficial liberalism and freedom and disorder in their design and spatial organisation actually produced underlying rigid order and control. As he so potently characterised the apparently haphazard layout of Manchester in the 1840s:

> Manchester is less built according to a plan . . . [and] is more the outgrowth of accident than any other city; and when I consider the eager assurances of the middle class, that the working-class is doing famously, I cannot help feeling that the liberal manufacturers, the 'Big Wigs' of Manchester, are not so innocent after all, in the matter of this sensitive method of construction.[5]

Engels argued that this 'self-serving' freedom of design produced a very ordered and ordering city, so rigorously segregating rich from poor that Manchester's overwhelming destitution was not only sustained by it, but hidden from bourgeois sight as well. Thus the design of space could serve to analyse a whole socio-economic system. While Joyce curiously argues that Engels failed to see the directing powers of society in the built form of cities (when in fact Engels spent much time highlighting exactly that),[6] Joyce plausibly concludes, again echoing Engels' arguments about false consciousness, that aesthetics functioned in liberal discourse to legitimate a well-regulated *moral* city, in much the way that medicine legitimated – and indeed, produced – the regulatory structures of the mid-nineteenth-century 'sanitary' city. Thus, 'aesthetics' and 'architecture' must occupy a central place in understanding early twentieth-century urban life, just as sanitary reform does in understanding that of the nineteenth century, both for the practical reason that it helps us understand the failures of the housing market, and for the ideological one that it helps us understand why contemporaries preferred aesthetic to sociological language.

Defining the problem, asking the question: the space of home

Technically speaking, there was no housing shortage in the most abstract sense in Germany in the late nineteenth century. In fact, Karl Christian Führer describes it as a time of housing plenty, though with short crises.[7] There was, however, a terrible shortage of small flats in the big cities, units which poorer people could rent with any degree of permanence, and without threat to their physical safety. This left contemporaries struggling to define the nature of the problem, and competing to determine the parameters of the knowledge which should be used to solve it. The huge influx of population into the cities had completely altered the modes of building in all capitalist societies. In pre-capitalist systems, for a largely static population, houses had been built quite often by the people who lived in them, or their ancestors. However, the rapid influx of people into the cities created a sudden demand for an enormous amount of housing, while suggesting no new models beyond the Parisian–Viennese apartment block for providing it.[8] Both a spatial–stylistic model was lacking, as well as a way of integrating housing of this type into governmental and capitalistic discourses and systems.

Housing surplus, housing shortage
This failure of the market is significant, because before the Great War, economists and architects alike genuinely struggled to understand

why the free market model failed so conspicuously to provide sufficient appropriate housing, when it seemed to work so well in other areas – such as the supply of food or clothing. They overlooked, just as most present-day historians overlook, the importance of design and space. Only in the late 1900s did academic economists start to challenge liberal economic orthodoxy on the housing market. They did this by constructing a model of a heavily sectorised *set* of markets which, while they all represented the general category 'housing', were separated by distinct, and large, jumps in cost, rather than on a gradual continuum of both production and consumption. In doing so, they tacitly recognised that types of market reflected types of space and types of class. The work of Emil Lederer, one of early twentieth-century Germany's leading economists, is illustrative in this regard, arguing that there was not one contiguous housing market from shack to palace, but several unrelated housing markets, each discrete from the other. Thus the consumers of single-room, high-occupancy dwellings would never, under any reasonable circumstances, become consumers of large, suburban villas. They were different, unrelated markets, but classic economics described them as points on a graduated scale of the same market. The 'quantum' leap, rather than gradual change, required to move between the two different markets was not understood up to that point – economically or aesthetically. The new economists who attempted to transform the *laissez faire* model of the market from the late 1900s offered an improved economic analysis of the problem, but had little to say on design – except that using current designs, there was no solution whichever way the housing market was constructed, as flats were too luxurious and expensive.[9] An inability to generate political, architectural and capital reformulations, combined with a severe economic depression, led to a stall in already meagre small-housing production which was to have deep political, social and stylistic consequences.

It is important to understand the implications of this distorted housing market which troubled so many contemporaries, because it illustrates the struggle contemporaries had in linking their ideas about, say, capitalism and the market, and their ideas about, say, design. Between 1885 and 1900, the population of Munich grew by 90%, from 261,981 to 499,932, and Munich was not an unusual city in Germany in that respect.[10] Crudely envisioned, production of accommodation met this demand fully, and in 1900 there was a 5% unoccupancy rate in Munich's apartments – a cause of some worry to the City Council.[11] Similar figures were reported across the Reich. On the surface, the free market was working well: supply matched demand, as evidenced by empty dwellings. In classic economic theory, this excess of supply over demand should suppress prices, and benefit the consumer.

However, it was precisely during the first statistical calculations of this surplus in housing that the city government instituted widespread subsidies for social housing construction through the Verein für die Verbesserung der Wohnungsverhältnisse in München (VVWM; Association for the Improvement of Housing Conditions in Munich). The VVWM was a quasi-autonomous body, juridically separate from the Corporation, but actually integral to it, and headed by Mayor Borscht. So at a time of 5% dwelling unoccupancy, bourgeois politicians began discussing the construction of extra housing. Although they did not, at this stage, propose any specific architectural reform, they did argue that such reform was necessary in general, based on their growing realisation of the inappropriate nature of existing housing. They said that it was necessary to invent a new form of dwelling: the *Kleinwohnung*, or 'small dwelling'. It should meet the social control aspirations of doctors and hygienists, produce sufficient profit to be produced by the private sector and be sufficiently cheap that the working classes might afford it. In design terms, this was a phenomenally tall order. Until a design could be evolved to solve this riddle, public policy in this area could not proceed.

This gap between homelessness and surplus of homes was a paradox to which contemporaries (especially rich contemporaries) persistently drew attention: why were city governments subsidising housing, when empty flats were everywhere to be seen, and when property companies were regularly going bust because they could not rent them? The answer was largely architectural. The forms of housing which were built in the 1880s and 1890s across Germany were typified by imitation of the apartment block models of mid-century Vienna and Paris, in which external order and regularity was paramount and legislation focused on the issue of street widths, and consistent height of buildings and floors. Little attention was paid to the internal layouts and functions of such buildings, which rapidly became subdivided, diseased, dangerous slums, likened most frequently to rabbit warrens and mazes. In short, space was divided in an abstract way, with little regard to function. Space was abstract and absolute, rather than relative and function-specific.

This was because the speculators always built for what they perceived to be the most stable market – the bourgeoisie. Thus they built highly decorated blocks of large flats. Even despite a series of catastrophic bankruptcies throughout the 1880s when the economic bubble after German unification burst, they did not seem to learn. Project after project failed to let to their intended markets (supply massively exceeding demand) and, after failure, were made to bare profit by subdividing the interiors of large flats intended for the bourgeoisie into the smallest of dwelling units. Frequently, each room of a spacious bourgeois apartment was 'turned into' a flat – a process that was more about relabelling than any meaningful sort of structural remodelling. The situation in Berlin was typical: one contemporary investigator estimated that there were 41,963 dwellings with only one heated room, *and* which had an occupancy of between five and thirteen people. This practice did not go unnoticed by the people crammed into them. As some workers in Hamburg, overheard by the secret police, commented on the contemporary building style in 1895:

> Three workers were overheard to make the following remarks: that the building type of the larger flats has really got out of hand in the last few years, even though the owners can see the damage it causes. There are always more and more of those sorts of palaces being built, in which no-one can ever live given the current employment conditions. They [the three workers] want to build different flats, namely housing designed to suit the circumstances of the working classes, and as near as possible to the city. The current workers' housing lies an hour-and-a-half or two hours from their workshops, and if one wants to live there more cheaply, one has to pay for the horse omnibus. If one does not want to do that, one has to take a beautiful house in the Steinstraße or Niedernstraße palaces, which are popularly referred to as 'hell on earth', and which are notorious for cholera.[12]

Having no other *architectural* model, bourgeois capitalists across Germany repeated their follies, building houses which, no sooner were they completed were redundant for their intended market, and full of industrial workers living in rooms with 4 m high, plaster-moulded ceilings, but no water, no toilets, no cooking facilities, often no windows, no heat source (big rooms were often subdivided, cutting out both window and heating), no fire protection and so on. Typical of this would be the structure in Figure 4.1, which is easily recognisable from almost any continental city. Grandiose it may be, and yet, as one contemporary observed: 'the newer building already shows signs of decay throughout. The mortar is breaking up on every floor; the ornamentation has become damaged . . . A satisfactory condition cannot be achieved in such mass rental buildings . . . such decoration, even when not so pronounced, is expensive and a burden to the owner. Contrast this with the smaller buildings behind which, despite their age, show far fewer signs of decay.'[13]

4.1 Typical 1890s Viennese Apartment Block. This type of apartment block was typical of those constructed in Continental cities in the 1880s and 1890s. Built for the bourgeoisie, they often ended up subdividing the flats and renting rooms to working-class families. The buildings fell into disrepair – as this one has done, with the elaborate plaster mouldings falling off by the 1900s.

Describing the 'home' at the turn of the century: numbers and words
This gap between the paradigms of architectural production and the social consequences of architectural need was a major motor in producing the aesthetic reform discourse which underpinned the turn-of-the-century attack on Historicism in architecture, but contemporaries struggled to formulate the problem effectively. The period before the First World War should probably be characterised

by this quest fully to 'know' the current housing situation, for what contemporaries really wrestled with was finding a way to *de*scribe to understand what currently happened inside private properties, and *pre*scribe what should happen there.

In particular, the threshold of the private property was widely regarded as a distinctly impervious 'frontier' for the state and its agents. In Britain it was often up to private individuals like Rowntree and Booth to give this human tragedy the quantifiable explanations which might legitimate state action. In Germany, the lead rather came from state employees. The closest substitutes were the emergent strands of Wilhelmine academic thought known as 'national economics' and *Kathedersozialismus*, or 'the socialism of the professors'. These individuals (which represented neither a coherent bloc nor a coherent ideology) did argue for a rationally driven attempt to solve the problem, but they tended to do so from a deeply nationalist perspective, and from the heart of the Wilhelmine establishment.[14]

Stimulated by academic discussions such as these, and driven also by the machinations of populist politicians of both left and right who used housing as a potent issue to mobilise support, corporations across German-speaking Europe began to investigate the problem in a systematic way, beginning to challenge the convenient ignorance and blindness which Engels criticised to such devastating effect. So, Bavaria established a Central Office of Housing Inspection in 1906, and the Munich Corporation ordered an investigation into every dwelling in the city (the *Wohnungsuntersuchung*) between 1904 and 1907, before establishing its own Housing Office in 1911. Investigations such as these genuinely shocked the city authorities which carried them out, although Engels may well have critiqued the 'genuineness' of their surprise. As he said, as we saw above: 'I cannot help feeling that the liberal manufacturers, the "Big Wigs" . . . are not so innocent after all, in the matter of this sensitive method of construction.' In the case of Munich, for example, investigators discovered that 25.1% of all dwellings were subdivisions of larger dwellings – not whole houses broken up, but divisions within spaces already conceived of as apartments.[15] Mazes were being constructed inside mazes.

Research was being done, however, to try to understand the consequences of current spatial practices in economic terms – to try to translate space into numbers. Organisations like the VVWM set themselves the task of estimating some of the cost implications of the current building styles, and was one of a clutch of organisations which began to use statistical analysis to argue for a distinctive, innovative form of dwelling: the *Kleinwohnung*, or 'small flat'. The VVWM estimated in 1899 that most flats in Munich were being built in Parisian- or Viennese-style blocks with five rooms, excluding kitchen – like those criticised by the Hamburg workers above. Furthermore, the VVWM emphasised that highly insecure tenancies meant that poorer families were being evicted in order to charge higher rents in a rapidly inflationary, uncontrolled market system – rent in Munich for a two-room flat with kitchen rose by nearly 20% between 1907 and 1912; more quickly for smaller flats, and more slowly for larger ones.[16] If an unscrupulous landlord could secure a higher rent with new tenants, then evictions would soon follow.

Thus, when the municipal authorities in Munich undertook their major investigation in the mid-1900s, and began to cross the threshold into the private sphere, they found that 40% of families with two or more children had moved in the previous twelve months.[17] According to VVWM analysis, a flat of two rooms in total with a window in each could not be had for under 200 Marks a year in 1899 – well beyond the means of most workers. A flat with two rooms, each with a window, and access to a toilet (their model dwelling) was over 300 Marks in 1899.[18] In the *Wohnungs-Zeitung* (*Housing News*) for the week of 16 December 1908, at the height of a desperately hard winter, there were only two flats with two rooms or fewer advertised for the whole of Munich (compared to whole rows of flats with four, five and six rooms), priced at 25 Marks and 30 Marks per month, respectively. Neither had heating in both rooms, neither had running water in them at all. This would mean between 300 and 360 Marks a year, for a two-room flat with no toilet, not heated throughout and with no water.[19]

A couple of months later, the situation was worse still. The *Wohnungs-Anzeiger* (*Housing Advertiser*) of 1 February 1909 again had only two such small flats, priced at 28 and 40 Marks per month (336 or 480 Marks a year) respectively, and on 1 April, only one small flat was listed (a different one), at 40 Marks. Alongside this one *Kleinwohnung* were twenty-nine flats with five or six rooms.[20] This 480 Marks p.a. should be measured against a Reich average wage in industry and handicrafts of 928 Marks p.a., thereby making the average skilled worker pay over half his or her wages for the tiniest – and most unsuitable – of dwellings. Workers in industry and handicraft were considered well paid, and the many millions in service or unskilled labour would earn far beneath this. In fact, in 1907, in an industrial city like Bochum, 35.8% of workers earned less than 900 Marks p.a. No wonder that *per capita* consumption of meat, bread, potatoes and fruit fell across the Reich in the period between 1900 and 1910 – and no wonder either that the number of days lost in strikes grew from about 2 million p.a. in 1900–4 to around 11 million p.a. between 1905 and 1913. In Munich, 27% of wage labourers and their families lived in one room without toilet or kitchen, and 36% in one room plus kitchen, while the figures for white-collar workers (which included transport workers and shop employees) were 22% and 49%, respectively.[21] Huge numbers of people were being charged large amounts of money to be crammed into unsafe housing. Family life and physical health in this situation was bound to suffer. Political stability would eventually be threatened.

When the Munich Corporation ordered the inspection of the city's dwellings as part of its quest fully to know the state of the subjects it hoped to order, it started with all its own properties, as it, like most German Corporations, was a substantial property-owner in its own right. It discovered that in the 18th City District (the industrial area of Giesing), for example, the city was landlord of fifteen substantial properties, all residential blocks housing more than 100 people each. The inspector could not count residents accurately, because he was not sure how to define 'resident', as many people used the buildings only to sleep during the day and he did not know how to count people living in stairwells, sheds, cellars and hallways. Seven of these fifteen blocks had no toilets in them at all. The inspector openly admitted bemusement about where the residents of these buildings had been disposing of their urine and faeces.[22] While hygiene and money were frequent ways to define the problem, at the turn of the century, however, some commentators were beginning to define the problem in terms of architectural design – even if they were still a long way from specifying a plausible solution. A popular South-German paper close to the Centre Party, the *Neue Bayerische Zeitung*, called for the development of the *Kleinwohnung* – by implication, purpose-built and cheap. Only this could remedy the ratio of toilets to citizens of 1:41, which made Munich, according to one front page headline, the '*Dreckhaupstadt Deutschlands*': 'Muck capital of Germany.'[23]

The real horror of housing in Germany at the end of the nineteenth and the beginning of the twentieth centuries is perhaps best understood in experiential descriptions rather than statistics – which often hid wide variations, moderating the lived-out devastation which engulfed so many people's lives by including the richer quarters.[24] No statistic could capture the distress felt by the Bezirks-Inspektor (District Inspector) of the 16th Bezirk (Untere Au) of Munich, who reported to his superiors – apparently unprompted – in July 1909 that sometimes he felt unable to go on with his job, so great was the suffering which he had to confront every day:

> The awful suffering of the housing emergency has been growing – insofar as I can tell – for some time on a terrible scale. Hardly a day has gone by since November in which families have not come to me after days of desperate searching. Families are daily broken up, and compelled to live in stables and under bridges with up to ten children, sleeping on the floor in the hay among the horse droppings. Another man whose wife is dead is forced to live in a cellar with no light or heating with his six children, and he is about to be evicted from what I hesitate to call this *Wohnung* [dwelling/flat]. He is preparing to move to a lumber yard and sleep under the planks, and hopes to be allowed to make himself a shack. At any rate, it is so urgently to be wished that even these people of low worth [*minderwertigen Menschen*] should be given accommodation which matches their worth as people.[25]

Strong words, conveying beautifully and very personally just some of the potential horror of life in the big city. That a German administrator should produce such a letter to the city government's executive is perhaps indicative of the true shock and horror which he felt in the execution of his duties, entering the spaces of the poor.

Technologies of space: land versus architecture

While contemporaries were increasingly successful at defining the problem – whether using the potent symbolism of popular journalism, or the dry statistics of statistical investigation – they proved less successful in proposing realistic solutions to it, because they could not devise a suitable approach to space that would satisfy both the poor who needed rehousing, nor the middle classes who would have to pay for it. There were roughly three political approaches to housing which contemporaries might take: they either argued ideologically that the state should not act at all; or that the state should act, but only to direct and encourage the market; or that the state should act, but that the 'space' of most importance was an abstraction of land, not about what was built on top of it. The refusal of the state to undertake responsibility to solve the problem was important – but even when the state did undertake to do something, there remained another obstacle. A central difficulty was housing campaigners' insistence on explaining the problem to themselves and to others in the rhetoric and metaphors of land, not the technical exigencies of architecture. This focus on land, rather than what was built on top of it, is worth some substantial exploration, for it had important consequences.

There was not even consensus on whether anything should be done at all – on whether the extant city needed any reform of the spatial principles on which it was organised. Extreme liberals – who represented a substantial minority of the political class in turn-of-the-century Germany – argued that nothing whatsoever should be done by the state (or, more frequently, the city), and that the market would resolve the issue. Any intervention by the state would distort the market, and therefore cripple the functioning of the entire market system. As the Association of Construction Companies wrote in an open letter in 1902:

> Numerous voices, almost exclusively from the laity, scream 'housing emergency'. But the deployment of state or city money would be an attack on the private life of the citizen. Experiences in Berlin and Spandau [a suburb of Berlin], where there was a particularly conspicuous temporary lack of *Kleinwohnungen* in early 1901, have shown that in most cases, the problem came down to the ill will of the homeless, in that they would not undertake to occupy a home.[26]

Mayor Borscht of Munich read this note – his signature is on the front. As evidence for the 'ill will' of the homeless, the Association of Construction Companies cited the gas workers of Spandau who, when evicted from their works houses, 'found a dwelling in less than four hours'. Borscht, like most urban administrators, saw things differently. When addressing his own city's gas workers, he referred to a '*Wohnungskalamität*' – a housing calamity – and his different vision highlights the gap between national debate (which had little policy-making responsibility) and city governments (which were most closely involved with social intervention).[27]

A more moderate liberal position was to argue that the state should intervene to restructure the urban environment, but only in order to improve building regulations. Subsequently, it was argued, urban growth and gradual rebuilding driven by capitalist market mechanisms would eventually ensure improvement to housing. This was perhaps the most common line of argument among the political élites. In arguing for this regulatory framework, they did in fact deviate from extreme *laissez faire* liberalism, but they remained wedded to a Haussmannesque model of planning, in which the state provided a very general algorithm of widths, heights and depths, while other, unspecified, agents funded the working out and exploitation of it. Archetypal of this was the Hobrecht Plan for Berlin, which although it was regularly revised after its inception in 1861, essentially provided an infinite set of algorithms for an ever-expanding city.[28]

Finally, another substantial minority argued that Britain (and sometimes the Netherlands) offered the model solution to the problems, either in the terraced house or, after 1900, in the Garden City. This focus on British solutions is crucial, for several reasons. First, English and Welsh terraced housing is land-intensive compared to the tenement blocks which characterise continental (and Scottish) cities. This meant that any advocate of this solution had to accept, by implication, the reconstruction of the city elsewhere, far outside extant city frontiers; thus, it was geographically problematic and spatially radical. Secondly, it was an alien form of living, culturally strange and ideologically complex. Lastly, it was very, very expensive, and German workers were not nearly as well paid as their British counterparts, and so the British building society model which financed terraced housing would be unsuitable for building such expensive dwellings on the continent.

However, there was a powerful ideological motor driving forward this obsession with open space. Contemporaries frequently focused on *rhetorical* solutions about the fundamentally landed nature of German-ness, rather than the technical solutions of design reform, or the fiscal–political solutions of state intervention. However, the design and political solutions had to accompany each other, because the state could provide successful social housing only if it was cheap to construct and useful for its intended inhabitants: these are design questions. So a radical left-leaning housing reformer, prominent at Reich-level in the 1890s and 1900s, like Adolf Damaschke, would typically condemn the concentration of capital (in the form of income-giving land) in the hands of the few, and quote the terrifying statistics beginning to emerge from more thorough investigations into living conditions. While Damaschke did advocate radical tax reform (by shifting tax from income to property), this economic aspect of the problem (locating it in land-holding) did not necessarily provide Damaschke's primary stimulus to act, and therefore master the economics of design. He legitimised action because:

> in overfilled rear apartments without air and light, even the most highly gifted, noble race must waste away and degenerate in less than the span of a human lifetime![29]

This focus on race and degeneracy was far from unique to Germany, and underpinned much enquiry into the city across the West.[30]

Damaschke founded the German League for Land Reform, and expressed a strong preference for the Garden City idea and for what he felt to be pre-modern models, derived not least from Britain and the Bible. Again and again he and his allies emphasised land – land was the root of the German *Wesen* ('being' or 'nature'), and thus freeing up land was the challenge. However, economies with less restrictive land development policies, like Britain, still had acute housing problems, demonstrating that the problem was not the free use of space outside existing cities, but a different use of space inside them.

Perhaps the most influential 'high-brow' economist and social analyst of the housing question was Rudolf Eberstadt, and his richly illustrated works show well how refined the definition of the problem had become by the Great War.[31] But they also illustrate excellently how this emphasis on provision of surface area of land outside cities, rather than the design of what one puts on top of land inside them, led to such a genuine set of practical difficulties in formulating an answer to the housing question (political ones notwithstanding). Here again is an example of a reformer focusing on space, but the wrong space. Eberstadt and his many followers and colleagues approached economics and social problems with a set of *a priori* moderate liberal axioms. The first of these was that, whatever the type or scale of the problem, the solution probably existed in the private sector. Thus while he could criticise the worst excesses of land speculation, he would never entirely discard the idea that it was the role of the private sector to acquire and develop land. Furthermore, he argued that this private sector role was not an unpleasantness to be tolerated but was, instead, the absolute key to providing a solution to the housing problem. While the market might need reform (in that, for example, the state should sell the private sector more land at lower prices, with closer regulation of what might be built upon it), the market was in no sense the central problem. Eberstadt wrote in 1912:

> Now is the time to highlight a widespread misunderstanding. We often hear from the opponents of land speculation. However, I and authors following me could not speak in terms of a fundamental opposition to it. Just the opposite: we emphasise to the utmost the necessity of speculative undertakings in land acquisition and construction. We seek to foster it energetically. We oppose only that inflationary drive which stems from the use of certain building forms [apartment building] . . . which contradicts the natural laws of economics, and which stems (according to us) from a faulty system of town planning and street design.[32]

Here, rather than demanding innovation in apartment design, Eberstadt actually spelled out that the contemporary urban form of spatial appropriation was inappropriate – even unnatural.

At the time of Eberstadt's writings, there were beginning to be experiments in small social housing in the form of flats for the working classes. However, he and his followers argued fiercely that the purpose-built *Kleinwohnung* as it was currently being developed was completely unacceptable, insisting instead that the true solution lay in a radical reconfiguration of land-holding patterns outside existing cities. Eberstadt was obsessed with the idea of thinning population density according to the romantic, quasi-racist Garden City theories coming out of Britain.[33] Indeed, even the existing situation in Britain was to be admired. So, whereas Manchester had an average occupancy per building in 1910 of 4.9, and London of 7.9, Munich had 36.6, Hamburg 38.7 and Berlin 75.9, although German reformers seem to have had a very imperfect understanding of the problems left in the British housing system.[34] Such a reconfiguration of population density could be achieved only through complete redesign of the dwelling in its continental European form. This was an anti-urban, anti-technological argument that few technocrats could accept. It was a way of viewing land that few politicians could afford.

However, even if this way of viewing a solution to the housing problem was impractical, some of Eberstadt's criticisms of the high-density small flat as currently constituted in Central Europe were legitimate. As can be seen in Figure 4.2, showing some early attempts to design small flats for the working classes in Vienna, such dwellings were absolutely minuscule. Even such well-provisioned dwellings as these (there are toilets outside every flat, and every flat has a kitchen, albeit with no window) were exceptionally scarce. Furthermore, accommodation designed in this way was usually intended for what were termed *kinderreiche Familien* – 'child-rich' families. Such a close cramming together of people in living spaces of little more than one room would do little to alleviate the very real problems of rest, food hygiene, domestic violence, contagion, child abuse or fire which reformers identified in conventional dwellings for the poor. Designing the solution in this way was affordable, but gave little good reason for either the state or the poor family to enthuse about it.

If one examines the plan of the ideal solution to high-density housing design that Eberstadt developed with Hermann Muthesius, the influential civil servant the Prussian government had sent to

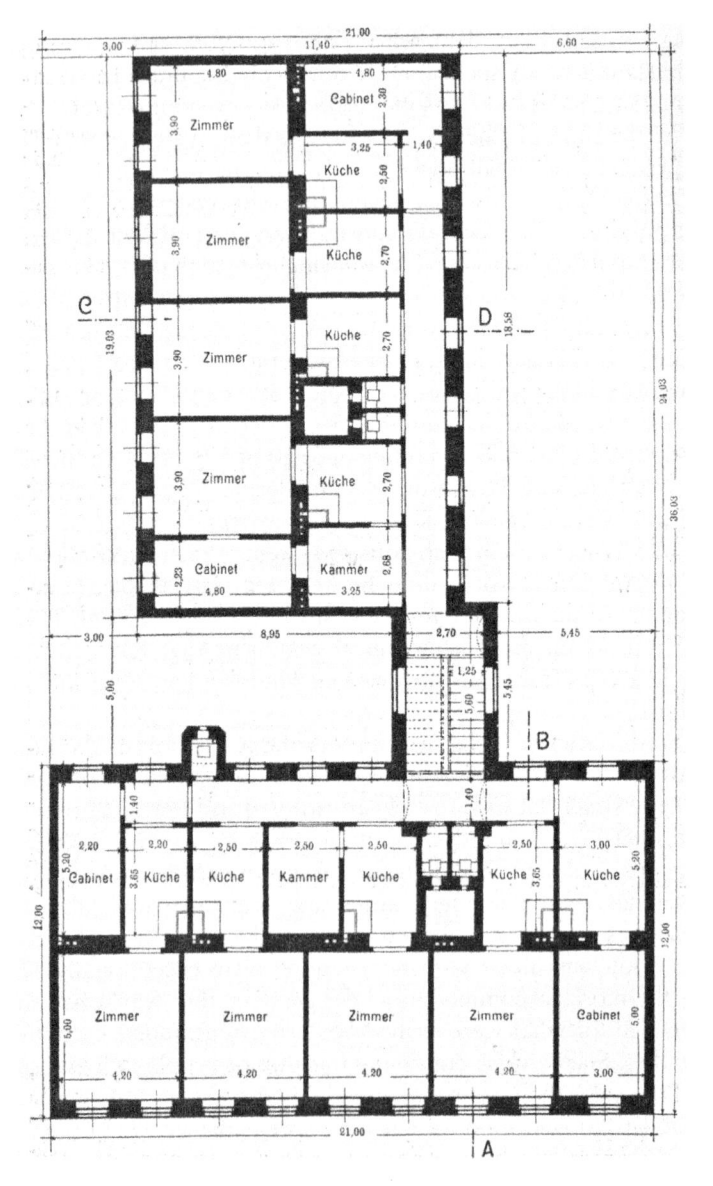

4.2 Plans for model small flats for the poor, Vienna, 1900s. These flats were built by a charity and the city of Vienna for working-class families. They offer one room and a tiny unventilated kitchen, with many of the flats wedged into a rear courtyard. Even when constructed, social housing like this did not match the ambitions of the working classes, or the reforming goals of the technocracy.

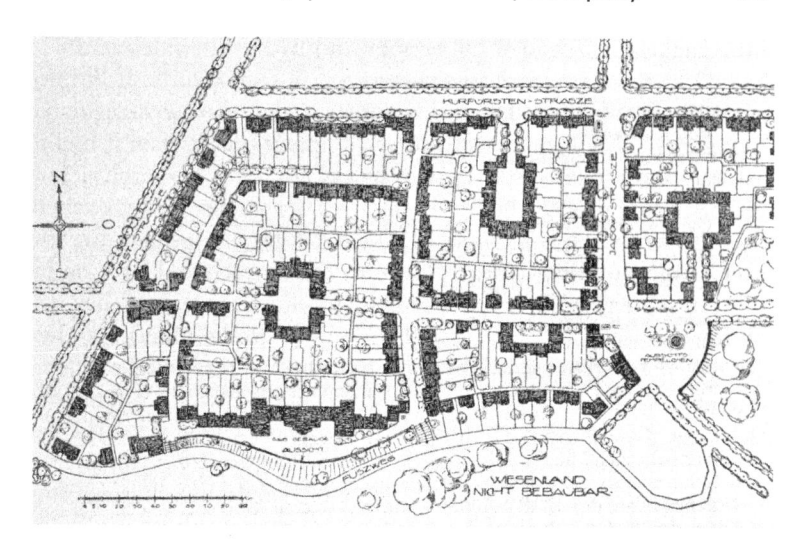

4.3 'Garden City' designs for housing reform, 1900s. This plan of the ideal solution to the housing question was developed by the Prussian government's chief expert on housing, Hermann Muthesius. It uses land extravagantly – so would have to be built miles from current cities (and therefore, employment). The plan is dominated by gardens and open land – the housing is shown merely as black blocks. Trees are shown in more detail. It is surrounded by meadowland, which would be protected from development. In the context of a solution to urban housing problems, this was a rural, nationalist fantasy.

Britain to produce a report on the housing problem (Figure 4.3), one can begin to see the sense of unreality and disbelief which must have accompanied many city administrators' encounters with proposals like this. The irregular plots of land, each designed to hold one house, were utterly inefficient, and completely alien to the spatial arrangement of cities like Paris, Vienna, Munich, Berlin or St Petersburg. In short, the 'national economists' seemed to have imagined that the private sector might somehow be induced, through complex arguments about the profitability of mortgages and mystical talk about the need to be in touch with the land, to provide the poorest people in society with middle-class villas utterly culturally alien to both residents and builders, on land miles away from industrial installations and service sector employment, in service of a set of ideological principles (the 'Garden City') which were far from universally shared.

Even when housing was built on the spatially generous model advocated by nationalists and Garden City reformers, it offered too little capacity to control the actions and lives of its inhabitants to appeal to the regulatory instincts of urban technocrats. It did not assist in producing what Joyce earlier called the 'well-regulated moral city'. If housing was to be government policy, then it had to assist in the project of governing. It was not a gift from the rich to the poor, but an intervention in the lives of the poor to make them live differently. Thus quantity of, and subdivision of, space given to each family in housing was central to the moral–regulatory ambitions of reformers. Give a poor family too little space, and they will all have to sleep (and wash, and eat and go to the toilet) together. Give them too much, and they will introduce non-familial residents as an extra source of income. Thus the technology of the quantity of space was central. In particular, reformers wanted to develop the stability of the family, and so opposed subletting to *Schlafgänger*, the custom whereby a room would be let out to single men sharing often four to the room, some of whom would work night shifts, and some day shifts. In fact, making workers' housing spacious actually encouraged such 'disorder' inside the home, because an abundance of space meant expense, and expense meant opening up the home to people from outside the family in order to fund it. Thus, rather than offering space as a coercive technological instrument in the social reformer's toolbox, expensive and spacious social housing solutions would, on the rare occasions they reached construction, actually encourage precisely the moral disorder among the poor that campaigners hoped to eradicate – and which led to the subdivision of bourgeois apartments. As already mentioned, a key problem was not that there was not enough housing, but that the available housing was not being used 'correctly'.

The introduction of non-familial residents into many homes was thought to lead to high levels of child abuse and sexual profligacy of other sorts. Whether 'abuse' is the right term is hard to say: a poor family would typically live in one room and, if they had two rooms, would often have a lodger. This problem would only be exacerbated should the number of rooms be increased, and the cost passed on to the poor. Such lodgers were often little more than migrant children, in German called *Schlafburschen* or *Schlafmädchen* – 'sleeping lads' or 'sleeping girls'. Beds were expensive rarities among the urban poor, meaning that people slept in all sorts of places and all sorts of configurations. Night shifts were common, so lodgers could be a good way of keeping small children tended while mothers went to work during the day. In periods of intense cold combined with economic stress, and in 'flats' (rooms or cellars or shacks) which were frequently unheated, putting people to sleep together was often the only form of heating available. People of all ages slept together – sexually and platonically, and on a spectrum of ways in between – for all sorts of reasons and in all sorts of relationships. This was precisely the sort of behaviour that the 'invention' of the bedroom in poor people's housing after the war was intended to tackle.

Proceedings against 'abusers' were frequent (although often, the abusers themselves were little more than children), and show how the dynamics of residential space might exacerbate the problems of poverty. Such cases were popular stories in newspapers, like this one from the *Berliner Lokalanzeiger* of 8 March 1908. 'Worker K' lived in one room plus kitchen with his two children, 11 and 8. He rented the room also to two '*Schlafburschen*' – 'lads who slept over'. The two lads and the two children slept in one room, while 'Worker K' and his wife slept in the kitchen. The 11-year-old child was eventually diagnosed with a 'hateful' (i.e. sexually transmitted) disease, found to be also present on Andreas Wojciechowsky, one of the boys renting the room during the day while the parents were out. Wojciechowsky was sentenced to fifteen months in prison.[35] Such stories were common, and the 'shame' of overcrowded housing was often a euphemism for abuse or sexual misconduct of some kind – the German word for the 'disgrace' (*Schande*) of the housing situation is related to that used to describe child abusers (*Kinderschänder*). However, Wojciechowsky's age is unspecified, and he is described as a '*Bursche*' – a lad – and his sentence was not particularly long by today's standards. This was a relatively frequent occurrence, and spacious, expensive housing solutions like those proposed by nationalist reformers would do little or nothing to prevent it, and much to encourage it.

It was in tackling problems like this that building design came to be seen as a central, pragmatic tool in the interventionist projects of the state. Furthermore, as it was urban governments in the early twentieth century which were responsible for dealing with the problems which housing difficulties caused (such as disease, fire or child abuse), it was with them that any projected solution was likely to come. When urban political and administrative élites fully realised the capacity of building design to facilitate social reform, they began imagining solutions to the housing problems which would address first a perceived need, secondly, widespread critiques of modernity and, lastly, the architectural and financial problems implicit in the aesthetic cul-de-sac of the Garden City-type solution. German cities' pre-war success in the area of housing was more modest than in that of their public buildings (like schools and hospitals), but is exemplary of the ways contemporary experts, technocrats and policy-makers might attempt to define a problem, and relate a solution to it. It also demonstrates the link between policy and the capacity to manipulate space.

Technology, rent and construction

This modesty of achievement before the war was partly because, as already discussed, city governments frequently faced stiff Liberal opposition to large-scale intervention. However, even when they did commit themselves to providing housing, projects often failed to achieve desired objectives even in the short term. This despite housing's emergence as a key area of concern – and despite extensive public disorder at moments of acute housing shortage, such as the winter of 1908–9 in Munich, or the summer of 1911 in Vienna. Of the two *Kleinwohnung* projects undertaken in Munich, it has been possible to identify only one as still standing. Small as it is, it is important, because it shows the 'workaday' architects of a city administration, a million miles from the 'manifesto cultures' emphasised in conventional architectural history, trying to join the technical, spatial, productive and aesthetic problems of housing to the social and economic ones of the modern governmental project.[36] Both projects were constructed primarily for poorly paid municipal employees. Although they at least had the advantage of job stability, many belonged to the poorest classes, in jobs like dung collecting, ticket collecting and portering. Many unskilled jobs in the private sector were paid daily, however, and these workers led a much more hand-to-mouth existence. As Schoener, the Housing Director, complained in 1908, 'the huge class beneath them are not heard'.[37]

Investigating the revolutionary approach to the production of space in the city's housing project is useful, though, as it highlights the failure to produce space in similar ways in other projects built by housing associations, charities and the private sector. That is to say, it shows that even when urban solutions (rather than the land reformers' extra-urban ones) were adopted, they could not offer sufficient benefit without innovation in design. The *Kleinwohnung* (small dwelling) complex by Building Officer Robert Rehlen on Thalkirchenerstraße in Munich was built at break-neck speed between November 1909 and November 1910 to address the terrible housing crises which became conspicuous in Munich in the winters of the pre-war recession years. Typically, the technocrats canvassed opinion from other German cities on what should be built – and rejected all their suggestions. Unlike most developments in other German cities at this time, it was not based on the model of the 'housing colony', influenced by English models.[38] The illustrations sent by Cologne Corporation show the half-timbered dream of the Cologne *Arbeiter-Kolonie* ('workers' colony') Ehrenfeld, and was standard practice in terms of its architectural–organisational principles – those of the *Kolonie* or *Cottage-Anlage* (cottage estate) – until well after the war, a practice which was always resisted in Munich. This would have made the flats expensive to build, and therefore rent. Rehlen seems to have rejected the wasteful use of space in other cities and focused on the technological task of producing a high level of facilities at a low cost. His block used standardised parts, and had shower-rooms in the basement.

The Thalkirchenerstraße project was, however, entirely differently conceived. The flats were designed to be either two or three rooms, plus toilet, but on a less grand scale and to a standard plan – this was their revolutionary element. The facilities were standardised, as were all the fittings, and the ground usage was denser, this one small square offering 177 flats. Flushing toilets were in each flat, but showers and baths were in the basement, and there was a communal laundry for the entire block and a playground installed in the middle. All this foreshadowed the communal provision of social, personal and domestic facilities which are usually stressed as being distinctive features of 1920s planned housing. Decoration was kept to a minimum, and only enough variation was introduced into the shape and masses to keep away any '*kasernenmäßiger*' ('barrack' or 'slum'-like) character.

This meant that rent could be kept to a minimum too – in 1910, it was 22.80 Marks for a two-room, and 34.20 Marks for a three-room flat.[39] As shown earlier in this chapter, in 1908 a two-roomed flat on the open market in Munich ranged between 28 and 40 Marks per month, with neither natural light nor heating in both rooms, nor a toilet, nor running water. This new workers' accommodation, built on innovative principles, marked a substantial improvement in quality of housing, with a reduction in rent of at least 19%, and quite possibly as much as 43% over the free market. It did this while improving on the problematic Viennese social *Kleinwohnung* (seen in Figure 4.3), but still respecting the contemporary conventions of block land parcelisation. Thus it *accepted* the ways that land was partitioned in the modern city (into blocks), and *accepted* the conventions of continental land use (having high-density flats built on it). It *rejected* the central plank in Garden City reform ideology, that populations should be dispersed and thinned. This was achieved partly by using cheaper credit obtainable by state agencies, and partly by innovative design.

This design solution can be contrasted with the large quantity of housing constructed by charitable organisations, and their attempts to reconfigure housing design. The VVWM (which, it will be remembered, was effectively an agency of the city government) conducted an experiment into lower-density housing on the Stadtlohnerstraße, but it was not a success. If one compares the costs of rental in the Thalkirchenerstraße project to the lower-density housing in Stadtlohnerstraße, the significance of both accepting the spatial configurations of the extant city, and design innovation, becomes yet clearer. The Stadtlohnerstraße project was largely paid for by the city between 1909 and 1911. Fischer, the architect, decided to build on *Einfamilienhaus* (one family per unit), *Flachbau* (low-rise) principles, though with subdivisions into flats. This meant that the cheapest flats were 30 Marks a month for two rooms, though only a very few of these were built. Most of them were 45 Marks a month for two rooms (versus 22.80 Marks on Thalkirchenerstraße), rising to 60 Marks a month for three rooms (versus 34.20 Marks on Thalkirchenerstraße). The rooms themselves were of a similar size to the Thalkirchenerstraße project, but land use was much less dense, ceilings higher, the interior fittings were not standardised throughout and external decoration was prominent, and therefore expensive.[40] Thus the standardised, high-density design way outstripped private housing in terms of facilities, at a cost to inhabitants that undercut both all private housing and other state-subsidised dwellings of a different design. The success and cheapness of the Thalkirchenerstraße project could not have gone unnoticed, because Munich showed itself more committed to what it came to call the *Kleinwohnung* than any other European city in the immediate postwar period.

From housing 'question' to design 'policy', 1917–30

Housing and political stability
During the war, housing construction – already slowing after 1912 – stopped. Production of subsidised small social housing units in Munich had risen from an average of 405 *Kleinwohnungen* per annum in 1906–9 to a peak of 4,210 per annum in 1912, when it started to fall quickly.[41] These peak figures are actually fairly similar

to the best years of the Weimar Republic, but much of this housing was designed on the principles of the Stadtlohnerstraße, and so not affordable by the poor. If reactions to difficult housing conditions in the period before the First World War were characterised by a humane concern for human suffering, during and after the war the situation was very different. It became clear to contemporaries that if a solution to the housing 'question' were not found, then it was unlikely that there would be political stability. It also became clear to some – though far from all – that most of the spatial and design solutions which provided the currency for debate before the war would not be capable of contributing to a realistic solution.

In the unusually bitter winter of 1908–9, when the City Council opened its properties to the homeless, and many thousands slept in Council offices, tram depots and school halls, the justifications for intervention were all humane. Words such as *Elend* (sorrow, misery, distress) and *Scham, tief beschämend* (shameful, disgraceful) were used. The unhappiness that people felt was personal and empathetic – albeit based on their own bourgeois ideals and morality. It was not preoccupied by worries of social upheaval. While bourgeois planners before the war feared that the architectural–social failures in housing would hinder their plans to produce an orderly, moral society, they never assumed that it would imperil its existence altogether – not even during times of civil unrest, such as the winter of 1908–9 in Munich or the summer of 1911 in Vienna.

But as the First World War drew to a close it was realised that attempts to solve the social problems caused by housing had failed on almost every level. Few could sustain either the design ambitions or the political assumptions which underpinned pre-war housing policy. Paradoxically, those that did try to sustain them dominate the historiography – people like Ernst May in Frankfurt or Adolf Loos (temporarily) in Vienna. Most, however, realised that political, architectural, financial and social reformulations of design and land policies were essential if society were to be preserved at all. Perhaps in some ways this is a distinct sign that modernity was indeed threatening, as the chaos of the end of the war showed that modernising societies had lost their impressive ability to accommodate huge technological and social changes while providing relative stability in political structures.

It seems that many Germans were frank about the likely outcome of the war from as early as spring 1917. The use of phrases such as 'Whatever may be the outcome of the present conflict, we certainly do not have to fear any boom in construction similar to that in 1870' seem to indicate a certain pointed neutrality towards the possibility of German victory.[42] Munich City Council enquired in late 1917 with other German cities what they planned to do about housing after the war. They, too, cannot realistically have been planning for victory. Other municipal authorities seem to have been more complacent. Bizarrely, 'Berlin believes it can assume that there would not be a sudden demand for *Kleinwohnungen*, but that should such arise, the property companies have plenty of land around the city'. (Note this emphasis again on 'free' land in the countryside.) However, Cologne, Bochum, Bremen and other cities were busy making more realistic plans.[43] The phrase most commonly used to describe what would happen at the end of the war was *Übergangswirtschaft* – literally, 'transitional economy' but, in fact, this was a sop to the patriots. It was code for 'impending crisis'.

Social, political and cultural élites, in Germany and across Europe, came to equate a solution to the housing problem with social calm and political stability in the post-war order. Munich's Director of Housing at the end of the war, Mayr, said he foresaw a new '*Schreckgespenst*' – terrifying spectre – of a housing emergency threatening all hope of building a society again after the war.[44] He said that without good housing the population would be dissatisfied and unhealthy, there would be domestic strife, violence and drunkenness. He added that every society reflected the families which made it up: where there was domestic strife and unrest, there would be social strife and unrest. In making this argument, he sketched out the triangle of control discussed at the beginning of this chapter: design was central to a project of moral regulation, and this moral regulation and aesthetics were central to policy-making. The disorder and disease of internal domestic spaces would be inverted and projected out into the public realm. Mayr felt that the solution was a total commitment to the *Kleinwohnung* ('small flat', rather than house) as an architectural form, 'ugly though it may be', and a financial–social–political boldness.[45] A year before the end of the war, he proclaimed what post-war housing policy would be:

> We have agreed a new goal of housing policy: every citizen should have a healthy, sufficiently big home, corresponding in price to his financial position. I hear straight away the objection, that this ideal solution is a Utopian demand, which stands no better chance of being solved than the social question as a whole. This objection is, of course, very comforting, and is most often heard from those who thereby relieve their consciences, put their hands in their laps, and quite happily let everything drift on.[46]

Gut, deputy director of the Housing Department at that stage, amplified this sense of fear and impending crisis. He wrote a proposal in September of 1918 warning of the terrible consequences housing shortages would bring in the immediate post-war period, and prophesied that housing would be the dominant socio-political question of the next decade.[47] This explosive and pessimistic policy document, marked 'Streng Vertraulich!' ('Highly Confidential!') seems to have had a deep effect on the Mayor, Borscht, who issued instructions based on:

> the escalation of this crisis to be expected especially because of the imminent demobilisation of our troops and the most terrifying dangers to the public peace which we can expect from this.[48]

In the same letter he also ordered the Municipal Building Office to convert all military properties in the city into housing, a surprisingly revolutionary act for Borscht to take on his own authority a month before the truce. In fact, this appropriation of space controlled by the Reich and dedicated to military use demonstrates that if we allow control of space to stand as a proxy index for central governmental authority, the revolution had already begun. Clearly the authority of the Reich government and the Wehrmacht was so degraded that local mayors could take decisions about military installations, appropriating them from the central government and re-inscribing them with civilian, social functions.

Housing, modernism and economic modernity

Mayr was replaced at the end of the war by a certain Schlicht, who seems to have realised that the problem was, in large part, to do with the technical aspects of building design, because he showed a revolutionary interest in the technicalities of housing design and production. He became actively involved in assessing possible new building types which might be suitable for building *Kleinwohnungen*, specifically the use of concrete. This would indicate the ever closer alignment of a social problem with an aesthetic or design one, as there would be no reason for someone like Schlicht to start this wild experimentation if previous models of construction were satisfactory. Schlicht and Building Officer Robert Rehlen (who had designed the block of flats on the Thalkirchenerstraße) ordered the construction in June 1918 of two experimental houses, one framed with wood, supporting '*Poroesbeton*' – porous concrete. The other would be framed with wood with metal plating – a sort of low-budget, low-technology reinforced concrete structure.[49]

Furthermore, in the closing days of the war, Mayor Borscht ordered the construction of ten *Probehäuser* (experimental houses), to be designed to last between ten and twenty years. The Municipal Building Office was asked to come up with a *Sparbauweise* – a money-saving method of building – which would provide housing for returning soldiers and their families and thereby stave off the inevitable social conflict which Mayr and Gut had warned of.[50] The city set its sights on *Sparbauten* (cheaper building technologies) despite heavy opposition from private architects, property owners and the Bavarian government.[51] The new municipal Gemeinnützige Wohnstättengesellschaft (Communal Housing Corporation) promoted similar projects in the summer of 1918. The spirit of open enquiry is in this example, by an architect called Böttge:

> Architect Böttge wants to try a new process for constructing *Kleinwohnungen*, a so-called 'poured concrete process' [*Betongussverfahren*]. The building authorities have just permitted this. About the execution, suitability for accommodation [*Bewohnbarkeit*] and costs of such houses, nothing is known; it is a totally new method we are trying here.
>
> Therefore, we must construct some experimental models. To enable this, the municipal Gemeinnützige Wohnstättengesellschaft has applied to the German Cement Association to ask for supplies of cement in these difficult times. This approach was entirely justified, as the Zementbund would have a great interest in this should poured concrete building become practicable, were our novel methods to be used across Germany. As yet, we have had no answer from them.[52]

This report illustrates the sense of total innovation with which these bureaucrats were approaching the problem. This is not to say that Munich invented it – but it shows that experimentation associated with *avant garde* architects were actually rather widespread after the war – which makes the focus on 'heroic' Modernists in the historiography all the more problematic. This sense of a technical–design imperative, combined with genuine, open ended enquiry about what forms future housing might take, is illustrated beautifully here. As with all of these experimental projects, it has not been possible to trace them further. Technical innovation in housing design was being placed at the centre of social policy, as the understanding of the link between the ways domestic space is produced, and effective social policy deepened.

The key project at the end of the war which was realised in Munich was the Alte Heide housing estate (Figure 4.4). It was managed by the Gemeinnützige Wohnstättengesellschaft, and represents a revolu-

4.4 Alte Heide Housing Estate, Munich. This estate was a revolution in social housing design. It was high-density, urban, cheap, well-provisioned, standardised, oriented around social facilities (in the centre of the plan). It effectively got rid of streets – even the Alte Heide Straße is little wider than one delivery vehicle.

tion in western housing design. After 1920, little is known of the Gemeinnützige Wohnstättengesellschaft. It built approximately 2,700 flats in difficult economic circumstances before the beginning of the financial meltdown which stopped all building projects right across Germany in 1921–22,[53] and by far the most significant one which it funded was Alte Heide.[54] Comprising 795 flats in its finished state, 600 were completed by December 1920.[55] The revolutionary features of this project were: the flats were very small, but all were of two rooms plus kitchen, and absolutely uniform throughout; fittings were standardised; and they were laid out in a *Zeilenbau* ('row building') system, meaning that traffic circulation and pedestrian circulation were entirely separated, as the plan in Figure 4.4 shows – a phenomenon that would dominate social housing construction in the West for fifty years. The flats were not built on streets, but in rows oriented to maximise sun intake, minimise traffic noise and also fundamentally to recast the whole 'flavour' of the urban form, eradicating the hustle and hurry and noise pollution of traffic, and restoring calm tranquility to the residential areas of the poor. Such designs offered the population density (and therefore cost efficiency) of conventional urban planning, and saved money to build facilities like basement showers by effectively eliminating streets. They had communal facilities similar to those built by Rehlen on Thalkirchenerstraße (that is to say, showers were provided in the cellars of the buildings, there was a central laundry) but, additionally, the entire project was ordered around a nursery school and social welfare centre. These principles – separation of circulation spaces, standardisation, provision of communal facilities – would be the central features of all Modernist housing in the 1920s, and would remain so until the 1970s.

In context, this was truly innovative. For example, in Paris throughout the 1920s and 1930s the Office d'Habitations à Bon Marché built densely packed, traditional tenements. Vienna's building immediately after the war was characterised by the Garden City mentality which underpinned the *Cottage-Anlage*. The general plan drawn up by Adolf Loos asserted:

> To become settlers, we have to learn to live as settlers. What should a settlement house look like? . . . We must start with the garden. The garden is primary, the house is secondary.[56]

The mentality in Munich was very different. Alte Heide committed the city to what it came to call the *Kleinstwohnung* ('tiny flat') early on, and the Corporation strongly resisted any attempts to pressurise them into building Garden City-influenced projects. By the mid-1920s, however, the *Kleinstwohnung* was attracting considerable opposition, and the *Kleinwohnung* became the norm. The City Council shifted from c. 40m² average, to c. 55m² per dwelling. To achieve economies of scale, and to tackle the tensions engendered in the minds of the councillors by the politically volatile metropolis (they were aware that the German revolutions of 1918 had started in Munich, and understood that the city was as vulnerable to volatility from the right as from the left), Munich embarked on a programme of planned housing construction, as did most other cities across Germany. Unlike Frankfurt and Berlin, however, the Council opted for very high-density land use, multi-storey units and a large proportion of communally owned accommodation.

The Corporation was building large volumes of housing before 1928, but piecemeal. Realising that this would never solve the housing problems, or allow the level of social intervention and control to which they aspired, in 1928 it proposed the '12,000-Programme', to build that many houses in three years. The figure was not arbitrary. There were 12,000 families on the 'acute housing need' register; thus 12,000 homes would banish the housing crisis forever. To complement Alte Heide in the north of the city, they proposed four further large estates, one each at the remaining main entrance points to the city: Neu Ramersdorf, Walchenseeplatz, Neu Harlaching and Neuhausen. Of primary interest here are the areas in which the estates just somehow failed to be Modernist in the art-historical sense. This is because it is in these failures to be Modern*ist* that the German bureaucrats' nuanced relationship to modernity is most clearly demonstrated, and can be most clearly contrasted with the fundamentally antithetical attitudes towards modernity of the mainstream of Modernism. Furthermore, this 'failure' to follow the paths of art-historical development also shows how the technocracy were using design to manipulate economics. It also acts as a corrective to the problematic focus on 'Heroic' Modernists, because most housing construction in Germany was similar to that in Munich, in that it was relatively conservative compared to Munich (though relatively radical compared to the period before the First World War).[57]

For example, none of the estates in Munich used flat roofs, as it was considered pointless given the unsuitability to climate which they evidenced, the storage space which was lost, the lack of insulation, the unavailability of standardised parts, the lack of expertise in laying them and their expense. In that sense, the buildings were destined to lack perhaps *the* distinctive feature of Heroic Modernism although, equally, this made the buildings fairly typical for social housing in Germany. Flat roofs remained rare. In some ways, this equating of Modernism with the flat roof is unfair; most of the modernist architects who get most of the attention did in fact also use pitched roofs in many, sometimes even most, of their buildings, and so their historians have been partly to blame. They tend not to be shown. So, for example, the famous Hufeisen at the oft-cited Berlin Britz estate is flat roofed, but the large estate surrounding it is pitched.[58] The *Einfamilienhäuser* (family houses – as opposed to blocks of flats) estates by May in Frankfurt were also flat roofed, but his largest estate, Bornheimer Hang, and the only one which actually offered high-density housing, has pitched roofs throughout. This estate is almost never shown.

Perhaps most significantly, the estates in Munich were designed to house an *extant* social order, not engineer the uniformity of a future or hypothetical one. Modernist architecture is often described as 'functionalist', but if it was functionalist, then it intended to use space to *ascribe* functions to people, rather than *follow* existing models of social life (as seen in the second half of Chapter 3). Munich's housing designs were designed to reconcile existing Germans with an existing modernity, not to define a hypothetical humanity for a hypothetical society. They were not intended to produce a fundamentally new sort of citizen, but to equip citizens to live comfortably with a new sort of society. Naturally, the demographics of the city meant that most of the flats fell into the category of small flats for cheap rent to poorer families. Yet some of them were designed to be rented to more middle-class (or at least, petty bourgeois) groups, and some were intended for families with many children. These attempts to produce vertical social integration within the same environment achieved some success.

This reconciliation with an extant order can be seen in the ways that different cities produced socialised facilities in their housing designs. Such facilities were included in Munich, but in the case of laundries they were optional. It caused resentment in some projects in Germany and Austria that the laundry bills were added to the rent whether they residents wished it or not. This uniform application of laundry charges (as in Frankfurt) assumed that poorer women would each do their own washing, whereas in fact many women grouped their laundry together to allow them to work – or, having only few clothes, it was simply unnecessary for them to wash sufficiently often to justify the fees charged to them. When Munich's councillors and architects went on a fact-finding mission to Frankfurt they secretly interviewed the housewives who lived there. They had made a formal request to May to speak to them, and this seems to have been ignored. So they went behind May's back, and found some themselves – women whose opinions appear in their conclusions. Some Frankfurt women complained to Munich's councillors that they did not feel that they got their 3 Marks per month's worth out of the laundry, but had to pay for it anyway. The centrally heated blocks incurred a charge of 8 Marks per month, which the residents did not like as they felt it removed control of their budgets and meant that they could not save money in hard times by turning the heating off and sleeping in the same bed, which was their custom in difficult periods.[59] However, infrequent washing of clothes, and intergenerational and mixed-sex sleeping arrangements were precisely the sorts of behaviours which architects hoped to eliminate, but it seems that different architects were willing to tolerate different degrees of autonomy in the people for whom they designed.

The city of Munich's rejection of the ideologies of a high degree of normified ways of living was evidenced in the writings of Mayor Scharnagl regarding the methods by which the corporation was striving to overcome the difficulties in designing modern housing, when he stressed that:

> The City of Munich is fully aware of this [problem of designing a new way of life], and is currently engaging itself in the tricky task of showing how to use technology for the completion of the home, and at the same time do justice to the diverse relationships inherent in the social organisation of this city.[60]

This has already been discussed in relation to the kitchens in Chapter 3. The city government's repeated stress – for example, in a letter to the research party from Birmingham – was on a refusal to typify, a refusal to engineer for a typified citizen:

> The endeavour of the City Council and the responsible board of dwelling was to build lodgings which may at the same time be used by an industrial worker as well as a lower official or employee or a small trader . . . So the city of Munich has no real artisans' dwellings as they are usual in manufacturing districts.[61]

Statistics of the surface area of flats built show that, while the weight of production was in the small flat, the Council always tried to balance this production to reflect the diversity of the city.[62] This is particularly conspicuous in the even distribution of flat size in the Siedlung Neuhausen. This was the estate of which the Council was proudest, and with justice. It is beautiful, and has continued to be a very successful housing project, just behind the Hauptbahnhof and stretched along the main rail entrance to the city. The relatively even spread of floor areas of the flats demonstrates an interest in using housing policy for the purposes of integration and social cohesion, as opposed to, for example, Alte Heide, where all the apartments are under 55m^2, and therefore rent to only one sector of society: the poorest. Thus housing like this was intended to reflect social composition, rather than transform it. With regard to the distribution of housing sizes, the Council is seen to be rejecting the normifying ambitions of the ideologies underpinning most Modernist housing projects; it rejected the ambition to create a 'new man' or a 'new humanity', and instead evidenced a desire to use its designs to reform the experience of the present one. The Corporation wanted socially diverse housing estates, and largely achieved this. However, the activity of designing housing does not just interface with society in terms of the spaces it produces. Uneconomic spatial solutions could exacerbate the very problems which reformers hoped to eliminate (see the graph of economics of production on p. 182). Thus the mode of production which a particular design solution deploys is of central importance. While most attention has been given to housing solutions which deployed innovative modes of production – such as

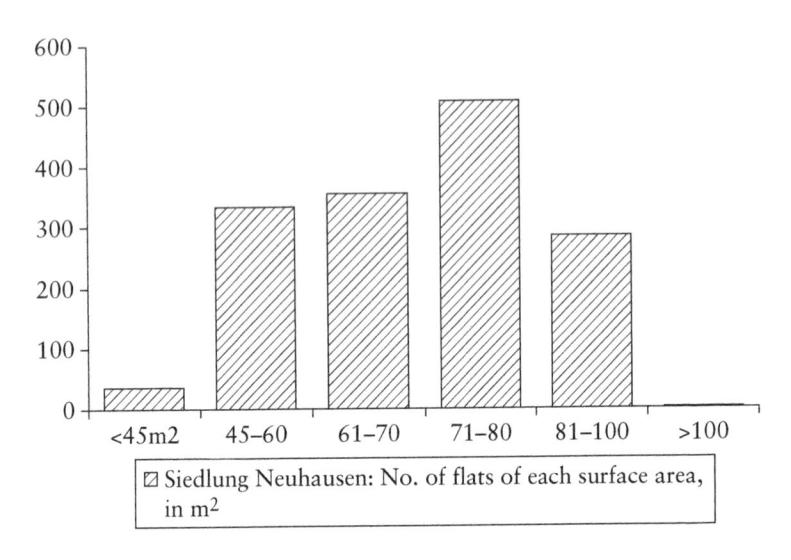

```
600
500
400
300
200
100
  0
     <45m2  45-60  61-70  71-80  81-100  >100
```

☒ Siedlung Neuhausen: No. of flats of each surface area, in m²

socialised manufacture of components or flat roofs – in fact, the most successful designs for housing were ones which engaged with capitalism in innovative ways, rather than ones which tried to replace it.

In the process of physically producing flats, every City Council had to make a decision about what sort of economic system it wished to stimulate in the design of the housing it produced. Three options were available, each of which corresponded to a political ideology: socialised production managed by the city; small businesses and craftspeople paid to produce the dwellings; or large capitalist construction corporations. The Munich city government and its allied technocrats – like those of most German cities – never seriously considered manufacturing some building elements itself, as May had done in Frankfurt. May had set up his own socialised manufacturing plants, thereby creating yet another level of normed building elements which were usable in only one particular project, or type of project, but which had no wider application in housing construction beyond the city of Frankfurt. Thus, despite coming from a mentality which stressed science, rationality and norms, Frankfurt's administrators ended up with parochial, local, unique projects. May had insisted on public production, but had allowed private ownership of the final products (leaving many homes empty as they were too expensive); Munich demanded public ownership, but private production.[63] When the city reviewed research into this way of building by a team of architects, they found socialised production uneconomical:

In Frankfurt-am-Main, it was found that in the new building there conducted according to the innovative 'May System', construction was 24.6% more expensive than conventional building. Furthermore, these buildings caused more economic disadvantage because they were not impermeable to weather, and so had more expensive maintenance costs . . . Despite typification and normification [of components], this system was 8.20 Marks per cubic metre more expensive than conventional methodology.[64]

Note the reference to 'economic disadvantage because they were not impermeable to weather'. The understatement is amusing: the buildings were not watertight and this meant that they were 'economically disadvantageous'. Frankfurt had been paying a lot for leaky, draughty flats. Clearly communalised production was not a design solution fit for the job. Effective policy was again undermined by a poverty of design.

There were powerful interest groups which campaigned for the use of small companies and craftsmen in the '12,000-Programme'. There were vigorous campaigns to do this from small businesses' organisations, some members of the BVP (the Bavarian wing of the Centre Party) and Stadtrat Fiehler (the NSDAP leader in the Council and Mayor of Munich from April 1933).[65] However, the city resolutely stuck to its intention to employ only big private construction firms like Stöhr, Moll and Gebrüder Rank. Furthermore, the Municipal Building Department resolved to use fittings which were already standardised, and which could be used in all of the estates. This policy had in fact underpinned the entire programme. As the socialist Director of Housing commented:

> With the planned new *Großsiedlungen* we aim to achieve the utmost economies of scale and reductions in costs through the thorough typification of the buildings and the flats within them, through the application of normified fittings throughout the entire project, and through securing as contractual partners large companies, and placing large scale orders with big firms and manufacturers. Only by these methods can we achieve the necessary cheapening of the means of production themselves, while guaranteeing that the solidity of the buildings is not compromised.[66]

They did, however, have reservations about this method of proceeding:

> The ultimate goal of the creation of housing must be some sort of industrialisation of the building process . . . We are not, however, of the opinion that the industrialisation should be so complete as, for

example, in America, where entire buildings can just be ordered from a catalogue. Where in Germany the way of the industrialisation of the entire building process has been trodden, as for example in Frankfurt-am-Main or in Berlin with the *Occidentbauweise* [a Dutch-patented industrial building technique], or where houses according to the Wagner or Frank system have been built on a large scale, they have not achieved the intended reduction in costs or economies of scale, because they have involved their own norms, and have not taken advantage of the typification already in existence.[67]

Innovative, socialist norms were too expensive, as was employing small businesses. However, designing capitalism into structures could enhance the delivery of policy objectives.

Using *new* norms also caused problems in that not every difficulty could be foreseen – the classic Burkean critique of rational innovation – and the buildings ended up not being watertight. Employing small businesses was politically attractive – probably the most attractive model in Munich. But beside being expensive, the estates could not be constructed on sufficient scale to tackle the housing problem. However, the archetypally modernising economic organisation of the large private company working to norms generated by profit optimisation was cheap. The Munich Corporation decided to build through large construction companies. In embracing capitalism, they embraced modernity. Given the way that the city government had constituted the board of the GeWoFAG (Gemeinnützige Wohnungsfürsorge AG – Communal Housing Provision Company), this policy was almost inevitable: three of its sixteen members were directors of banks, and three more were directors from Germany's biggest construction companies.[68] Significantly, the parts in Munich were standardised according to the coincidental and profitable manufacturing imperatives of advanced capitalism, not according to the socially idealistic ones of a restructured, made-to-measure modernity. This could be the general picture in Germany; the problem is that what research there is remains closely focused on the few architects and cities which socialised their own production. It is in the fundamentally banal, almost mannerist application of Modernist styles to its housing projects that Munich revealed its willingness to accept modernity, to work with the everyday, the transient, the fleeting – and, significantly, to accept the existing geographic location of the city and the dynamics of production of advanced capitalism. Thereby the Corporation displayed its willingness to work with modernity rather than an uncompromising desire to destroy or supersede it: the city designed modernity in, and did not plan it out.

Conclusion

Every formulation of economic or social policy had a spatial, design or procurement consequence. The processes by which buildings and spaces were produced – in this case, housing – impacted profoundly on the capacity of the state (in either its local or national form) to formulate and deliver effective policy. German technocrats and administrators sought to bring together the governmental, economic and architectural paradigms available to them, and stretch them as far as they would go in order to enrich (and also control and regulate) the lives of the citizen.

The sorts of men who worked in municipal administration mostly never assumed, however, that they could completely overcome key features of modernity like capitalism, or set an agenda for a society entirely on their own terms. They seem to have regarded those who thought that they could – whether Garden City planners before the war, or Heroic Modernists after it – as impractical and naïve. Before the war, they explored the possibilities which a departure from the dominant model of apartment building might offer in terms of enabling socially reforming projects, and developing a suitable aesthetic–technological response which would improve on the one-room-per-family idea, but also be cheap enough to build.

Before the First World War, Munich's administrators, politicians, journalists, trades unions and so on focused on a humane imperative for design reform, and afterwards on a socio-political one. It was an area in which they demonstrated they were ready to experiment, challenging the *laissez faire* liberal ethos without advocating globalising revolutionary alternatives; challenging the traditional form of the nineteenth-century apartment building without committing to the abstract (and leaky) Modernism of Frankfurt. The re-interpretations of the domestic form which were built on the Thalkirchenerstraße proved to the Council that its reconfigurations of the dwelling were cheap and effective, and apparently stiffened their resolve to build densely, using standardisation and with the provision of social facilities. This was a habit which they perpetuated after the war, offering Germany's first housing estate on the most modern town planning principles, and planning the country's first reinforced concrete tower block at the war's close. Unfortunately for the posterity of their work, they omitted to do this inside the art-historical canon of Modernism.

Unlike the architects that feature in the 'manifesto culture' which dominates architectural history, city planners like those in Munich tried to respond to an extant world, rather than positing a new one – geographically, temporally, or ideologically.[69] Even their revolutions were quiet ones: the social funding of housing in 1904; their rejection of historicism and adoption of the 'form follows function' credo in schools; their occupation of military buildings before the war's end; their principled insistence on high-density housing; their separation of vehicular and pedestrian circulation spaces; their adoption of large-scale standardisation; their experimentation with poured and reinforced concrete. All of this was done with a quiet, though public, resolution, and in a spirit of compromise with the social, cultural and economic structures which they felt would best help them realise their ambitions – be they big business, or the state. The focus was always on being at the cutting edge of the achievable, and they avoided problems requiring long-term systematic social restructuring for success. Preis' assertion that 'we want to keep our distance from all experimentation' was aimed directly at the ceaseless and seemingly unending practical innovation which seemed to emerge from American ultra-capitalism, and also the more radical 'blue sky' revolutionary visions emerging from the (usually leftist) 'manifesto cultures' of France, Italy, Frankfurt, Vienna and Berlin. Preis summed up a theme for the whole period when he said to the Council:

> This policy document also takes a position à propos the economic and modern building technique, and comes to the conclusion that the efforts to find a more economic way of building must be supported, but only in a step-by-step way, with a constant and cautious evaluation of the experiences elsewhere, and with constant regard to local peculiarities which may influence the outcome.[70]

There is little drama in such a way of proceeding, but it probably represents where most history has taken place.

So when they found that standardisation was useful, they accepted it, but on the terms of corporate capitalism not socialised production. Theirs was a borrowed or adopted standardisation, not the product of their own idealism or political agenda. One BVP councillor asserted that the question of normification was not one for the Council Chamber, but for experts,[71] and the Council ignored all the pleas to reject the new emphasis on division of labour, standardisation, large corporations and large contracts.[72] Throughout the period, the city's governors and experts showed a resolution to innovate, sometimes dramatically, but only as far as was necessary to fulfil their reforming ambitions and not a step further. They were prepared to explore, and even generate, unusual housing solutions and architectural answers if they could see a use and a measurable, balance-sheet gain from doing so. An aesthetic or design solution not linked directly to a nameable and achievable short- and medium-term social objective did not, however, interest them. I will venture one thing further: I suspect that this was fairly typical in Germany, and this means that we need to look again at the culture of that society, and look not for the bold heroes of Modernism, nor the daemons of reactionary cultural conservatism, but at the fairly stolid middle ground. There we will see that policy, design and space operate together to produce social change and continuity over time.

Notes

1 For example, Michael Harloe, *The People's Home? Social Rented Housing in Europe and America* (Oxford, 1995), which does not have any pictures in its 600 pages; Martin Daunton (ed.), *Councillors and Tenants: Local Authority Housing in English Cities, 1919–1939* (Leicester, 1984) does have images, but is still primarily statistical and political in a formal sense; so does Zimmermann's *Von der Wohnungsfrage zur Wohnungspolitik: die Reformbewegung in Deutschland, 1845–1914* (Göttingen, 1991), though he does make up for this in the volume he edited in 1997, *Europäische Wohnungspolitik in vergleichender Perspective 1900–1939* (Stuttgart). Or see the essays in a recent collection on urban history, Martin Daunton (ed.), *The Cambridge Urban History of Britain: Volume III, 1840–1950* (Cambridge, 2000): Colin Pooley, 'Patterns on the Ground: Urban Form, Residential Structure and the Social Construction of Space', pp. 429–465; J.A. Yelling, 'Land, Property and Planning', pp. 467–493; Peter Scott, 'The Evolution of Britain's Urban Built Environment', pp. 495–523; Abigail Beach and Nick Tiratsoo, 'The Planners and the Public', pp. 525–550.
2 Tournikiotis, *The Historiography of Modern Architecture*.
3 Kathleen James-Chakraborty, *German Architecture for a Mass Audience* (London, 2000), p. 4–6.
4 Joyce, *The Rule of Freedom*, p. 145.
5 Friedrich Engels, *The Condition of the Working Class in England* (1845), in Richard LeGates and Frederic Stout, *The City Reader* (London, 1996), pp. 46–55 (p. 50).
6 Joyce, *The Rule of Freedom*, p. 155.
7 Karl Christian Führer, 'Managing Scarcity: The German Housing Shortage and the Controlled Economy, 1914–1990', *German History* 3 (1995), pp. 326–354.
8 Vanessa Schwartz, *Apartment Stories: City and Home in Nineteenth-Century Paris and London* (London, 1999); David van Zanten, *Architectural Institutions and the Transformation of the French Capital, 1830–1870* (Cambridge, 1994).

9 Emil Lederer, 'Bodenspekulation und Wohnungsfrage', *Archiv für Sozialwissenschaften und Sozialpolitik* 25 (1907), pp. 613–648. For more on this innovative economics, see Elisabeth Allgoewer, 'Emil Lederer: Business Cycles, Crises and Growth', *Journal of the History of Economic Thought* 3 (2003), pp. 327–348.
10 Preis, *Beseitigung der Wohnungsnot*, Appendixes, p. 5.
11 Preis, *Beseitigung der Wohnungsnot*, Appendixes, p. 5.
12 Evans, *Kneipengespräche im Kaiserreich* , pp. 65–66.
13 Rudolf Eberstadt, *Neue Studien über Städtebau und Wohnungswesen* (Jena, 1912), pp. 163–165.
14 See Repp's study of this milieu, *Reformers, Critics, and the Paths of German Modernity: Anti-Politics and the Search for Alternatives, 1890–1914* (London, 2000), throughout.
15 Robert Rehlen, 'Kleinwohnungsbauten', *München und seine Bauten* ed. by BAIVn, pp. 427–431 (p. 427).
16 Preis, *Beseitigung der Wohnungsnot*, p. 15.
17 Gerhard Neumeier, 'Königlich-bayerisch Wohnen?', in Friedrich Prinz and Marita Krauss (eds.), *München – Musenstadt mit Hinterhöfen: Die Prinzregentenzeit, 1886–1912* (Munich, 1988), pp. 119–123 (p. 122).
18 VVWM, Antrag, betreffend die Wohnungsfrage in München, n.d. [c. September 1898– July 1899]. SAM-WA-23.
19 *Wohnungs-Zeitung*, 14 December 1908. SAM-WA-23.
20 *Wohnungs-Anzeiger*, 1 February 1909, 1 April 1909. SAM-WA-23.
21 Volker Berghahn, *Imperial Germany, 1871–1914: Economy, Society, Culture and Politics* (Oxford, 1994), Statistical Appendix, Table nos. 14 (average wages), 20 (food consumption), 11 (strike days lost), 18 (percentage of workers in salary brackets) and 65 (Munich housing statistics).
22 Bezirks-Inspektor des 18. Stadtbezirks an den Magistrat der Königlichen Haupt- und Residenzstadt München, 1 Juni 1904, Betreff: Wohnungsaufsicht. Mit einem Verzeichnis. SAM-WA-39/1.
23 'Münchener Wohnungsbilder', *Neue Bayerische Zeitung*, 29 December 1898, front page. SAM-WA-23. Indeed, this figure, being an average, must have covered huge extremes, from middle-class homes with one or more toilets per household to poorer ones, in which whole blocks of flats had not one single access point to running (and therefore, flushing) water.
24 For this sort of analysis, see Gerhard Neumeier, *München um 1900: Studien zur Sozial- und Wirtschaftsgeschichte einer deutschen Großstadt vor dem Ersten Weltkrieg* (Frankfurt, 1995).
25 Bezirks-Inspektor des 16. Stadtbezirkes an den Magistrat der Königlichen Haupt- und Residenzstadt München, 8 July 1909. SAM-WA-23.
26 Innungs-Verband Deutscher Baugewerksmeister an die Staats- und Städtischen Behörden in Deutschland. Eingabe betreffend die Beschaffung billiger gesunder Arbeiterwohnungen, 30 August 1901. SAM-WA-23.

27 Resolution der Versammlung der Gasarbeiter der Stadt München an Hohen Magistrat der Kgl. Haupt- und Residenzstadt München. 7 August, 1908. SAM-WA-23.
28 Claus Bernet, 'The Hobrecht Plan (1862) and Berlin's Urban Structure', *Urban History* 3 (2004), pp. 400–419.
29 Adolf Damaschke, *Die Bodenreform: Grundsätzliches und Geschichtliches zur Erkenntnis und Überwindung der sozialen Not* (16th edn., 1916), in Kevin Repp, *Reformers, Critics and the Paths of German Modernity: Anti-Politics and the Search for Alternatives, 1890–1914* (London, 2000), p. 86.
30 Robert Nye, 'The Bio-Medical Origins of Urban Sociology', *Journal of Contemporary History* 4 (1984), pp. 659–675.
31 For a sketch of these economists' (known collectively as the Nationalökonomen) response to the housing question, see Stefan Fisch, *Stadtplanung im 19. Jahrhundert*, pp. 99–115, and Brian Ladd, *Urban Planning and Civic Order in Germany, 1860–1914* (London, 1990), pp. 139–185. This analysis is based on Rudolf Eberstadt, *Rheinische Wohnverhältnisse* (n.p., 1903); *Die Spekulation im neuzeitlichen Städtebau* (n.p., 1907); *Handbuch des Wohnungswesens und der Wohnungsfrage* (Jena, 1910); *Unser Wohnungswesen und die Notwendigkeit der Schaffung eines preußischen Wohnungsgesetzes* (Münster, 1910); *Neue Studien über Städtebau und Wohnungswesen* (Jena, 1912); *Städtebau und Wohnungswesen in Holland* (Jena, 1914).
32 Eberstadt, *Neue Studien*, p. 161.
33 These ideas are discussed on pp. 34–36. See Voigt, 'The Garden City as Eugenic Utopia'; Matless, 'Nature, the Modern and the Mystic'; Welter, *Biopolis*.
34 Eberstadt, *Handbuch des Wohnungswesens*.
35 Albert Südekum, *Großstädtisches Wohnungselend* (Berlin and Leipzig, c. 1909), pp. 41–42.
36 Mary Ann Caws, *Manifesto: A Century of -Isms* (Lincoln, NE, 2001); Janet Lyon, *Manifestos: Provocations of the Modern* (Ithaca, NY, 1999).
37 Sitzung der weiteren städtischen Wohnungskommission, 4 November 1908. SAM-WA-23.
38 See plans 'Arbeiter-Kolonie am Ehrenfeld der Stadt Köln' and the *Verwaltungsbericht 1902 der Stadt Nürnberg*. SAM-WA-23.
39 BAIVn, *München und seine Bauten*, pp. 652–653.
40 BAIVn, *München und seine Bauten*, pp. 432–436.
41 Magistrat der Königlichen Haupt- und Residenzstadt München an das K. Staatsministerium des Innern. Betreff: Vorarbeiten für den Wohnungsbau im Kriege und nach dem Kriege. SAM-WA-18.
42 Grund- und Hausbesitzer-Verein München, e.V., *Denkschrift zur Übergangswirtschaft im Wohnungswesen*, March 1917. SAM-WA-18.
43 Ergebnis der umfrage in den groesseren Städten Bayerns und des übrigen Deutschlands über die dort getroffenen oder beabsichtigten Massnahmen

gegen eine Wohnungsnot nach dem Kriege. N.d. (c. end 1917–early 1918?). SAM-WA-18
44 Wohnungsreferent Mayr, *Warum brauchen wir in München eine städtische Siedlungs-Gesellschaft?*, 'Im 4. Kriegsjahr [1918]'. SAM-WA-18.
45 Mayr, Referat VII [Wohnungswesen], *Denkschrift zur Neugestaltung des staedt. Wohnungsamtes*, October 1917, pp. 2, 4, 7, 15. SAM-WA-18.
46 Mayr, Referat VII [Wohnungswesen], *Denkschrift zur Neugestaltung des staedt. Wohnungsamtes*, October 1917, pp. 1–2.
47 Albert Gut, *Wohnungsfrage und Demobilmachung*, 18 September 1918. SAM-WA-18.
48 Borscht an das Referat II, Betreff: Wohnungsfrage und Demobilmachung, 8 October 1918. SAM-WA-18.
49 Schlicht and Rehlen, Lokalbaukommission, an das Referat II, Betreff: Zulassung eines neuen Kleinwohnungsbausystems im Rahmen der baupolizeilichen Verordnungen, 28 August 1918. SAM-WA-18.
50 Borscht an das Referat II, Betreff: Wohnungsfrage und Demobilmachung, 8 October 1918.
51 Niederschrift über die 1te öffentliche Sitzung des Wohnungsausschußes der Landeshauptstadt München vom 15. Oktober 1919. SAM-RSP-692/7.
52 Bericht über die Sitzung des Aufsichtsrates der Gemeinnützigen Wohnstätten-Gesellschaft München m-b.H. vom 24. Juli 1918. SAM-B&R-305/8a.
53 Wohnungsreferent Karl Preis an Herrn OB Scharnagl, Herrn rechtsk. BM Küfner, die Mitglieder des Wohnungsausschußes, sämtliche Stadtratsfraktionen, die Mitglieder des Haushaltsausschußes, Herrn Korreferenten Gasteiger, das Finanzreferat, die Direktion der staedt. Spar- und Girokasse, 20 December 1931. SAM-B&R-1455.
54 There was a nominal autonomy for the project under the Baugenossenschaft Alte Heide (Alte Heide Building Association), but the file SAM-B&R-305/8a makes it clear that there was no functional autonomy of the Baugenossenschaft from the Gesellschaft, and nor was there any practical separation between the Gesellschaft and the council.
55 Geschäftsbericht für das Jahr 1920. SAM-B&R-305/8a.
56 Blau, *The Architecture of Red Vienna*, pp. 88–133. Quote from pp. 99–101.
57 Anthony McElligott, 'Workers' Culture and Workers' Politics on Weimar's New Housing Estates: A Response to Adelheid von Saldern', *Social History* 15 (1990), pp. 104–105; Ben Lieberman, 'Testing Peukert's Paradigm: The "Crisis of Classical Modernity" in the "New Frankfurt", 1925–1930', *German Studies Review* 2 (1994), pp. 287–303.
58 This can be seen in aerial photographs, such as that on p. 167 of William Curtis, *Modern Architecture since 1900* (Oxford, 1982).
59 Bericht über die Reise der Mitglieder der Stadtratskommission beim Wohnungsamt nach Nürnberg und Frankfurt a.M. vom 22.-24. November 1926. SAM-WA-63.

60 Karl Scharnagl, 'Geleitwort', in *Amtlicher Katalog. Ausstellung 'München 1928: Heim und Technik'* (Munich, 1928), p. 13.
61 Referat VII [Wohnungsreferat], 'Principles for Judging the Housing Question', in response to Scharnagl, 29 July 1930, letter requesting the Housing Department to explain why the town had no working-class housing as Vienna had. SAM-B&R-993.
62 Jahresbericht des Vorstandes der Gemeinnützigen Wohnungsfürsorge Aktiengesellschaft München 1930, p. 5. SAM-B&R-1458.
63 Adelheid von Saldern argues that expensive housing requiring mortgages 'privatised' the German working class, dissolving its consciousness and identity. However, too few of these houses were built to exert such a bold effect. 'The Workers' Movement and Cultural Patterns on Urban Housing Estates in Rural Settlements in Germany and Austria during the 1920s', *Social History* 3 (1990), pp. 333-354.
64 Preis, *Beseitigung der Wohnungsnot*, p. 101.
65 See exchange of correspondence between the Handwerkskammer von Oberbayern, the Stadtrat, the Magistrat and Stadtrat Fiehler, March and April 1930. SAM-B&R-1458.
66 Preis, *Beseitigung der Wohnungsnot*, p. 98.
67 Preis, *Beseitigung der Wohnungsnot*, p. 99.
68 Jahresbericht des Vorstandes. Gemeinnützige Wohnungsfürsorge Aktiengesellschaft München 1929, p. 5. SAM-B&R-1458.
69 Caws, *Manifesto*; Lyon, *Manifestoes*.
70 Generaldebatte um die '12.000 Wohnungen'. Sitzung des Wohnungsausschußes, 14 March 1928. SAM-WA-64.
71 Stadtrat Gasteiger, Generaldebatte um die '12.000 Wohnungen' Sitzung des Wohnungsausschußes, 14 March 1928. SAM-WA-64.
72 J. Würz, Dr Knoblauch and Dr Etzel, Handwerkskammer von Oberbayern and A. Wagner, Allgemeine Gewerbeverein München to the Magistrat der Landeshauptstadt München, 22 May 1928; Handwerkskammer von Oberbayern, 'Durchführung der mit oeffentlichen Darlehen finanzierten Wohnungsbauten, insbesondere des Sonderbauprogramms München 1927 [*sic*], hier Vergebungswesen; Handelskammer von Oberbayern an das Direktorium A und B des Stadtrates München, betrifft: Wohnungsbauprogramm der Stadt München. SAM-WA-64.

Conclusion: Germany, space and modernity

The book started out in the Introduction by identifying three intellectual themes which it wished to address: the importance of space and ideas about space in understanding urban history; the complex ways that the category of modernity is modelled in contemporary discourse; and, indirectly, the metanarratives of German history. The subsequent chapters focused on the people who manipulated urban space in the service of a particular set of goals – especially on those working for the Corporation of Munich. By discussing a German history with neither National Socialism nor a Holocaust as a dominant theme or an end-point, a Germany at home with modernity and the city emerged. One might argue that 'of course' German bureaucrats were supportive of the city and modernity, and instinctively used modern means to reform those aspects of urban life which they did not like. However, many more people attended their schools, lived in their social housing, visited their exhibitions and sought cures in their hospitals than committed themselves to antidemocratic political philosophy or radical racism. This is not sufficiently reflected in the scholarship. Thus, in this book, as in an increasing amount of others, the subsequent catastrophe remained a silent presence in the room, and a different German mainstream came to the fore.

However, Chapter 1 explored the different ways of critiquing modernity and the metropolis in early twentieth-century Germany which, although critical, did not depart from the values of liberal humanism. Focusing on criticism of the city would allow any consistent irrational or extreme antipathy to emerge, but none could be found. Across Europe, the early twentieth-century state took its most active, most interventionist form in the institutions of urban government. Thus the historically neglected personnel of city administration were called upon – or called upon themselves – to define a set of problems to be solved, a set of solutions to solve them and pronounced

Conclusion: Germany, space and modernity 193

themselves as the appropriate agents in this process. They did this with gusto, and their location in the mainstream is demonstrated by their enthusiastic adoption of the widespread metaphor of the city as a landscape of nerves and anxiety, of agoraphobia, hustle and restlessness and potential social, moral and political disorder.

Out of this critique came two ways of rendering the city knowable and curable: one specific to Germany – the *Heimat* metaphor – and one universal across the West – town planning. With the rhetoric of *Heimat*, urban planners tapped into popular responses to urbanisation and modernity, and in developing a discourse of 'city building' or town planning, they produced a rational system in which this anxiety could be handled. Both were coping mechanisms, and thoroughly modern ones at that. The *Heimat* metaphor commodified and popularised a past that never was – and in that process of commodification, this 'past' became absolutely modern. Just as the discourses of nerves and psychology were modern, so too was the expert, systematic, statist, manipulative framework of knowledges which these city administrators developed to render the city manipulable. And rather than rest in their offices and rely on their authority as experts to legitimise their activities, they actively promoted their world view through exhibitions. The popularity of these exhibitions highlights that these bureaucrats were neither peripheral nor floating in some detached bureaucratic realm. Theirs was a dialectical technocracy. And, in doing all this, the administrators, experts and governors of Munich were fairly typical both of Germany in particular, and the rest of the West in general. While the historian must always acknowledge the particular and the unique in all that is human, nothing that these German bureaucrats and administrators did would have been thought of as bizarre or unthinkable in the town halls of Lyon, Glasgow or Chicago.

This carefully crafted critique of the city as potentially anxious, pathogenic, confused, riddled with class conflict was also balanced for contemporaries by a real willingness to fête aspects of the urban – including its hustle and bustle. Chapter 2 showed that this was not simply a process of making a declaration about personal freedom here, or an exclamation about clean water there. City governors had to become urban in identity and assumptions, and had to take their citizenry with them if they were to succeed. They had to overcome substantial obstacles in order to do this. They could not rest on their status as the agents of some 'process' of modernisation or progress. They had to define the world to themselves and to others and invent a vocabulary to do so. They had to move people away from a picture of the city and its hinterland which had served in Europe for hundreds of years – in German, the words would be *Stadt* and *Umland*: city and the country around it.

In place of this, they constructed a convincing model of the urban in which the city did not function merely as a servant for the surrounding country, offering functions which it could not provide itself, such as the exchange of goods or the administration of justice. Rather, the administrators and governors started to transform the landscape which constituted their horizons and identify with other cities. They started to grow their metropoles outward; they built a model of the surrounding countryside as something empty, useless, redundant, awaiting the benefits of urban civilisation. In the case of Munich's administrators, it meant they had to move away from seeing themselves as existing in relation to a state (or nation, or administrative area, or an economy) called Bavaria, and exchange a horizon of Alps for one of other cities. They pushed the city outwards, aggressively incorporating surrounding towns, pitching outposts into open countryside, replacing the conventional symbols of the bounded city – such as the toll-booth and the cemetery – with a new symbolism speaking of the dynamic city – such as schools, gasworks and industrial estates. The German words for 'housing estate' were variously *Siedlung* or *Kolonie*: settlement or colony. It seems that these administrators and experts constructed the un-urban other as empty and redundant, legitimising their civilising mission of colonies and settlements. Finally, these technocrats wanted to celebrate their triumph in the same ways the church, the court and the bourgeoisie had glorified their own hegemonies: by imprinting themselves on the city's visual image. While town halls were important buildings in nineteenth-century European cities, they tended to refer to past times in their symbolic grammar – but the resolve to build in a distinctively novel style for Munich's huge Technical Town Hall complex indicates a new confidence in the technocratic future, a confidence which citizens seem to have come to share. And so here we have a Germany which is not just 'tick-box' modern, technological only inasmuch as it serves perverse purposes, but which is genuinely at home in modernity. Furthermore, this position *vis-à-vis* modernity reconciled the ordered and the disordered aspects of modern metropolitan life, and the historian can access this reconciliation in the rather unlikely 'heroes' of this piece: a group of bureaucrats and local politicians.

Yet the discussion and manipulation of the urban environment did not take place merely to offer the public or the historian a barometer of how some Germans imagined the city, and themselves in it. These technocrats wanted to control and to order: they wanted to intervene. To do this, they had to manipulate physical space, and Chapter 3 focused on interior spaces. In crossing the threshold, they rendered available to themselves a whole range of implements with which to manipulate the citizen. By constructing the interiors of buildings in certain ways, they could design a place of prolonged encounter between themselves and the people they hoped to help/control. Their motives were mixed. On the one hand, it would be implausibly cynical to regard the efforts to improve hospitals, rebuild orphanages, care for the elderly or rehouse the poor as being devoid of genuine compassion, public service and love of humanity. But on the other, this technocratic class in Germany seemed to link these truly humane projects to a set of perceived disorders, or visions of the ideal citizen. In doing so, they intentionally designed the interior spaces of these buildings to have an effect on the citizen – to make the sick collaborate with the healers, to make the orphan feel bonded and loved, to make the old feel comforted and grateful to the City Council. This process reached its apotheosis in the post-war small flat, where architects across industrialised Europe redoubled the coercive capacity of space in a sphere which, until then, had been closed to them: the private home of the poor. The competing models of kitchens in dwellings did not *suggest* a model of behaviour or social interaction: they *imposed* one. This capacity of space to organise and coerce means that historians should pay more attention to space as a material force, and should be less timid about asserting that some things are (or were) 'real'. Although the spaces were created through the interplay of contested imaginings and symbolic hierarchies, once created in brick, concrete and iron they compelled a certain response for years afterwards. To misquote Marx: 'Men make their own history, but do not make it in spaces chosen by themselves, but in spaces directly found, given and transmitted from the past.'

But although designers and architects and administrators and bureaucrats could act with some confidence when they could identify problems, the difficulties they experienced in defining spatial or design solutions to the problems they identified illustrate the limits of their capacities. It also asks questions of historians about their epistemological categorisation of the history of the built environment as an aspect of the connoiseurial tradition of art history. While many factors contributed to the difficulty of resolving the housing problem – such as the enduring commitment to a small state – even when those financial and political problems were surmounted in the period before the war and social housing was built, architects were not able to find a technological solution to the problems posed by poor living conditions. Thus while the language which underpins architecture should be considered as 'aesthetic', the design processes and end-products should also be treated by historians much more materially: architecture should be viewed as a primary technology of space, and be integrated into historical causality in the same way that other technologies have been. Thus, when contemporaries struggled to define a form of housing that pleased a liberal consensus on the role of the state, matched expert imaginings of the ideal community and satisfied the people who would have to live in it, the role of 'aesthetics' in the connoiseurial sense must be radically enlarged, and the historian must adduce with greater firmness the 'facts' of the plan, the reasons it was accepted or rejected and the material artefact that was produced.

Thus when cities are historically investigated as real and material, not just imagined and eternally negotiable, many more dynamic aspects of space's role in stimulating or retarding change over time will be identified. When modernity is located in a middle ground, neither entirely risky and fun and endlessly ethereal, nor solely mechanistic and organising and impersonal, it will be closer to the lived experience of most Germans in the early twentieth century, as they described it. It will also contribute more fully to a discussion of high modernity across the industrialised world. And if the entirely casual relationship between modernity and Modernism is highlighted, both space and modernity in the early twentieth century will become clearer objects of investigation, freed from a restrictive canon. Should these paths – started some twenty years ago – be followed in German history, a very different character in contemporary historical studies may emerge.

Bibliography

Unpublished sources

SAM (Stadtarchiv München)
A&M (Ausstellungen und Messen): 648
B&R (Bürgermeister und Rat): 305/8a, 306/2a, 993, 1455, 1638
GW (Gaswerke): 278
HBA (Hochbauamt): 489, 502, 645/i, 727
KA (Kulturamt): 618/1, 618/2
KH (Krankenhäuser): 44
KHS (Krankenhaus Schwabing): 15/1
KrAnst (Kranken-Anstalten): 200
NLG (Nachlaß Grässel): 51, 60, 360, 367, 373, 374, 397, 399, 400, 403, 407, 408.
RSP (Ratsitzungsprotokolle): 692/7
WA (Wohnungsamt): 18, 23, 39/1, 63, 64
ZA-KH-KHS (Zeitungsausschnitte-Krankenhäuser-Krankenhaus Schwabing)
ZA-KH-UK-DK (Zeitungsausschnitte-Krankenhäuser-Universitätskliniken-Dermatologische Klinik)
ZA-KH-Ver-KHTK (Zeitungsausschnitte-Krankenhäuser-Verschiedenes-Krankenhaus an der Thalkirchenerstraße)

Dissertations

Bernhart, Janet. *Art Beyond Art's Sake: Modernism and Politics in Munich, 1890–1924* (unpublished doctoral dissertation, Harvard University, 1981).
Cintron, Leslie. *Preserving National Culture: The National Trust and the Formation of British National Heritage, 1895–2000* (unpublished doctoral dissertation, Harvard University, 2000).
Pokorny, Rita. *Die Rationalisierungsexpertin Irene M. Witte (1894–1976): Biografie einer Grenzgängerin* (unpublished doctoral dissertation, Technische Unversität Berlin, 2003).

Voglmaier, Edelgard. *Hans Grässel: Architekt und städtischer Baubeamter in München* (unpublished doctoral dissertation, Technische Universität München, 1992).

Published sources

Agrest, Diana, Conway, Patricia and Kanes Weisman, Leslie. *The Sex of Architecture* (New York, 1996).
Allgoewer, Elisabeth. 'Emil Lederer: Business Cycles, Crises and Growth', *Journal of the History of Economic Thought* 3 (2003), pp. 327–348.
Allison, K. 'The Provision of Allotment Gardens in East Yorkshire', *Northern History* 37 (2000), pp. 275–292.
Amt für Statistik und Datenanalyse der Landeshauptstadt München (ed.). *1875–1975: 100 Jahre Statistik in München* (Munich, 1974).
Angermair, Elisabeth. 'Münchener Kommunalpolitik. Die Residenzstadt als expansive Metropole', in Friedrich Prinz and Marita Krauss (eds.), *Musenstadt mit Hinterhöfen: Die Prinzregentenzeit 1886–1912* (Munich, 1988), pp. 36–43.
——'München als süddeutsche Metropole – Die Organisation des Großstadtausbaus 1870 bis 1914', in Richard Bauer (ed.), *Geschichte der Stadt München* (Munich, 1992), pp. 307–335.
Ankum, Katharina von (ed.). *Women in the Metropolis: Gender and Modernity in Weimar Culture* (London, 1997).
Anon. *Munchen* (Munich, 1895).
——*München* (Berlin, 1910).
——*München* (n.p., 1910).
——*Münchens Niedergang als Kunststadt* (n.p., 1902).
——*Hans Grässel: Eine biographische Übersicht* (Munich, 1930).
Applegate, Celia. *A Nation of Provincials: The German Idea of Heimat* (Berkeley, CA, 1990).
Architekturmuseum Schwaben (ed.). *Wohnarchitektur der 20er Jahre* (Augsburg, 1999).
Bane, Suda and Lutz, Ralph (eds.). *The Blockade of Germany After the Armistice, 1918–19: Selected Documents* (Stanford, CA, 1942).
Banham, Reyner. *Theory and Design in the First Machine Age* (Oxford, 1994 [1960]).
Barg, Hartwig. *Hans Roß, 1873–1922: Zur Heimatschutz- und Reformarchitektur in Schleswig-Holstein* (Hamburg, 1992).
Barnes, Ralph. *Motion and Time Study* (2nd edn., New York, 1940).
Baudelaire, Charles. *The Painter of Modern Life and Other Essays* (London, 1995).
Baudrillard, Jean. 'Simulacra and Simulations', in Jean Baudrillard, *Selected Writings*, ed. Mark Poster (Stanford, CA, 1988), pp. 166–184.
Bauman, Zygmunt. *Modernity and the Holocaust* (Cambridge, 1989).
Baumgartner, Alois. *Sehnsucht nach Gemeinschaft: Ideen und Strömungen im Sozialkatholismus der Weimarer Republik* (Munich, 1977).

Bäuml-Stosiek, Dagmar. 'Großstadtwachstum und Eingemeindungen: Städtische Siedlungspolitik zwischen Vorsicht und Vorausschau', in Friedrich Prinz and Marita Krauss (eds.), *Musenstadt mit Hinterhöfen: Die Prinzregentenzeit 1886–1912* (Munich, 1988), pp. 60–68.

Bayerische Akademie der schönen Künste (ed.). *Süddeutsche Bautradition m 20. Jahrhundert* (Munich, 1985).

Bayerischer Architekten- und Ingenieurverband e.V. (ed.) (BAIVd). *München und seine Bauten bis 1912* (Munich, 1984).

Bayerischer Architekten- und Ingenieurverein (ed.) (BAIVn). *München und seine Bauten* (Munich, 1912).

Bayerisches Landesamt fir Denkmalpflege (ed.). *Bauen in München 1890–1950* (Munich, 1980).

Beach, Abigail and Tiratsoo, Nick. 'The Planners and the Public', in Martin Daunton (ed.), *The Cambridge Urban History of Britain: Volume III, 1840–1950* (Cambridge, 2000), pp. 525–550.

Beblo, Fritz. 'Der Einfluß des Krieges und der Nachkriegszeit auf das Stadtbild und den Stadtplan Münchens', in *Das Bayerland* 6 (1925), pp. 180–184.

——*Hochbauten der Stadtgemeinde München den letzten fünf Jahren* (Munich, 1926).

——*München: Neue Stadtbaukunst* (Berlin, 1928).

——*Das technische Rathaus in München* (Munich, 1930).

Becker, Winfried. 'Die nationalsozialistische Machtergreifung in Bayern: Ein Dokumentarbericht Heinrich Helds aus dem Jahr 1933', *Historisches Jahrbuch* 2 (1992), pp. 412–435.

Beckstein, Hermann. *Städtische Interressenpolitik: Organisation und Politik der Städtetage in Bayern, Preussen und im Deutschen Reich, 1896–1923* (Düsseldorf, 1991).

Beecher, Catharine. *A Treatise on Domestic Economy for the Use of Young Ladies at Home and at School* (New York, 1989 [1841]).

Beecher, Catharine and Beecher Stowe, Harriet. *The American Woman's Home, or, Principles of Domestic Science* (New York, 1869).

Behrendt, Walter Curt. *Der Sieg des neuen Baustils* (Stuttgart, 1927).

Benjamin, Walter. *Walter Benjamin: Illuminations*, ed. Hannah Arendt, trans. Harry Zohn (London, 1992).

——'On Some Motifs in Baudelaire', in *Illuminations* (London, 1970), pp. 152–196.

——*The Arcades Project* (London, 1999).

Benninghaus, Christina. 'Mothers' Toil and Daughters' Leisure: Working-Class Girls and Time in 1920s Germany', *History Workshop Journal* 50 (2000), pp. 45–72.

Berghahn, Volker. *Imperial Germany, 1871–1914: Economy, Society, Culture and Politics* (Oxford, 1994).

Berman, Marshall. *All that is Solid Melts into Air: The Experience of Modernity* (London, 1999).

Bernet, Claus. 'The Hobrecht Plan (1862) and Berlin's Urban Structure', *Urban History* 3 (2004), pp. 400–419.

Betts, Paul. 'The New Fascination with Fascism: The Case of Nazi Modernism', *Journal of Contemporary History* 4 (2002), pp. 541–558.

——*The Authority of Everyday Objects: A Cultural History of West German Industrial Design* (Berkeley, CA, 2004).

Blackbourn, David. *Class, Religion and Local Politics in Wilhelmine Germany: The Centre Party in Württemberg before 1914* (London, 1980).

Blau, Eve. *The Architecture of Red Vienna* (London, 1999).

Blössner, August. *Fünfundzwanzig Jahre Münchener Stadterweiterung* (Munich, 1918).

——*Verhandlungen und Planungen zur städtebaulichen Entstehung der Stadt München von 1871 bis 1933* (Munich, 1949).

Bock, Irmgard. 'Pädagogik und Schule: Stadtschulrat Kerschensteiner', in Friedrich Prinz and Marita Krauss (eds.), *Musenstadt mit Hinterhöfen: Die Prinzregentenzeit 1886–1912* (Munich, 1988), pp. 213–219.

Bollerey, Franziska and Hartmann, Christiana. 'A Patriarchal Utopia: The Garden City and Housing Reform in Germany at the Turn of the Century', in Anthony Sutcliffe (ed.), *The Rise of Modern Urban Planning, 1800–1914* (London, 1980), pp. 135–164.

Borden, Iain. 'The Politics of the Plan', in Iain Borden and David Dunster (eds.), *Architecture and the Sites of History* (Oxford, 1995), pp. 214–226.

Bormann, Norbert. *Paul Schultze-Naumburg, 1869–1949. Maler, Publizist, Architekt: Ein Kulturreformer der Jahrhundertwende zum Kulturpolitiker im Dritten Reich* (Essen, 1989).

Borscht, Wilhelm. *Bauordnung für die Königliche Haupt- und Residenzstadt München* (Munich, 1896).

Boydston, Jeanne, Kelly, Mary and Margolis, Ann. *The Limits of Sisterhood: The Beecher Sisters on Women's Rights and Woman's Sphere* (London, 1988).

Boyer, John. *Culture and Political Crisis: Christian Socialism in Power, 1897–1918* (Chicago, 1994).

Bredt, Ernst. *München als Kunststadt* (Munich, 1907).

Breitling, Peter. 'The Role of the Competition in the Genesis of Urban Planning in Germany and Austria in the Nineteenth Century', in Anthony Sutcliffe (ed.), *The Rise of Modern Urban Planning, 1800–1914* (London, 1980), pp. 31–54.

Briesen, Detlef. 'Berlin – Die überschätzte Metropole: Über das system deutscher Hauptstädte zwischen 1850 und 1940', in Gerhard Brunn and Jürgen Reulecke (eds.), *Metropolis Berlin: Berlin im Vergleich europäischer Hauptstädte, 1871–1939* (Bonn, 1992), pp. 39–78.

Brüggemeier, Franz-Josef. 'Schlafgänger, Schnapskinos und schwerindustrielle Kolonie: Aspekte der Arbeiterwohnungsfrage im

Ruhrgebiet vor dem Ersten Weltkrieg', in Jürgen Reulecke *et al.* (eds.), *Fabrik, Familie, Feierabend: Beiträge zur Sozialgeschichte des Alltags im Industriezeitalter* (Wuppertal, 1978), pp. 139–172.

Burchell, Graham, Gordon, Colin and Miller, Peter (eds.). *The Foucault Effect: Studies in Governmentality* (London, 1991).

Burleigh, Michael. *Death and Deliverance: 'Euthanasia' in Germany, 1900–1945* (Cambridge, 1995).

Calinescu, Matei. 'Modernity, Modernism, Modernisation: Variations on Modern Themes', in Christian Berg, Frank Durieux and Geert Lernout (eds.), *The Turn of the Century: Modernism and Modernity in Literature and the Arts* (New York, 1995), pp. 33–52.

——*Five Faces of Modernity: Modernism, Avant-Garde, Decadence, Kitsch, Postmodernism* (Durham, NC, 1999).

Campbell, Joan. *The German Werkbund: The Politics of Reform in the Applied Arts* (Princeton, NJ, 1978).

Carey, John. *The Intellectuals and the Masses: Pride and Prejudice amongst the Literary Intelligentsia, 1880–1939* (London, 1992).

Caws, Mary Ann. *Manifesto: A Century of -Isms* (Lincoln, NE, 2001).

Clarke, Georgia and Crossley, Paul. *Architecture and Language: Constructing Identity in European Architecture, 1000–1650* (London, 2000).

Clinton, Catherine. *The Other Civil War: American Women in the Nineteenth Century* (New York, 1984).

Collins, George and Crasemann Collins, Christine. *Camillo Sitte and the Birth of Modern City Planning* (London, 1965).

Confino, Alon. *The Nation as a Local Metaphor: Württemberg, Imperial Germany and National Memory, 1871–1918* (London, 1997).

Cott, Nancy. *The Bonds of Womanhood: 'Woman's Sphere' in New England, 1780–1835* (New Haven, CT, 1977).

Cowling, David. *Building the Text: Architecture as Metaphor in Late Mediaeval and Early Modern France* (Oxford, 1998).

Curtis, William. *Modern Architecture since 1900* (Oxford, 1982).

da Costa Meyer, Esther. 'La Donna è Mobile', *Assemblage* 28 (1995), pp. 6–15.

Dal Co, Francesco. *Figures of Architecture and Thought: German Architecture and Culture, 1880–1920* (New York, 1990).

Damaschke, Adolf. *Die Bodenreform: Grundsätzliches und Geschichtliches zur Erkenntnis und Überwindung der sozialen Not* (16th edn., 1916).

Daunton, Martin (ed.). *Councillors and Tenants: Local Authority Housing in English Cities, 1919–1939* (Leicester, 1984).

——*The Cambridge Urban History of Britain: Volume III, 1840–1950* (Cambridge, 2000).

Davis, Belinda. *Home Fires Burning: Food, Politics, and Everyday Life in World War One Berlin* (London, 2000).

Debord, Guy. *The Society of the Spectacle* (London, 1992 [Paris, 1967]).

Dirks, Nicholas, Eley and Geoff Ortner, Sherry. *Culture/Power/History: A Reader in Contemporary Social Theory* (Princeton, NJ, 1994).
Dockal, Eva. 'J.J.P. Oud als Architekt des "Neuen München"? Eine verpasste Chance', *Zeitschrift für Kunstgeschichte* 1 (2001), pp. 103–115.
Doering, Oscar. 'Zwei Münchener Baukünstler: Gabriel von Seidl, Georg von Hauberisser', *Die Kunst dem Volke*, 51/2 (1924), pp. 2–32.
Donald, James. 'Metropolis: the City as Text', in Robert Bocock and Kenneth Thompson (eds.), *Social and Cultural Forms of Modernity* (Cambridge, 1992), pp. 418–470.
Donovan, Josephine. *Feminist Theory: The Intellectual Traditions of American Feminism* (New York, 1985).
Dorschel, Ruth, Kornacher, Martin, Stiglbrunner, Ursula and Stäbe, Sabine. 'Wohnreform – mehr als Licht, Luft und Sonne: Die ersten Baugenossenschaften in München', in Friedrich Prinz and Marita Krauss (eds.), *Musenstadt mit Hinterhöfen: Die Prinzregentenzeit 1886–1912* (Munich, 1988), pp. 124–131.
Dreysse, D.W. *May Siedlungen: Architekturführer durch Acht Siedlungen des neuen Frankfurt 1926–1930* (Frankfurt, 1987).
Eberstadt, Rudolf. *Rheinische Wohnverhältnisse* (n.p., 1903).
——*Die Spekulation im neuzeitlichen Städtebau* (n.p., 1907).
——*Handbuch des Wohnungswesens und der Wohnungsfrage* (Jena, 1910).
——*Unser Wohnungswesen und die Notwendigkeit der Schaffung eines preußischen Wohnungsgesetzes* (Münster, 1910).
——*Neue Studien über Städtebau und Wohnungswesen* (Jena, 1912).
——*Städtebau und Wohnungswesen in Holland* (Jena, 1914).
Elsaesser, Thomas. *Metropolis* (London, 2000).
Englert, Ferdinand. *Münchener Bauordnung* (Munich, 1895).
Evans, Richard. *The German Working Class 1899–1933* (London, 1982).
——*Death in Hamburg: Society and Politics in the Cholera Years, 1830–1910* (London, 1987).
——*Kneipengespräche im Kaiserreich: Stimmungsberichte der Hamburger Politischen Polizei, 1892–1914* (Hamburg, 1989).
——*Rereading German History, 1800–1996: From Unification to Reunification* (London, 1997).
Farr, Ian. 'Populism in the Countryside: The Peasant Leagues in Bavaria', in Richard Evans (ed.), *Society and Politics in Wilhelmine Germany* (London, 1978), pp. 136–159.
——'From Anti-Catholics to Anti-Clericalism: Catholic Politics and the Peasantry in Bavaria, 1860–1900', *Social Studies Review* 13 (1983), pp. 249–269.
Fehl, G. and Rodriguez-Lores, J. (eds.). *Städtebau um die Jahrhundertwende: Materialien zur Entstehung der Disziplin Städtebau* (Cologne, 1980).
Feldman, David and Stedman Jones, Gareth (eds.). *Metropolis – London: Histories and Representations since 1800* (London, 1989).

Fisch, Stefan. 'Theodor Fischer in München 1893–1901 – der Stadtplaner auf dem Weg zum Beamten', in Ekkehard Mai, Hans Pohl and Stephan Waetzoldt (eds.), *Kunstpolitik und Kunstförderung im Wandel der Sozial- und Wirtschaftsgeschichte* (Berlin, 1982), pp. 245–259.
——*Stadtplanung im 19. Jahrhundert: Das Beispiel München bis zur Ära Theodor Fischer* (Munich, 1988).
——'Neue Aspekte der Münchener Stadtplanung zur Zeit Theodor Fischers (1893–1901) im interurbanen Vergleich', in Wolfgang Hardtwig and Klaus Tenfelde (eds.), *Soziale Räume in der Urbanisierung: Studien zur Geschichte Münchens im Vergleich 1850 bis 1933* (Munich, 1990), pp. 174–191.
Fischer, Theodor. *Stadterweiterungsfragen: Mit besonderer Rücksicht auf Stuttgart* (Stuttgart, 1903).
——*Wohnhausbauten* (Munich, 1912).
——*Für die deutsche Baukunst* (Munich, 1917).
——*Sechs Vorträge über Stadtbaukunst* (Munich, 1922).
——*Stadt – München* (Munich, 1928).
Fischer, Wend. *Die andere Tradition: Architektur in München von 1800 bis Heute* (Munich, 1982).
Foucault, Michel. *History of Sexuality*, Vol. I (London, 1979).
——*Discipline and Punish: The Birth of the Prison* (London, 1977).
Frank, Josef. *Architektur als Symbol: Elemente neuen deutschen Bauens* (Vienna, 1931).
Frederick, Christine. *Household Engineering: Scientific Management in the Home* (London, 1920 [Chicago, 1919]); first German edn., *Die Rationelle Hausaltsführung: Betriebswissenschaftliche Studien*, trans. Irene Witte (Berlin, 1922).
Friedrich Engels. *The Condition of the Working Class in England* (London, 1971 [1845]).
Friedrich, Otto. *Before the Deluge: A Portrait of Berlin in the 1920s* (New York, 1995).
Frisby, David. *The Alienated Mind. The Sociology of Knowledge in Germany, 1918–1933* (London, 1983).
——*Fragments of Modernity: Theories of Modernity in the Works of Kracauer, Simmel and Benjamin* (Cambridge, 1985).
——*Simmel on Culture: Selected Writings*, ed. with Mike Featherstone (London, 1997).
——*Cityscapes of Modernity: Critical Explorations* (Cambridge, 2001).
Fritz, Karl. *München als Industriestadt* (Berlin, 1913).
Fritzsche, Peter. 'Nazi Modern', *Modernism/Modernity* 1 (1996), pp. 1–22.
——*Reading Berlin 1900* (London, 1996).
Fröhlich, Elke and Broszat, Martin. 'Politische und soziale Macht auf dem Lande: Die Durchsetzung der NSDAP im Kreis Memmingen', *Vierteljahreshefte fur Zeitgeschichte* 4 (1977), pp. 546–572.

Führer, Karl Christian. 'Managing Scarcity: The German Housing Shortage and the Controlled Economy', *German History* 3 (1995), pp. 326–354.
Gasser, Manuel. *München seit 1900* (Munich, 1977).
Gasteiger, Michael. *Die christliche Arbeiterbewegung in Süddeutschland* (Munich,1908).
——*Bauverein* (Munich, 1919).
——*Die Not in München* (München, 1923).
Gay, Peter. *Weimar Culture: The Outsider as Insider* (London, 1974).
Gessner, Dieter. 'Agrarian Protectionism in the Weimar Republic', *Journal of Contemporary History* 12 (1977), pp. 759–778.
GeWoFAG. *Die Siedlungen der Gemeinnützigen Wohnungsfürsorge AG München* (Munich, 1928).
Giedion, Siegfried. *Walter Gropius: Work and Teamwork* (New York, 1954).
——*Space, Time and Architecture: The Growth of a New Tradition* (Cambridge, MA, 1980 [1941]).
Gieryn, Thomas. 'What Buildings Do', *Theory and Society* 31 (2002), pp. 35–74.
Gilbert, James. *Perfect Cities: Chicago's Utopias of 1893* (London, 1991).
Gilbreth, Frank and Gilbreth, Lillian. *Applied Motion Study: A Collection of Papers on the Efficient Method to Industrial Preparedness* (New York, 1917).
Gill, Valerie. 'Catharine Beecher and Charlotte Perkins Gilman: Architects of Female Power', *Journal of American Culture* 2 (1998), pp. 17–24.
Gleber, Anke. 'The Secret Cities of Modernity: Topographies of Perception in Georges Rodenbach, Robert Walser and Franz Hessel', in Christian Berg, Frank Durieux and Geert Lernout (eds.), *The Turn of the Century: Modernism and Modernity in Literature and the Arts* (New York, 1995), pp. 380–390.
Goldhagen, Daniel Jonah. *Hitler's Willing Executioners: Ordinary Germans and the Holocaust* (London, 1996).
Goldhagen, Sarah Williams and Legault, Réjean. *Anxious Modernisms: Experimentation in Postwar Architectural Culture* (London, 2000).
Gordon, Jean and McArthur, Jan. 'Popular Culture, Magazines and American Domestic Interiors, 1898–1940', *Journal of Popular Culture* 22 (1989), pp. 35–60.
Gottdiener, Mark and Lagopoulos, Alexandros (eds.). *The City and the Sign: An Introduction to Urban Semiotics* (New York, NY, 1986).
Graham, Laurel. 'Domesticating Efficiency: Lillian Gilbreth's Scientific Management of Homemakers, 1924–1930', *Signs: Journal of Women in Culture and Society* 3 (1999), pp. 633–675.
Grässel, Hans. *Die Erhaltung des Charakters der Stadt München* (Munich, 1917).
——*Das neue Altersheim St Joseph der Stadt München* (Munich, 1929).

Gronberg, Tag. *Designs on Modernity: Exhibiting the City in 1920s Paris* (Manchester, 1998).

Gross, David. 'Space, Time and Modern Culture', *Telos* 50 (1981–82), pp. 59–78.

——*The Past in Ruins: Tradition and the Critique of Modernity* (Amherst, MA, 1992).

Habel, Heinrich. 'Späte Phasen und Nachwirken des Historismus', in Bayerisches Amt für Denkmalpflege (ed.), *Bauen in München, 1890–1950* (Munich, 1980), pp. 26–40.

Habel, Heinrich, Merten, Klaus, Petzet, Michael and Quast, Siegfried von. *Münchener Fassaden: Bürgerhäuser des Historismus und des Jugendstils* (Munich, 1974).

Habermas, Jürgen. *The Structural Transformation of the Public Sphere: An Inquiry into a Category of Bourgeois Society* (Cambridge, 1989).

Hagemann, Karen. *Frauenalltag und Männerpolitik: Alltagsleben und gesellschaftliches Handeln von Arbeiterfrauen in der Weimarer Republik* (Bonn, 1990).

——'Von "guten" und "schlechten" Hausfrauen: Möglichkeiten und Grenzen der Rationalisierung im großstädtischen Arbeiterhaushalt der Weimarer Republik', *Historische Mitteilungen der Ranke Gesellschaft* 8 (1995), pp. 65–84.

Hamerschmidt, V. *Anspruch und Ausdruck in der Architektur des späten Historismus in Deutschland 1860–1914* (Munich, 1985).

Hanson, Julienne. *Decoding Homes and Houses* (Cambridge, 1998).

Hardtwig, Wolfgang. 'Soziale Räume und politische Herrschaft: Leistungsverwaltung, Stadterweiterung und Architektur in München, 1870 bis 1914', in Wolfgang Hardtwig and Klaus Tenfelde (eds.), *Soziale Räume in der Urbanisierung: Studien zur Geschichte Münchens im Vergleich 1850 bis 1933* (Munich, 1990), pp. 60–151.

Harlander, Tilman. 'Notwohnen und Selbsthilfe in der Großstadtperipherie der 20er Jahre: Beispiele aus Österreich, Deutschland, Italien und Griechenland', in Clemens Zimmermann (ed.), *Europäische Wohnungspolitik in vergleichender Perspective 1900–1939* (Stuttgart, 1997), pp. 60–84.

Harloe, Michael. *The People's Home? Social Rented Housing in Europe and America* (Oxford, 1995).

Harrington, Anne. *Reenchanted Science: Holism in German Culture from Wilhelm II to Hitler* (Princeton, NJ, 1996).

Hartmann, Barbara. 'Zweckbau als öffentliche Aufgabe . . . Die Stadt als Bauherr', in Friedrich Prinz and Marita Krauss (eds.), *Musenstadt mit Hinterhöfen: Die Prinzregentenzeit 1886–1912* (Munich, 1988), pp. 107–113.

Hayden, Dolores. *The Grand Domestic Revolution: A History of Feminist Designs for American Homes, Neighborhoods, and Cities* (London, 1981).

Heinze, Karen. ' "Schick, selbst mit beschränkten Mitteln!" Die Anleitung zur alltäglichen Distinktion in einer Modezeitschrift der Weimarer Republik', *WerkstattGeschichte* 7 (1994) pp. 9–17.

Henderson, Susan. 'A Revolution in the Woman's Sphere: Grete Lihotzky and the Frankfurt Kitchen', in Debra Coleman, Elisabeth Danze and Carol Henderson (eds.), *Architecture and Feminism* (New York, 1996), pp. 221–253.

Hepp, Corona. *Avantgarde: Moderne Kunst, Kulturkritik und Reformbewegungen nach der Jahrhundertwende* (Munich, 1992).

Herf, Jeffrey. *Reactionary Modernism: Technology, Culture and Politics in Weimar and the Third Reich* (Cambridge, 1984).

Herman, Arthur. *The Idea of Decline in Western History* (New York, 1997).

Herrmann, Wolfgang. *Gottfried Semper: In Search of Architecture* (London, 1984).

Heynen, Hilde. *Architecture and Modernity: A Critique* (London, 1999).

Hiesinger, Catherine Bloom (ed.). *Art Nouveau in Munich* (Munich, 1988).

Hillier, Bill and Hanson, Julienne. *The Social Logic of Space* (Cambridge, 1984).

Hiscock, Karin. 'Modernity and "English Tradition" : Betjeman at the Architectural Review', *Journal of Design History* 3 (2000), pp. 193–212.

Hofmann, Wolfgang. *Zwischen Rathaus und Reichskanzlerei: Die Oberbürgermeister in der Kommunal- und Staatspolitik des deutschen Reichs 1890–1933* (Stuttgart, 1987).

Hoser, Paul. *Die politischen, wirtschaftlichen und sozialen Hintergründe der Münchener Tagespresse zwischen 1918 und 1934: Methode der Pressebeeinflussung* (Frankfurt am Main, 1990).

Hues, Timothy. *Thomas Theodor Heine, Fin-de-Siècle Munich and the Origins of Simplicissimus* (New York, 1996).

Hvattum, Mari and Hermansen, Christian (eds.). *Tracing Modernity: Manifestations of the Modern in Architecture and the City* (London, 2004).

Jacobeit, Wolfgang, Lixfeld, Hannjost and Bockhorn, Olaf (eds.). *Völkische Wissenschaft: Gestalten und Tendenzen der deutschen und österreichischen Volkskunde in der ersten Hälfte des 20. Jahrhunderts* (Vienna, 1994).

James-Chakraborty, Kathleen. *German Architecture for a Mass Audience* (London, 2000).

Jaques, Paul. 'German Neo-Classicism and the Modern Movement', *Architectural Review* 152 (1972), pp. 176–180.

Jazbinsek, Dietmar. 'The Metropolis and the Mental Life of Georg Simmel: On the History of an Antipathy', *Journal of Urban History* 1 (2003), pp. 102–125.

Jefferies, Matthew. *Politics and Culture in Wilhelmine Germany: The Case of Industrial Architecture* (Oxford, 1995).

Jelavich, Peter. *Munich and Theatrical Modernism: Politics, Playwriting and Performance, 1890–1914* (London, 1985).
——*Berlin Cabaret* (London, 1996).
Jencks, Charles. *Modern Movements in Architecture* (London, 1985)
——*The Language of Post-Modern Architecture* (6th edn., London, 1991).
Jenkins, Jennifer. *Provincial Modernity: Local Culture and Liberal Politics in Fin-de-Siècle Hamburg* (Ithaca, NY, 2003).
Jobst, G. and Langen, G. *Die halbländische Vorstadt-Siedlung* (Munich, 1918).
Jobst, Gerhard. *Bauliche Einzelheiten des Kleinhauses* (Munich, 1921).
Johnston, Norman. *Forms of Constraint: A History of Prison Architecture* (Chicago, 2000).
Joyce, Patrick. *The Rule of Freedom: Liberalism and the Modern City* (London, 2003).
Kahn, Julius. *Münchens Großindustrie und Großhandel* (Munich, n.d. [c. First World War]).
Kentgens-Craig, Margaret. *The Bauhaus and America: First Contacts, 1919–1936* (Cambridge, MA, 2001).
Kerkhoff, Ulrich. *Eine Abkehr vom Historismus, oder, Ein Weg zur Moderne: Theodor Fischer* (Stuttgart, 1987).
Kern, Stephen. *The Culture of Time and Space, 1880–1919* (Cambridge, MA, 1983).
Kerschensteiner, Georg. *Begriff der Arbeitsschule* (Leipzig, 1912).
——'Einfluß der Volksschulorganisation in München auf den Schulhausbau', in *Münchener städtische Baukunst aus den letzten Jahren* (München, 1912).
Kershaw, Ian. *Popular Opinion and Political Dissent in the Third Reich: Bavaria, 1933–1945* (Oxford, 1985).
Keunen, Bart. 'The Aestheticisation of the City in Modernism', in Christian Berg, Frank Durieux and Geert Lernout (eds.), *The Turn of the Century: Modernism and Modernity in Literature and the Arts* (New York, 1995), pp. 392–408.
Kish Sklar, Kathryn. *Catharine Beecher: A Study in American Domesticity* (New Haven, CT, 1973).
Klotz, Heinrich (ed.). *Ernst May und das neue Frankfurt, 1925–1930* (Berlin, 1986).
Klueting, Edeltraud. 'Vorwort', in Edeltraud Klueting (ed.), *Antimodernismus und Reform: Beiträge zur Geschichte der deutschen Heimatbewegung* (Darmstadt, 1991), pp. vii–xii.
Kocka, Jürgen. 'Asymmetrical Historical Comparison: The Case of the German *Sonderweg*', *History and Theory* 1 (1999), pp. 40–50.
Köhnke, Klaus. 'Soziologie als Kulturwissenschaft: Georg Simmel und die Völkerpsychologie', *Archiv für Kulturgeschichte* 1 (1990), pp. 223–232.
Krabbe, Wolfgang. 'Die Anfänge des "sozialen Wohnungsbaus" vor dem Ersten Weltkrieg: Kommunalpolitische Bemühungen urn eine Lösung

des Wohnungs Problems', *Vierteljahreshefte für Sozial- und Wirtschaftsgeschichte*, 71(1984), pp. 30–58.

——*Kommunalpolitik seit Industrialisierung: Die Entfaltung der städtischen Leistungsverwaltung im 19. und frühen 20. Jahrhundert: Fallstudien zu Dortmund und Münster* (Stuttgart, 1985).

Kramer, Lore. 'Rationalisierung des Haushaltes und Frauenfrage – Die Frankfurter Küche und zeitgenössische Kritik', in Heinrich Klotz (ed.), *Ernst May und das neue Frankfurt, 1925–1930* (Berlin, 1986), pp. 77–84.

Kuhn, Gerd. *Wohnkultur und kommunale Wohnungspolitik in Frankfurt am Main, 1880–1930: Auf dem Wege zu einer pluralen Gesellschaft der Individuen* (Bonn, 1998).

Kuhn, W. *Kleinsiedlungen aus Friderizianischer Zeit* (Stuttgart, 1918).

——*Kleinbürgerliche Siedlungen in Stadt und Land* (Munich, 1921).

Kushner, Howard. 'Suicide, Gender and Fear of Modernity in Nineteenth Century Medical and Social Thought', *Journal of Social History* 3 (1991), pp. 461–491.

Ladd, Brian. *Urban Planning and Civic Order in Germany, 1860–1914* (London, 1990).

Lamb, Stephen and Phelan, Anthony. 'Weimar Culture: The Birth of Modernism', in Rob Burns (ed.), *German Cultural Studies* (Oxford, 1996), pp. 53–100.

Landsberg, O. 'Conferences of German Municipal Statisticians', *Publications of the American Statistical Association* 12 (1911), pp. 661–664.

Langewiesche, Dieter. 'Wanderungsbewegungen in der Hochindustrialisierung: Regionale, interstädtische und innerstädtische mobilität in Deutschland', *Vierteljahresschrift fur Sozial- und Wirtschaftsgeschichte* 64 (1977), pp. 1–40.

Laqueur, Walter. 'Fin-de-Siècle: Once More with Feeling', *Journal of Contemporary History*, 1(1996), pp. 5–47.

Latour, Bruno. *We Have Never Been Modern* (London, 1993).

Läufer, Bernd. *Jakob van Hoddis: Der Variete-Zyklus. Ein Beitrag zur Erforschung der frühexpressionistischen Großstadtlyrik* (Frankfurt am Main, 1992).

le Bon, Gustave. *The Crowd: A Study of the Popular Mind* (London, 1896).

Le Rider, Jacques. *Modernité viennoise et crises de l'identité* (Paris, 1990).

Lederer, Emil. 'Bodenspekulation und Wohnungsfrage', *Archiv für Sozialwissenschaften und Sozialpolitik* 25 (1907), pp. 613–648.

Lees, Andrew. 'Critics of Urban Society in Germany', *Journal of the History of Ideas* 1 (1979), pp. 61–83.

——*Cities Perceived: Urban Society in European and American Thought, 1820–1940* (Manchester, 1985).

——*Cities, Sin and Social Reform in Imperial Germany* (Ann Arbor, MI, 2002).

Lefebvre, Henri. *The Production of Space*, trans. Donald Nicholson-Smith (Oxford, 1991 [Paris, 1974]).
LeGates, Richard and Stout, Frederic. *The City Reader* (London, 1996).
Lekan, Thomas. *Imagining the Nation in Nature: Landscape Preservation and German Identity, 1885–1945* (London, 2004).
Lenman, Robin. *Die Kunst, die Macht und das Geld: Zur Kulturgeschichte des kaiserlichen Deutschland*, trans. Reiner Grundmann (Frankfurt, 1994).
Lenman, Robin and Osborne, John Sagarra (eds.). 'Imperial Germany: Towards the Commercialisation of Culture', in Rob Burns (ed.), *German Cultural Studies* (Oxford, 1996), pp. 9–52.
Levine, Robert, Martinez, Todd, Brase, Gary and Sorenson, Kerry. 'Helping in 36 US Cities', *Journal of Personality and Social Psychology* 67 (1994), pp. 69–82.
Lewis, Michael. *The Politics of the Gothic Revival: August Reichensperger* (Cambridge, MA, 1993).
Lieberman, Ben. 'Testing Peukert's Paradigm: The "Crisis of Classical Modernity" in the "New Frankfurt", 1925–1930', *German Studies Review* 2 (1994), pp. 287–303.
——*From Recovery to Catastrophe: Municipal Stabilisation and Political Crisis in Weimar Germany* (Oxford, 1998).
Lilley, Keith. 'On Display: Planning Exhibitions as Civil Propaganda or Public Consultation?', *Planning Perspectives* 3 (2003), pp. 3–8.
Lübbren, Nina. *Rural Artists' Colonies in Europe, 1870–1910* (Manchester, 2001).
Lutz, Tom. *American Nervousness, 1903: An Anecdotal History* (Ithaca, NY, 1991).
Lyon, Janet. *Manifestos: Provocations of the Modern* (Ithaca, NY, 1999).
Mai, Ekkehard, Paul, Jürgen and Waetzoldt, Stephan (eds). *Das Rathaus im Kaiserreich: Kunstpolitische Aspekte einer Bauaufgabe des 19. Jahrhunderts* (Berlin, 1982).
Makela, Maria. *The Munich Secession: Art and Artists in Turn-of-the-Century Munich* (London, 1990).
Mallgrave, H.F. (ed.). *Otto Wagner: Reflections on the Raiment of Modernity* (Santa Monica, CA, 1993).
Marcus, Sharon. *Apartment Stories: City and Home in Nineteenth Century Paris and London* (Berkeley, CA, 1999).
Mark Jarzombek, *The Psychologizing of Modernity: Art, Architecture and History* (Cambridge, 2000).
Markus, Thomas. *Buildings and Power: Freedom and Control in the Origins of Modern Building Types* (London, 1993).
Marx, Karl and Engels, Friedrich. *The Communist Manifesto* (Oxford, 1998).
Masaryk, Tomàs. *Suicide and the Meaning of Civilisation* (London, 1970 [Vienna, 1881]).

Masterman, Charles. 'Realities at Home', in Charles Masterman (ed.), *The Heart of Empire: Discussions of Problems of Modern City Life in England. With an Essay on Imperialism* (London, 1901), pp. 1–52.

Matless, David. 'Nature, the Modern and the Mystic: Tales from Early Twentieth-Century Geography', *Transactions of the Institute of British Geographers* 3 (1991), pp. 272–286.

Mayne, Alan. *The Imagined Slum: Newspaper Representations in three Cities, 1870–1914* (Leicester, 1993).

Mayne, Alan and Murray, Tim (eds.). *The Archaeology of Urban Landscapes: Explorations in Slumland* (Cambridge, 2001).

McElligott, Anthony. 'Workers' Culture and Workers' Politics on Weimar's New Housing Estates: A Response to Adelheid von Saldern', *Social History* 15 (1990), pp. 104–105

——*Contested City: Municipal Politics and the Rise of Nazism in Altona, 1917–1937* (Ann Arbor, MI, 1998).

McLeod, Mary. 'Architecture or Revolution: Taylorism, Technocracy and Social Change', *Art Journal* 2 (1983), pp. 132–147.

McPhail, Clark. *The Myth of the Maddening Crowd* (New York, 1981).

Mebes, Paul. *Architektur und Handwerk im letzten Jahrhundert*, 2 vols. (Munich, 1908).

Megele, Max. *Baugeschichtlicher Atlas der Landeshauptstadt München* (Munich, 1951).

Mengin, Christine. 'H.B.M. et "Siedlungen": étude comparative du logement social en France et en Allemagne (des debuts a la crise de 1929)', in Clemens Zimmermann (ed.), *Europäische Wohnungspolitik in vergleichender Perspective 1900–1939* (Stuttgart, 1997), pp. 130–152.

Miller Lane, Barbara. *Architecture and Politics in Germany, 1918–1915* (Cambridge, MA, 1968).

——'Government Buildings in European Capitals 1870–1914', in Hans Teuteberg (ed.), *Urbanisierung im19. und 20. Jahrhundert: Historische und Geographische Aspekte* (Cologne, 1983), pp. 517–560.

Miller, Simon. 'Urban Dreams and Rural Reality: Land and Landscape in English Culture, 1920–1945', *Rural History* 6 (1995), pp. 89–102.

Minden, Michael and Bachman, Holger (eds.). *Fritz Lang's Metropolis: Cinematic Visions of Technology and Fear* (Rochester, NY, 2000).

Mitchell, Dean. *Governmentality: Power and Rule in Modern Society* (London, 1999).

Mitchell, Timothy. *Rule of Experts: Egypt, Technopolitics, Modernity* (Berkeley, CA, 2002).

Moeller, Robert. *German Peasants and Agrarian Politics, 1914–1924: The Rhineland and Westphalia* (Chapel Hill, NC, 1986).

Moore-Coyer, R. 'From Great Wenn to Toad Hall: Aspects of the Urban–Rural Divide in Inter-War Britain', *Rural History* 10 (1999), pp. 105–124.

Mosse, George. *The Crisis of German Ideology: Intellectual Origins of the Third Reich* (New York, 1961).
Müller-Wulckow, Walter. 'Deutsche Baukunst der Gegenwart' series:
——*Bauten der Arbeit und des Verkehrs* (Berlin, 1929).
——*Bauten der Gemeinschaft* (Berlin, 1929).
——*Wohnbauten und Siedlungen* (Berlin, 1929).
——*Die deutsche Wohnung* (Berlin, 1932).
Mumford, Eric. *The CIAM Discourse on Urbanism, 1928–1960* (Cambridge, MA, 2000).
Muranga, Manuel. *Großstadtelend in der deutschen Lyrik zwischen Arno Holz und Johannes Becker* (Frankfurt am Main, 1987).
Murphy, Graham. *Founders of the National Trust* (London, 2002).
Muthesius, Hermann. 'Das Farbrikdorf Port Sunlight bei Liverpool', *Zentralblatt der Bauverwaltung* 23 (1899), pp. 133, 146–147.
——*Style-Architecture and Building-Art: Transformations of Architecture in the Nineteenth Century and its Present Condition*, trans. Stanford Anderson (Santa Monica, CA, 1994 [Mühlheim an der Ruhr, 1903]).
——*Das englische Haus* (Berlin, 1904).
——'Die Entwicklung des künstlerischen Gedankens im Hausbau', in Centralstelle für Arbeiterwohlfahrtseinrichtungen (ed.), *Die künstlerische Gestaltung des Arbeiterwohnhauses* (Berlin, 1906).
——*Kleinhaus und Kleinsiedlung* (Munich, 1920).
Nash, Roderick. 'The American Invention of National Parks', *American Quarterly* 3 (1970), pp. 726–735.
Nead, Lynda. *Victorian Babylon: People, Streets and Images in Nineteenth-Century London* (London, 2000).
Nerdinger, Winfried (ed.). *Richard Riemerschmid vom Jugendstil zum Werkbund: Werke und Dokumente* (Munich, 1982).
——*Theodor Fischer: Architekt und Städtebauer, 1862–1938* (Berlin, 1988).
Neumeier, Gerhard. *Visions of Modernity: American Business and the Modernisation of Germany* (Oxford, 1994).
——*München um 1900: Wohnen und Arbeiten, Familie und Haushalt, Stadtteile und Sozialstrukturen, Hausbesitzer und Fabrikarbeiter, Demographic und Mobilität: Studien zur Sozial- und Wirtschaftsgeschichte einer deutschen Großstadt vor dem Ersten Weltkrieg* (Frankfurt, 1995).
Ney, Robert. 'Degeneration, Neurasthenia and the Culture of Sport in Belle Epoque France', *Journal of Contemporary History* 1 (1982), pp. 51–68.
Nolan, Mary. ' "Housework made Easy": The Taylorized Housewife in Weimar Germany's Rationalized Economy', *Feminist Studies* 3 (1990), pp. 549–578.
Nolte, Paul. 'Georg Simmels historische Anthropologie der Moderne: Rekonstruktion eines Forschungsprogramms', *Geschichte und Gesellschaft* 2 (1998), pp. 225–247.
Nordau, Max. *Degeneration* (English edn., New York, 1895).

Nye, Robert. 'The Bio-Medical Origins of Urban Sociology', *Journal of Contemporary History* 4 (1984), pp. 659–675.
Oechslin, Werner. *Otto Wagner, Adolf Loos and the Road to Modern Architecture* (Cambridge, 2002).
Offer, Avner. *The First World War: An Agrarian Interpretation* (Oxford, 1990).
Palmowski, Jan. *Urban Liberalism in Imperial Germany: Frankfurt am Main 1866–1914* (Oxford, 1999).
Pawley, Martin. *Architecture versus Housing* (London, 1971).
Peach, Mark. 'Wohnfords, or German Modern Architecture and the Appeal of Americanism', *Utopian Studies*, 2 (1997), pp. 48–65.
Pelt, Robert van and William Westfall, Carroll. *Architectural Principles in the Age of Historicism* (London, 1993).
Peukert, Detlev. 'Das Janusgesicht der Moderne', in *Max Webers Diagnose der Moderne* (Göttingen, 1989), pp. 55–69.
——*The Weimar Republic: The Crisis of Classical Modernity* (London, 1991).
——'The Genesis of the "Final Solution" from the Spirit of Science', in Thomas Childers and Jane Caplan (eds.), *Re-Evaluating the Third Reich* (London, 1993), pp. 234–252.
Pfammatter, Ulrich. *The Making of the Modern Architect and Engineer: The Origins and Development of a Scientific and Industrially Oriented Education* (Boston, 2000).
Pfister, Rudolf. *Theodor Fischer: Leben und Wirken eines deutschen Baumeisters* (Munich, 1968).
Pohl, Karl-Heinrich. *Die Münchener Arbeiterbewegung: Sozialdemokratische Partei, Staat und Gesellschaft 1890–1914* (Munich, 1992).
Pommer, Richard and Otto, Christian. *Weißenhof 1927 and the Modern Movement in Architecture* (London, 1991).
Pooley, Colin. 'Patterns on the Ground: Urban Form, Residential Structure and the Social Construction of Space', in Martin Daunton (ed.), *The Cambridge Urban History of Britain: Volume III, 1840–1950* (Cambridge, 2000), pp. 429–465.
Posener, Julius. *From Schinkel to the Bauhaus: Five Lectures on the Growth of Modern German Architecture* (London, 1972).
——*Berlin auf dem Wege zu einer neuen Architektur: Das Zeitalter Wilhelm II* (Munich, 1979)
Preis, Karl. *Die Beseitigung der Wohnungsnot in München: Denkschrift und Anträge des städt. Wohnungsreferenten vom 24. Dezember 1927* (Munich, 1927).
Radkau, Joachim. 'Die wilhelminische Ära als nervöses Zeitalter, oder: die Nerven als Netz zwischen Tempo- und Körpergeschichte', *Geschichte und Gesellschaft* 2 (1994), pp. 211–241.
——*Das Zeitalter der Nervosität: Deutschland zwischen Bismarck und Hitler* (Munich, 1998).

Repp, Kevin. *Reformers, Critics and the Paths of German Modernity: Anti-Politics and the Search for Alternatives, 1890–1914* (London, 2000).
Robinson, Jennifer. *The Power of Apartheid: State, Power and Space in South African Cities* (Oxford, 1995).
Robinson, Louis. 'The German Städtetag', *Annals of the American Academy of Political and Social Science* 31 (1908), pp. 169–172.
Rohkrämer, Thomas. 'Antimodernism, Reactionary Modernism and National Socialism: Technocratic Tendencies in Germany, 1890–1945', *Contemporary European History* 1 (1999), pp. 29–50.
——*Eine andere Moderne? Zivilisationskritik, Natur und Technik in Deutschland 1880–1933* (Paderborn, 1999).
Rohmeder, A.F. *München als Handelstadt in Vergangenheit, Neuzeit und Gegenwart* (Munich, 1905).
Röhrs, Hermann. 'Georg Kerschensteiner', *Prospects: The Quarterly Review of Comparative Education* 3–4 (1993), pp. 807–822.
Rollins, William. *A Greener Vision of Home: Cultural Politics and Environmental Reform in the German Heimatschutz Movement, 1904–1918* (Ann Arbor, MI, 1997).
Rowe, Peter. *Modernity and Housing* (Cambridge, MA, 1993).
Rudloff, Wilfried. 'Notjahre — Stadtpolitik in Krieg, Inflation und Weltwirtschaftskrise, 1914 bis 1933', in Richard Bauer (ed.), *Geschichte der Stadt München* (Munich, 1992), pp. 336–369.
Rutherford, Janice. *Selling Mrs. Consumer: Christine Frederick and the Rise of Household Efficiency* (Athens, GA, 2003).
Ryan, Deborah. *Daily Mail Ideal Home Exhibition: The Ideal Home through the Twentieth Century* (London, 1997).
Sackett, Robert. *Popular Entertainment, Class, and Politics in Munich, 1900–1923* (London, 1982).
Saldern, Adelheid von. 'The Workers' Movement and Cultural Patterns on Urban Housing Estates in Rural Settlements in Germany and Austria during the 1920s', *Social History* 3 (1990), pp. 333–354.
——'Social Rationalisation of Living and Housework in Germany and the United States in the 1920s', *History of the Family* 2 (1997), pp. 73–97.
——*The Challenge of Modernity: German Social and Cultural Studies, 1890–1960* (Ann Arbor, MI, 2002).
——'*Volk* and *Heimat* Culture in Radio Broadcasting During the Period of Transition from Weimar to Nazi Germany', *Journal of Modern History* 76 (2004), pp. 312–346.
Savage, Mike and Warde, Alan. *Urban Sociology, Capitalism and Modernity* (London, 1993).
Scharnagl, Karl. *Wir und der Städtebau* (Munich, 1948).
Schilling, Donald. 'Politics in a New Key: The Late Nineteenth Century Transformation of Politics in Northern Bavaria', *German Studies Review* 1 (1994), pp. 33–57.
Schmitz, Walter. *Die Münchener Moderne: Die literarische Szene in der Kunststadt um die Jahrhundertwende* (Stuttgart, 1990).

Schorske, Carl. *Fin-de-Siècle Vienna: Politics and Culture* (London, 1981).
Schosser, Erich. *Presse und Landtag in Bayern von 1850–1918* (Munich, 1968).
Scott, Peter. 'The Evolution of Britain's Urban Built Environment', in Martin Daunton (ed.), *The Cambridge Urban History of Britain: Volume III, 1840–1950* (Cambridge, 2000), pp. 495–523.
Schubert, Dirk. 'Theodor Fritsch and the German (*völkische*) Version of the Garden City: The Garden City Invented Two Years before Ebenezer Howard', *Planning Perspectives* 19 (2004), pp. 3–35.
Schutte, Jürgen and Sprengel, Peter (eds.). *Die Berliner Moderne* (Stuttgart, 1987).
Schütte-Lihotzky, Margarete. *Warum ich Architektin wurde* (Salzburg, 2004).
Schwartz, Frederic. *The Werkbund: Design Theory and Mass Culture before the First World War* (London, 1996).
Schwartz, Vanessa. *Apartment Stories: City and Home in Nineteenth-Century Paris and London* (London, 1999).
Schwarzer, Mitchell. *German Architectural Theory and the Search for Modern Identity* (Cambridge, 1995).
——'History and Theory in Architectural Journals: Assembling Oppositions', *Journal of the Society of Architectural Historians* 3 (1999), pp. 342–348.
Segel, Harold. *Turn-of-the-Century Cabaret: Paris, Barcelona, Berlin, Vienna, Cracow, Moscow, St. Petersburg, Zurich* (New York, 1987).
Silagi, Michael. 'Henry George in America and Europe', *American Journal of Economics and Sociology* 3 (1993), pp. 369–384.
Simmel, Georg. 'The Metropolis and Mental Life', in *Simmel on Culture*, eds. David Frisby and Mike Featherstone (London, 1997), pp. 174–185.
——*Simmel on Culture: Selected Writings*, ed. David Frisby with Mike Featherstone (London, 1997).
Sitte, Camillo. *Der Städtebau nach seinen künstlerischen Grundsätzen* (Vienna, 1972 [3rd edn., 1901]).
Smith-Rosenberg, Carroll. *Disorderly Conduct: Visions of Gender in Nineteenth-Century America* (New York, 1985).
Soja, Edward. *Post-modern Geographies: The Reassertion of Space in Critical Social Theory* (London, 1989).
Spence, Mark. *Dispossessing the Wilderness: Indian Removal and the Making of the National Parks* (Oxford, 2000).
Steinborn, Peter. *Grundlagen und Grundzüge Münchener Kommunalpolitik in den Jahren der Weimarer Republik: Zur Geschichte der bayerischen Landeshauptstadt im 20. Jahrhundert* (Munich, 1968).
Steinmetz, Georg. *Grundlagen für das Bauen in Stadt und Land*, 3 vols. (Munich, 1916–28).

Bibliography 215

Steinmetz, George. *Regulating the Social: The Welfare State and Local Politics in Imperial Germany* (London, 1993).
Stern, Fritz. *The Politics of Cultural Despair: A Study in the Rise of the Germanic Ideology* (London, 1961).
Sternhell, Zeev. *The Birth of Fascist Ideology: From Cultural Rebellion to Political Revolution* (Princeton, NJ, 1994).
Stieber, Nancy. *Housing Design and Society in Amsterdam: Reconfiguring Urban Order and Identity, 1900–1920* (Chicago, 1998).
Südekum, Albert. *Großstädtisches Wohnungselend* (Berlin and Leipzig, c. 1909).
Summerson, John. *The Classical Language of Architecture* (London, 1964).
Sutcliffe, Anthony. *Towards the Planned City: Germany, Britain, the United States and France, 1780–1914* (Oxford, 1981).
——'Urban Planning in Europe and North America before 1914: International Aspects of a Prophetic Movement', in Hans Teuteberg (ed.), *Urbanisierung im 19. und 20. Jahrhundert: Historische und geographische Aspekte* (Cologne, 1983), pp. 441–474.
——(ed.). *Metropolis 1890–1940* (London, 1984).
Swett, Pamela. *Neighbours and Enemies: The Culture of Radicalism in Berlin, 1929–1933* (Cambridge, 2004).
Swift, Charles. 'The Ideal Home: 1900–1920', *Journal of American History* 81(1994), pp. 1247–1251.
Tafuri, Manfredo. '*Sozialpolitik* and the City in Weimar Germany', in *The Sphere and the Labyrinth*, ed. Manfredo Tafuri (Cambridge, MA, 1987), pp. 197–233.
Tafuri, Manfredo and Dal Co, Francesco. *Modern Architecture* (New York, 1979).
Tatar, Maria. *Lustmord: Sexual Murder in Weimar Germany* (London, 1995).
Taylor, Jeremy. *The Architect and the Pavilion Hospital: Dialogue and Design Creativity in England, 1850–1914* (Leicester, 1997).
Teeuwisse, Nicolas. *Vom Salon zur Secession: Berliner Kunstleben zwischen Tradition und Aufbruch zur Moderne, 1871–1900* (Berlin, 1985).
Tenfelde, Klaus. 'Stadt und Land in Krisenzeiten: München und das Münchener Umland zwischen Revolution und Inflation, 1918 bis 1923', in Wolfgang Hardtwig and Klaus Tenfelde (eds.), *Soziale Räume in der Urbanisierung: Studien zur Geschichte Münchens im Vergleich 1850 bis 1933* (Munich, 1990), pp. 37–59.
Theweleit, Klaus. *Male Fantasies*, 2 vols. (Cambridge, 1987, 1989).
Thies, Ralf and Jazbinsek, Dietmar. 'Berlin – das europäische Chicago: Über ein Leitmotiv der Amerikanisierungsdebatte zu Beginn des 20. Jahrhunderts', in Clemens Zimmermann and Jürgen Reulecke (eds.), *Die Stadt als Moloch? Das Land als Kraftquell? Wahrnehmungen und Wirkungen der Großstädte um 1900* (Basel, 1999), pp. 53–94.

Tooze, J. Adam. *Statistics and the German State, 1900–1945: The Making of Modern Economic Knowledge* (Cambridge, 2001).
Tournikiotis, Panayotis. *The Historiography of Modern Architecture* (Cambridge, MA, 2001).
Turner, Bryan. 'Simmel, Rationalisation and the Sociology of Money', *Sociological Review* 1 (1986), pp. 93–114.
Vadé, Yves. 'Modernisme ou Modernité?', in Christian Berg, Frank Durieux and Geert Lernout (eds.), *The Turn of the Century: Modernism and Modernity in Literature and the Arts* (New York, 1995), pp. 53–65.
Vale, Lawrence. *Architecture, Power and National Identity* (London, 1992).
Vidler, Anthony. 'Agoraphobia: Spatial Estrangement in Georg Simmel and Siegfried Kracauer', *New German Critique* 54 (1991), pp. 31–45.
——'Technologies of Space/Spaces of Technology', *Journal of the Society of Architectural Historians* 3 (1999), pp. 482–486.
——'Agoraphobia: Psychopathologies of Urban Space', in *Warped Space: Art, Architecture and Anxiety in Modern Culture*, ed. Anthony Vidler (London, 2001), pp. 25–50.
Voigt, Wolfgang. 'The Garden City as Eugenic Utopia', *Planning Perspectives* 3 (1989), pp. 295–312.
Wachsmann, Nikolaus. 'After Goldhagen: Recent Work on the Genesis of Nazi Genocide', *Journal of Contemporary History* 3 (1999), pp. 477–487.
Ward, Janet. *Weimar Surfaces: Urban Visual Culture in 1920s Germany* (London, 2001).
Waterhouse, Alan. *Boundaries of the City: The Architecture of Western Urbanism* (London, 1993).
Waters, Malcolm (ed.). *Modernity*, 4 vols. (London, 1999).
Weber, Max. *Economy and Society*. (New York, 1968 [1904]).
Wegner, Armin. 'Gesang von den Straßen der Stadt', in Waltraud Wende (ed.), *Großstadtlyrik* (Stuttgart, 1999).
Weindling, Paul. *Health, Race and German Politics between Unification and Nazism 1870–1945* (Cambridge, 1989).
Welter, Barbara. 'The Cult of True Womanhood', *American Quarterly* 18 (1966), pp. 151–174.
——*Dimity Convictions: The American Woman in the Nineteenth Century* (Athens, OH, 1976).
Welter, Volker. *Biopolis: Patrick Geddes and the City of Life* (London, 2003).
Whyte, William. 'How do Buildings Mean? Some Issues of Interpretation in the History of Architecture', *History and Theory* 45 (2006), pp. 153–177.
Wiedman, August. *The German Quest for Primal Origins in Art, Culture and Politics, 1900–1933: Die Flucht in Urzustände* (Lewiston, NY, 1995).

Bibliography

Wilhelm, Hermann. *Dichter, Denker und Fremdmörder: Rechtsradikalismus und Antisemitismus in München, 1900–1921* (Berlin, 1989).

Willett, John. *The New Sobriety: Art and Politics in the Weimar Period 1917–33* (London, 1978).

Wilson, Elizabeth. 'Looking Backward: Nostalgia and the City', in Sallie Westwood and John Williams (eds.), *Imagining Cities: Scripts, Signs, Memory* (London, 1997), pp. 127–139.

Windsor, Allan. *Peter Behrens: Architect and Designer* (London, 1981).

Wolf, Paul. *Praktische Baupflege in der Kleinstadt und auf dem Lande* (Berlin, 1923).

——*Wohnung und Siedlung* (Stuttgart, 1926).

Yelling, J.A. 'Land, Property and Planning', in Martin Daunton (ed.), *The Cambridge Urban History of Britain: Volume III, 1840–1950* (Cambridge, 2000), pp. 467–493.

Zanten, David van. *Architectural Institutions and the Transformation of the French Capital, 1830–1870* (Cambridge, 1994).

Zauner, Franz Paul. *München in Kunst und Geschichte* (Munich, 1914).

Zell, Clemens. *Geschichte der Elektrizitätsversorgung Münchens* (Munich, 1949).

Zelljadt, Katja. 'Presenting and Consuming the Past: Old Berlin at the Industrial Exhibition of 1896', *Journal of Urban History* 3 (2005), pp. 306–333.

Zimm, Alfred. 'Berlin als Metropole: Anspruch, Wirklichkeit, Tendenzen', *Beiträge zur Geschichte der Arbeiterbewegung* 3 (1992), pp. 3–15.

Zimmermann, Clemens and Reulecke, Jürgen (eds.). *Die Stadt als Moloch? Das Land als Kraftquell? Wahrnehmungen und Wirkungen der Großstädte um 1900* (Berlin, 1999).

Zimmermann, Klaus. *Von der Wohnungsfrage zur Wohnungspolitik: Die Reformbewegung in Deutschland, 1845–1914* (Göttingen, 1991).

——*Europäische Wohnungspolitik in vergleichender Perspective 1900–1939* (Stuttgart, 1997).

Zukowsky, John (ed.). *The Many Faces of Modern Architecture: Building in Germany Between the Wars* (London, 1994).

Index

Figures in **bold** refer to illustrations.

AEG 107–8
Aesthetics and material culture 195–6
　politics of 151–3
agglomeration 48–9
Agriculture, urban attitudes to 77
alienation 35, 114
Alte Heide housing estate 176–8, **177**
anti-pollution laws 108
apartment blocks 153, 155–6, **157**, 171–2
Applegate, Celia 28, 29, 30
Arcades Project (Benjamin, Walter) 12
architectural patronage 125
architecture
　definition of 150
　historians and 128, 150
　historiographical tradition 8–9
　as language 69
　messages 38–9
　National Socialist 38
　neo-classical 97
　propaganda 43
　and social policy 149
art, historical cannon of 128
artists, migration to countryside 82
Association of Construction Companies 162
avant garde, architectural 17, 27, 28–9, 133, 135, 176

Baudelaire, Charles 3, 4
Bauhaus 9
Baukunst vs. Architektur 43
Bauman, Zygmunt 2, 3, 70
Baumeister, Reinhard 52
Bayerische Staatszeitung (newspaper) 99
bedrooms, and social control 169
Beecher, Catharine 131–2, 133–4, 141
behaviour, control of 106–7
　in bedroom 169
　in kitchens 135–42
　political 110–15
Behrendt, Walter Curt 94
Behrens, Peter 41
beliefs and interpretation of space 7
belonging 25, 30
　and urban environment 20
　and *Heimat* 25–31
　production of 31–9, 117, 140
　destruction of through town planning 52, 54
Benjamin, Walter 3, 12, 50
Benninghaus, Christina 137
Berlin
　as symbol of modernity 10, 81–2
　political significance of 12–13
　planning of 30–1, 162
　exhibitions in 40
　housing conditions in 156, 162–3, 165

Berlin (cont.)
　housing construction in 44, 75, 107–8, 124, 174, 178, 179
'Berliner' modernity 13
Berman, Marshall 3, 4
Bertsch, Wilhelm 32, 87–8
Betts, Paul 9
Birchow hospital, Berlin 124
Birmingham 55–6, 79, 181
birth-control 137
Bochum 159, 174
borders, city 83–4
Borscht, Wilhelm 26, 43, 74, 76, 155, 162, 175, 176
Braunschweig 73
Bremen 73, 174
brick building and the historiography of Modernism 94
building control 107
building regulations 53, 162–3
buildings
　'character' and anonymity in 25, 34–5, 110–12, 119–20, 123, 139
　historians and 150
　as transformative agent 115–16
buildings, interior layout
　hospitals 121–6
　old people's homes 119–21
　orphanages 116–9
　schools 32-9
　social housing 126–42, 164–70
built environment, historical analysis of 8–10
Bund Heimatschutz 29, 32
bureaucracy, rise of 70, 71
bureaucratic logics 69
BVP (Bayerische Volkspartei) 79–80, 81–2, 183, 186

Calinescu, Matei 3, 27–8
capitalism 183–4
care homes 108
central heating 56, 119, 180
Central Office of Housing Inspection 158

Chamberlain, Houston Stewart 21, 49
Charlottenburg 75
Chicago World's Fair, 1939 40
child abuse 168–9
cholera 72, 73
chronocyclegraph, the 133
cities
　characterised as problematic 47
　communication between 72–3
　community of 67–8, 69–78, 78–82
　cooperation among 71–2
　critique of 67, 192–3
　enlargement of 84–5, 86, 89–90, 99, 194
　incorporation of peripheral areas 85
　and mental illness 25
　and modernity 11, 13
　opposition to universal model 79–82
　planning paradigms 30–1
　Sitte on 51, 52
　visits to 78–9
citizens
　definition of 143
　and the state 110–16
City Building According to its Artistic Principles (Sitte) 50–1
city councils 31–2
City Extension Plan 85
city governors, urban identity 193–4
city life 1, 31–2
city walls 84
civil servants and urban problems training course 112–13
civil unrest 173
Cologne 75, 174
colonial mentality among urban governors 68, 86–7, 91–2
communities of knowledge 72–3
concrete 175, 186
Confino, Alon 28, 29
Congress of the German Association of Housing Departments 81–2

Index

construction firms 183–4
countryside 82–3
  changing attitudes to 68
  colonisation of 85–8, 91–2
  as unproductive void 90–2
cultural history 3–4
cultural manipulation by city governments 41–3
cultural pessimism 21

Damaschke, Adolf 163–4
Davis, Belinda 78
Debord, Guy 3
decoration
  lack of in Modernism 96–7, 123–4
  opposition to decoration in social housing 156–7, 171–2
  of orphanages 117
  of schools 36, 37, 38
dependence, social: produced by urban living 24
Der Sieg des neuen Baustils (Behrendt) 94
design
  language of 151–3
  and social policy 185–7
Deutsche Städtetag (Conference of German Cities) 71–2
Deutsche Bauzeitung (journal) 117, 124–5
Deutscher Werkbund 41
Die Schönheit der Großstadt (The Beauty of the Metropolis) (Endell) 30–1
disease 4, 24, 122, 169
  mental and urban life 4, 24
  prevention of in cities 50, 107, 112, 169
  and space 174
  tackling in hospitals 121–2
disintegration caused by cities 48–9
domestic space, *see also* kitchen, the
  planning 109
  state intervention in 126–31, 142–4, 195
dwellings, occupancy 59, 165

Eberstadt, Rudolf 164–5
economic system and construction technologies in social housing 182–4
education 32, 43–4, 57, 106
Einfamilienhäuser (terraced housing) 179
elections, 1919 79
electricity 43, 53
Elektrizitätsverwaltung 93, **96**, 96–7
'End of the World, The', firework show, 1928 46–7
Endell, August 30–1
Engels, Friedrich 4, 152–3, 158
enlargement of city 84–5, 86, 89–90, 99, 194
environmental determinism 23
environmental protection 29–30
Erbauer (builder-creator) 36, 89, 118
estrangement
  in personal relationships 25–6
  social/class 112–13
Evans, Richard 72
exhibitions 14, 23, 193
  as critiques of modernity 44
  culture of 39–47, 76
  Home and Technology, 1928 41, 44–7, 139–42
  industry 42
  München 1908 41–4, 76
  organisation 42
  role of 39, 40–1, 59
  scale of 39–41
  visitor numbers 41, 44, 46, 47
  Weißenhof, 1927 41, 47
experiential disorder 4
experimental housing 175–6
experts
  mission 112
  rise of 70–1
exteriors, and landscape 34–5

firework displays 46–7
First World War 77–8, 90, 172, 173–5
Fischer, Theodor 32, 53, 172

flats 59, 74–5, 155–6, 159–60, 165, **166**, 177–8, 181–3, **182**, 195
food supplies 77–8
Ford, Henry 132
form, follows function 34–5
Foucault, Michel 3, 69, 70
Frankfurt
  building system 182–3
  Einfamilienhäuser (individual houses) 179
  kitchen model 128, **129**, 130–1, 135–7
  laundry charges 180
  Newspaper Tower 98
  social housing model 44, 55, 56, 57–8, 59, 73, 138–9, 144, 178
Frederick, Christine 131, 132, 133–5, **134**, 135–6, 140–1, 141, 143
freedom
  and city life 24
  and liberal ideology 69
  and social facilities 56–7
  and social housing 141–2
frescos 36, 37, 38, 117, 119
Frisby, David 49, 50
frontier mentality 83–4
Führer, Karl Christian 153
Fukayama, Francis 69
functionalism 9, 34–5, 179–80
furnishings 117
Fürstenriederstraße school 89

Garden Cities
  as model of town planning 55, 58
  as model for urban expansion 82–3
  land use and economics in 163, 164, 165, **167**, 167–8, 169, 172, 178
Gas Board 93
Gaswerkviertel 86
Geddes, Patrick 22, 30
Gemeinnützige Wohnstättengesellschaft (Communal Housing Corporation) 176–9

Gemeinschaft (community) 22, 112
Gemüt 113, 121
Gerber, Carl 98–9
German League for Land Reform 164
German-ness 163–4
Germany
  diversity within 12–13
  historiography 10–13, 21
Gesellschaft (society) 22, 112
GeWoFAG (Gemeinnützige Wohnungsfürsorge AG - Communal Housing Provision Company) 184
Giesing 160
Gilbreth, Frank and Lilian 132, 133, 136
Gliederung 89
Grässel, Hans 32–5, 83, 87–9, 91–2, 114–16, 117–18, 119, 120–1
Great Britain
  environmental protection 29–30
  Garden Cities 163, 165
  industrial estates 90–1
  land development policies 164
  National Trust 29
  planning paradigms 30
  town planning 21–2
Gross, David 28
Großstadt, acceptance of 99–100
Großstadtangst
  characteristics 22–3, 24–5
  culture of 24–5
  definition of 20–3
  relief of 23
Großstädte (metropolises)
  community of
  1890-1914 69–78
  1918-30 78–82
Großstadtfeindlichkeit (hatred of the big city) 20
Großstadtfreude (joy in the big city) 67–9
Großstadtkritik (criticism of the big city) 21, 22, 24–5, 25–6

Index

Großstadtmensch (urbanite: citydweller) 112
Gut, Albert 175, 176
guten Geschmack (good taste) 42

Habermas, Jürgen 70
Hagemann, Karen 137
Hamburg 72, 73, 77, 156, 165
Harbou, Thea von 48
Häring, Hugo 41
Hayden, Dolores 135–6
head and heart, reconciliation of 110–16, 120, 142–3
health 16
health regulations 108
Heiliggeistspital old people's home, Neuhausen 34, 119–20
Heim (home, dwelling), ideological aspects of 45
Heimat
  and alienation 35
  and art 82
  avant garde modernist use of 28–9
  commercialisation of 30, 193
  complex nature of concept 23, 25–6, 30
  definition of 25–6
  discourse 28–9
  Kitsch aspects 26–8, 30
  modern nature of 28
  movement 29–30
  in orphanages 118
  and planning 51
  producing 31–9
  role of 31
  as spatialised form of identity 30
  use of 59
Heimat League 27
Heimatgefühl (sense of belonging) 54
Heimatkunde (school subject: study of the *Heimat*) 38
Heimatlosigkeit (lack of feeling of belonging to the *Heimat*) 26
Helmreich R.R. 80, 81, 82
helping environments as form of social control 108–9

Herf, Jeffrey 11
Herman, Arthur 21
Hermansen, Christian 9
Hertling, George von 114–15
Heynen, Hilde 26
hinterlands 77–8
historical materialism 71
Hobrecht Plan 162–3
Hocheder, Carl 53
Holocaust, the 10, 70
Holy Ghost Old People's Home 117
Home and Technology Exhibition, 1928 41, 44–7, 139–42
homelessness 155, 173
The Homemaker and Her Job (Gilbreth) 133
homogeneity, stylistic in nineteenth-century cities 30–1
hospitals 93, 108, 109, 143, 195
  architectural brief 123
  decoration 123–4
  interior space 122
  internal layout 124
  personality 124–5
  planning 122–3
  role of 121–2
  as symbols of modernity 121
Household engineering: Scientific Management in the Home (Frederick) 131, 133–5, 135–6
household management 137
housing
  12,000-Programme 44–5, 47, 54–60, 178–80
  construction 170–1, 172–3, 178–84
  design 179–84
  design problem 151–2
  experimental 175–6
  forms 155–6, 195–6
  Home and Technology Exhibition, 1928 44
  living space 136–7, 168–9
  Lückenbebauung policy 59
  market 154–5, 164
  market forces and 162
  and modernity 45

housing (*cont.*)
  and moral disorder 168
  occupancy 59, 165
  and political stability 172–5
  rent 159, 171, 172, 180
  scientific management 126
  shortages 170, 175
  situation at the turn of the century 157–61
  and social policy 149–50, 185–7
  and social reform 168–9
  spatial arrangement 16, **167**, 167–8
  spatial policies 58
  standardisation 177
  state intervention 161–3, 169–70
  subdivision of 156, 158
  supply 153–6
housing colonies 171
Housing Committee 55
housing estates 55–7, 59, 176–80, 181–2, 185, 194
Housing Office 158
housing policy 44–7, 54–60, 174–5
housing question, the 73–6, 151–2
Howard, Ebenezer 21, 49, 58, 83
Hufeisen housing estate, Berlin 179
Humar, Josef 75–6
Hvattum, Mari 9
hygiene 160

Ideal Home exhibition, Earl's Court 40
identity
  in cities 30
  and modern systems 49
  of an expert class 71–6
Implerstraße school
  background 32–3
  exterior 33–5
  frescos 36, **37**, 38
  interior 35–8
  location 33
  messages 38–9
individuals, as type 110–11
industrial quarters, descriptions of 49
industrial zones 53, 90, 90–1

institutional buildings 117, 119–20
interior space, reconfiguring 109
interiors
  decoration 36, **37**, 38
  role of 35–6

James-Chakraborty, Kathleen 150
Jelinek, Joseph 141–2
Joyce, Patrick 152, 153, 168

Kathedersozialismus ('socialism of the professors') 158
Kerschensteiner, Georg 32, 43–4
kitchen, the
  American heritage 131–5, **134**, 135–6
  debate over 109–10
  Frankfurt model 128, **129**, 130–1, 135–7
  male 132
  Munich model 128, **130**, 130–1, 137–42
  as representational space 15–16
  state intervention in 195
Kitsch 26–8, 30, 128
Kleinwohnung (small flat for social housing) 155, 159, 160, 165, 170–2, 174, 178, 195
Klihm, Hans 113–14
Kolonien (colonies) 83
KPD (Communist Party) 60
Kramer, Lore 131
Krupp ordnance works 90–1
Küfner, Hans 47, 55, 58–9, 78, 80–1, 94

labour, division of 144
Laim, incorporation of 89
land use
  and race 163–4
  as solution to housing question 161–2
land speculation 59, 164
Landmann, Ludwig 131
landscape, buildings and 34–5
Lane, Barbara Miller 38
Lang, Fritz 48

Index

Langbehn, Julius 21
Laqueur, Walter 21
Latour, Bruno 2, 3, 70
laundries 56–7, 180
Le Corbusier 41, 140
League for the Heimat and Environment in Germany 27
Lederer, Emil 154
Lees, Andrew 29
Lefebvre, Henri 6–8
Leistungsverwaltung 93
leisure 134
Lekan, Thomas 27
Lieberman, Ben 12, 79
lifestyle reform 115–16
Lilley, Keith 39
living conditions 158–61, 196
lodgers 168–9
London 79
Loos, Adolf 173, 178
Lübbren, Nina 82
Lückenbebauung ('infill building') policy 59
Ludwig I, King 97

McElligott, Anthony 12
Manchester
  and British model of housing reform 75, 79
  and the development of industrial estates 90–1
  Engels' analysis of city plan of 152–3
  housing occupancy in 165
manifesto culture in history of architecture 185, 186
Mantel, Karl 45–6
manufacturing, socialised 182–3
Marx, Karl 3, 4, 195
Marxism 70
mass-produced goods 92
Masterman, Charles, and racialised thinking in Britain 21–2
May, Ernst
  architecture as social reform 138
  formal modernism 179
  influence of American business techniques on 133, 135–6
  influence of Ebenezer Howard on 58
  politics of 143, 144
  and position in historiography 173
  and standardised housing 131, 141, 182–3
  and users of social housing 139
Mayr, *Wohnungsreferent* (Housing Director) 174, 175, 176
medicine 106
Menschenzusammenballung ('clumping together of humans') 54
mental illness 24–5, 31
'The Metropolis and Mental Life' (Simmel) 24–5, 32–3
Metropolis (film) 48
metropolis, the, problems of 24, *see also Großstadt*; individual topics
Meyer, Erna 131, 137
military installations, conversion into housing 175, 186
Millionenstadt, the 51
Modernism 9–10, 34, 94, 128, 140, 144, 176, 178, 179–80, 181
Modernist architects 51, 55, 176, 179, 185
modernity
  acceptance of 99–100, 184
  benefits of 5
  and Berlin 13
  buildings as key features of 89–90
  catastrophist model 2–3
  celebration of 92–3
  and the city 11, 13
  critique 59, 192–3
  critiquing through exhibitions 44
  definition of 2–6
  disordering effects of 3–4, 20
  faith in 22
  German critiques of 20–1, 67, 192–3, *see also Großstadtangst*

modernity (*cont.*)
  in Germany 10–11, 26
  hospitals as symbols of 121
  and housing 45
  and Modernism 9
  negative themes 34
  and nostalgia 33–4
  ordering 2–3, 20
  and personal freedom 57
  positive themes 34
  responses to 14, 125–6
  and space 196
  tensions and contradictions 49
  and transcendental values 125–6
modes of production 133, 144, 181
monocentric cites 30–1
Moosach, incorporation of 86
Morris, William 152
Mosse, George 21
MSDP (Majority Social Democrats) 79, 81
Müller-Wulckow, Walter 94
Müller'sches Volksbad swimming pool complex 113
München 1908 exhibition 41–4, 76
Münchner Neueste Nachrichten (newspaper) 91–2, 96–7, 114–15
Munich
  16th Bezirk 160–1
  18th City District 160
  mundane nature of buildings 10
  as representative metropolis 2, 13
Municipal Building Department 83
Municipal Building Office 41, 42
municipal gasworks 85–8
Municipal Orphanage 34, 36
municipal statistics offices 74
Muthesius, Hermann 75, 79, 165, 167, **167**

National Socialism
  as anomaly 9–10
  architecture 38
  and modernity 10, 11
  nature, commercialisation of 29–30

Netherlands 163
Neu Harlaching housing estate 179
Neu Ramersdorf housing estate 179
Neue Bayerische Zeitung (newspaper) 160
Neuhausen housing estate 179
Newspaper Tower, Frankfurt 98
newspapers, on the Technisches Rathaus 96–100
Nietzsche, Friedrich 21
Nipperdey, Thomas 11
Nolan, Mary 132
nostalgia 27–8, 33–4
NSDAP (Nazi Party) 60, 97
Nuremberg 75
Nymphenburg canal municipal orphanage 116–18

Office d'Habitations à Bon Marché 178
old people's homes 34, 109, 117, 119–21, 143, 195
orphanages 34, 36, 109, 116–18, 143, 195
Oud, J.J.P. 41
overcrowding 168–9

Panoptikon, the 128
Paris 178
parlours 136–7
past, commercialisation of 27–8
personal freedom 57
Peukert, Detlev 2, 5–6, 10
planning, totalising ambitions of 107
planning competition, 1893 52–3
planning paradigms 30–1
political violence 55
pollution 53
population 13, 154
population density 165, 177–8
post-war housing policy 174–5
poverty 169
Preis, Karl 139, 186
prisons 109, 127
Production of Space, The (Lefebvre) 7

progress 71
propaganda 43, 68–9
psychology 116
public sphere, power and 70
Pullman's model city 40

race and racism 21–2, 163–4
Radkau, Joachim 25, 31
railways 91
rambling movement 36
Rapp Motorenwerke 92
rational households 137
rationalism 68–9
reality, production of in discourse on space 7–8
'Red' Vienna 57–8
Rehlen, Robert 32, 43, 170–1, 175
rent 159, 171, 172, 180
representational space 7, 8, 15–16
Ries, *Dirrektor der gas Ansalt* (Director of Gas Works) 85, 86–7, 88
roads 91
Robinson, Louis 71–2
Rohe, Mies van der 41
Rohkrämer, Thomas 11
roofs, flat 179
Ruskin, John 152

Saldern, Adelheid von 137, 191n63
Schachner, Richard 122
Scharnagl, Karl 45, 47, 55, 59, 80, 82, 140–1, 142, 180–1
Scheffler, Karl 28–9
Schlichtheit (simplicity) 42, 118
Schmid, Eduard, Mayor, 1919-24 80
Schoener, Housing Director 75, 79, 84, 170
schools 32, 88–9, 108, 117, 186
Schorske, Carl 50
Das Schulhaus (journal) 88–9
Schütte-Lihotzky, Margarete 131, 132, 133, 135–6, 137, 141, 144
Schwabing Hospital
architectural brief 123
decoration 123–4
internal layout 124
personality 124–5
planning 122–3
role of 121–2
Schwarzer, Mitchell 9
scientific management 126
scientific revolution, the 70
SDP (Social Democratic Party) 60, 73, 114
secret police reports 77, 78
self-expression 24
Selling Mrs. Consumer (Frederick) 135–6
Sendlinger Unterfeld 33, 35
sensory stimulation 24–5
Seraphischer Kinderfreund (journal) 117–18
Siedlung Neuhausen 181–2, **182**
Simmel, Georg
and freedom 57
influence on theory of modernity 3
and the modern state 32–3
and 'nerves' in urban life 24–5
and polarisation of urban life 48–9
Singer, Karl 74
Sitte, Camillo 14, 49–54, 55
skyscrapers 69
slums 155
social and class conflict 111
social care 43, 106
social democracy 114–15
social engineering 110–16
social facilities, shared 56
social infra-structure 24
social order, reconciliation with extant 179–80
social polarisation 48–9, 54, 59–60
social policy 176
architectural design and 185–7
language of 151–3
space and 149–51
Soja, Edward 116
Sonderweg thesis 10–11
space
definition of 6–8
determining possibilities of 144

space (cont.)
  Eberstadt's focus on 164
  importance of 168
  and modernity 196
  representational 7, 8, 15–16
  residential 168–9
  role of in gender relations 127
  and social policy 149–51
  state intervention in 195
  transforming role of 110
  types of 7
Spandau 162
Sparbauten (economical building methods) 176
spatial practice 7, 8, 16
spatial regulation 107–10
SPD 80, 114
Spengler, Oswald 21, 59
Stadtbild (image or impression of the city), the 58–9, 85, 87, 92
Stadtbildzersplitterung 54
Städtebau (town planning) 23, see also town planning
  background 47–9
  definition of 51
  housing policy 54–60
  human focus 50–1
  and planning 51
  Sitte's influence 49–54
  spatial solutions 54
Stadtlohnerstraße housing project 172, 173
Staffelbauordnung (Tiered Building Regulations) 53
standardisation 183–4, 186
state, the, role of 39–40, 110–16
state intervention 106
State Planning Authority 98
state power 70, 106
Steinmetz, George 12
Stern, Fritz 21
Stimmung (mood or atmosphere) 36
strikes 160
Stübben, Josef 53
Stuttgart 139
  Weißenhof exhibition, 1927 41, 47

subletting 168
surface area, flats 181–2, **182**
symbolic environments 8
symbolism 87–8, 127

Taylor, Frederick 132
Technisches Rathaus (Technical Town Hall) 93–6, **95**, 194
  responses to 96–100
technology 45–7, 93, 140–2
Technik 45–7
Thalkirchenerstraße gasworks 85
Thalkirchenerstraße hospital 93
Thalkirchenerstraße housing project 170–1, 172, 185
Tiered Building Regulations (Staffelbauordnung) 53
time and motion analysis 132–3
toilets 43, 156, 160, 165, 171
toll-booths 83–4, 194
Tönnies, Ferdinand 112
tourism 90
Tourniktiotis, Panayotis 8–9, 150
tower blocks 185
town planning 21–2, 31, 193, see also Städtebau
tradition, as defining feature of modernity 28
traffic 52
Trafford Park, Manchester 90–1
trams 91, 107
transcendental values, and Weimar politics 125–6
transitional economy 174
transport 107
12,000-Programme 44–5, 47, 54–60, 178–80
typification in housing construction 141

Übergangswirtschaft (post-war transitional economy) 174
Uebel, Hans 43
Ulm 80
United States of America 126–7
  kitchen heritage 131–5, **134**, 135–6
  National Parks 29

Index

Unterer Anger, the 94
Urban Growth in its Technical, Regulatory and Economic Dimensions (Baumeister) 52
urban history 2
urban identity 82, 193–4
urban underworld 49
urbanisation 20
USPD (Independent Social Democrats) 79, 81–2
utopianism 3

values, ascribed to space 7
Versöhnung (social reconciliation) 142–3
Vidler, Anthony 4, 24–5, 50
Vienna
  and German politics 12
  housing models in 44, 55, 56
  culture of 50
  critique of architecture in 51, 165, **166**
  as model of modernity 57-9
  housing crisis in 170, 173, 178
  and Modernist architecture 188
Völkischer Beobachter (newspaper) 97, 98–9
Volkstümlichkeit (folksiness) 27
VVWM (Verein für die Verbesserung der Wohnungsverhältnisse in München/Association for the Improvement of Living conditions in Munich) 74, 155, 158–9, 172

wages 159–60, 163, 170
Wagner, Martin 98
Wagner, Otto 50

Walchenseeplatz housing estate 179
Wanderschaft (ramblers) 36, 38
Waterhouse, Alan 107–8
Weber, Max 69, 70
Wedekind, Frank 27
Wegner, Armin 29
Weimar Republic
  planning in 14
  Heimat discourse in 27
  urban/rural conflict in 77
  social policy in 79–80
  local politics in 81
  role in historiography of Germany 128
Weißenhof exhibition, 1927 41, 47
Welter, Volker 22
Wembley Park, London 91
Whyte, William 17n17
wildlife, relationship with 36, 37, 38–9
Witte, Irene 131, 133, 137
Wohnungs-Anzeiger (Housing Advertiser) 159
Wohnungs-Zeitung (Housing News) 159
Wohnungsuntersuchung, the 158
women
  characterisation 127, 135–6, 138, 141–2, 143
  and laundry 180
  and the rational household 137
  role of 109–10, 143
  single 140
World's Fairs 40

Zeilenbau ('row housing system for housing estates') system 177